BLANDINGS THE BLEST

For Wodehouse devotees and for newcomers
alike, a whole new world of primal innocence is
opened up by this splendid companion to the
Wooster saga. In the words of Richard Usborne,
'the *belle epoque*, eternal hammock weather,
the snakeless meadow, the embroilments of
Mayfair in mossy country vicarage life,
reverence to butlers, gardeners and pigmen,
irreverence to reverends, peers, policemen,
magistrates, headmasters, boys, babies, dogs,
cats and sacred cows . . .' and above all the
language, 'fluent with mad alienations, most
savoury similes, but innocent, vulnerable and
often wonderfully vivid'.

**Also by the same author,
and available in Coronet Books:**

Wooster's World

Blandings The Blest and The Blue Blood

A Companion to
The Blandings Castle Saga of
P. G. WODEHOUSE, LL.D.
with A Complete Wodehouse
Peerage, Baronatge & Knightage

Geoffrey Jaggard

CORONET BOOKS
Hodder and Stoughton

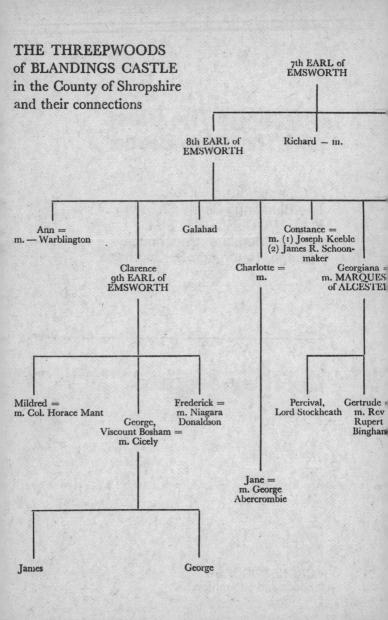

THE THREEPWOODS
of BLANDINGS CASTLE
in the County of Shropshire
and their connections

7th EARL of
EMSWORTH

8th EARL of
EMSWORTH   Richard — m.

Ann =
m. — Warblington   Galahad   Constance =
m. (1) Joseph Keeble
(2) James R. Schoon-
maker

Clarence
9th EARL of
EMSWORTH   Charlotte =
m.   Georgiana =
m. MARQUES
of ALCESTEI

Mildred =
m. Col. Horace Mant   Frederick =
m. Niagara
Donaldson   Percival,
Lord Stockheath   Gertrude =
m. Rev
Rupert
Bingham

George,
Viscount Bosham =
m. Cicely

Jane =
m. George
Abercrombie

James   George

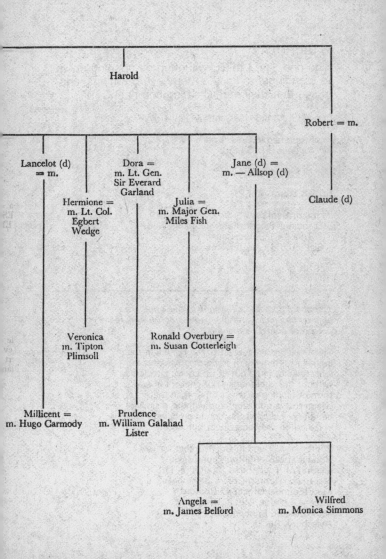

to NICHOLAS
who one day, I think, will often be popping down
to Blandings, to keep a merry eye on things, and
to see that they are 'all sitting comf'ably'.

Copyright © 1968 by Geoffrey Jaggard

First published in Great Britain 1968
by Macdonald & Co Ltd.

Coronet edition 1984

British Library C.I.P.

Jaggard, Geoffrey
  Blandings the blest and the blue blood.
  I. Title   II. Wodehouse, P. G.
  823' .912[F]   PR6045.053

  ISBN 0-340-35910-2

Printed and bound in Great Britain for
Hodder and Stoughton Paperbacks, a
division of Hodder and Stoughton Ltd.,
Mill Road, Dunton Green, Sevenoaks,
Kent (Editorial Office: 47 Bedford
Square, London, WC1 3DP) by
Hunt Barnard Printing Ltd.,
Aylesbury, Bucks.

It was the Threepwood family of Blandings who, with their family connections and friends, first inspired me to collect those data which later ambition developed into a complete Companion-Concordance covering the whole Wodehouse corpus. Here then, in primal state and pomp, are the Threepwoods, serenely maintaining in their Shropshire Eden the standards and responsibilities, the peace and grandeur, the fun and games of an England that was, and nevermore will be.

That grey and noble pile in the Welsh Marches, which so often down the years has lured the Wodehouse mind and imagination, to our advantage, away from Mayfair and less happier realms, seems to pronounce, from its pleasant setting at the head of the Vale of Blandings, a strange benediction upon a county which, in literature at least, has been singularly unblest. What the late A. E. Housman, or Mary Webb, in their time made of the goings-on in this corner of their chosen and dedicated shire is anyone's guess. The east wind that withers the souls of lightfoot lads on Wenlock Edge never has the temerity to invade Lord Emsworth's rose-garden. No pigman employed by the baronets of Much Matchingham has ever been known to hang himself for love in the apple orchard (though there are not wanting those who wish that some of them would). Nor has any tenant farmer on the Blandings rent-roll ever plunged to his death in a mere, with the biggest splash heard since the brindled calf fell into the water. What has gone wrong? Have we been misled down the years? Is Shropshire not, after all, the land of heavy clay and heavier hearts? Or is Blandings Vale populated by a race of fairy changelings from Belloc's Sussex where, to the banging of pewter beer mugs, they sing loud and macaronic choruses in praise of Saint Dunstan. For what it is worth I hazard a simpler solution. The star-crossed lads of Blandings, when racked by maiden wiles, have an ever-ready antidote. A woman is only a woman, but Ovens' home-brewed is a drink.

For the rest of the present book, it seemed equitable here to embody a complete survey of the Wodehouse Peerage, Baronetage and Knightage. It covers the whole corpus from 1900 to the present day; but it should not be imagined that it reflects only the six reigns during that period. It has period flavours of Regency days and much further back—of Whitehall Palace in King Charles II's time, of Henry V and Agincourt, of the Lionheart, of the Conqueror and even of King Arthur. The Wodehouse Peerage, *per se*, deserves indeed a special study. It must be unique in English literature—and not only for its proliferation. If not absolutely precise, the ratio of the various degrees of nobility is uncannily approximate to real life. To create, over a period of some sixty-five years, a complete hierarchy of peers and peeresses, baronets, knights and their ladies, without serious solecisms, maintaining a virtually correct incidence between the dukes and marquesses, earls, barons and the lesser degrees, is itself an extraordinary achievement. It has made it possible, for instance—indeed practicable—to borrow here the standard presentation established by *Whitaker's Almanack*.

To continue over sixty-five years of social re-alignment to add to the peerage in what was and is, by any apparent standards, a falling market for the blue-blooded, argues an insight into the English-speaking mind which without doubt will receive due attention from literary critics of the future. It is but one more example of that exquisite social judgment that has placed more than one generation deeply in debt to an author who, patently, knows his English and his Americans better than do the sociological experts. In the interests of literary history, I should perhaps add that when I began, years ago and somewhat lightheartedly, to compile the list, there appeared a certain shortage of some of the degrees of nobility (though later creations have tended to redress the balance). Obviously, where a noble lord had a son and heir who bore a subsidiary title the father must be a marquess or earl—a fact subsequently confirmed in correspondence with the author. In this way, e.g. the Alcester and Malvern marquessates were established. It remains only to add that, as with the Peerage, the noble mansions listed under 'Even Statelier', the superior major-domos of 'A Bulk of Butlers' and the convivial water-holes discovered in 'Taverns in the Town' also cover the whole Wodehouse corpus to date.

I am grateful to all those readers who have been kind enough to write to me appreciatively about *Wooster's World* and especially to those who, like Freddy and Denise Salfeld, Anthony Lejeune, Lord King's Norton, Macdonald Hastings, Norman Painting, R. B. D. French, Martin Holmes, Richard Usborne and Leslie Mead, have suggested emendations or given valuable help on points involving research. My gratitude as always is also due to A. W. Rhodes, as well as to Nick Mason, for their most welcome and enthusiastic help, and to Ben Goodden whose phenomenal memory, on his reading the text of *Blandings the Blest*, notably assisted my faltering steps.

Brockworth,
Glos.

A COMPLETE WODEHOUSE

PEERAGE

BARONETAGE, AND KNIGHTAGE

WITH

STRAYS FROM THE ALMANACH DE GOTHA

VINTAGE ROYALTY

Pharaoh King of Egypt
Helen of Troy
King Solomon
Queen of Sheba
Sisera
Queen Jezebel
King Cophetua
King Lear
Cleopatra Queen of Egypt
King Herod the Tetrarch
Emperor Tiberius
Emperor Vespasian

Queen Boadicea
Emperor Caligula
Emperor Galba
Emperor Vitellius
Emperor Marcus Aurelius
Attila the Hun
King Arthur
Emperor Charlemagne
Claudius King of Denmark
Prince Hamlet of Denmark
Tsar Ivan the Terrible
Queen Isabella of Aragon
    and Castile

ROYAL HOUSE OF ENGLAND

King Edward the Confessor
King Harold II
King William I
King Henry I
King Henry II
King Richard I
King Edward III
King Henry V
King Henry VII

King Henry VIII
Queen Mary I
Queen Elizabeth I
King Charles I
King Charles II
Queen Victoria
H.R.H. Albert,
    Prince Consort
King Edward VII

H.R.H. the Duke of
  Connaught
King George V

King Edward VIII
King George VI
Queen Elizabeth the Queen
  Mother

ROYAL HOUSE OF SCOTLAND

King Duncan I
Macbeth, Mormaer of Moray,
  King of Scots

Queen Gruoch
King Robert the Bruce
King James VI

DUKES

His Grace the Duke of
  Axminster
  Bootle
  Chiswick
  Devizes
  Dunstable
  Gorbals & Strathbungo
  Hampshire
  Havant

His Grace the Duke of
  Kirkcudbrightshire
  Lochlane
  Mull
  Pevensey
  Ramfurline
  Waveney
  Wigan

MARQUESSES

The Most Hon. the Marquess of
  Alcester
  Broxham
  Buxton
  Cricklewood
  Hunstanton
  Malvern
  Peckham

EARLS

The Rt. Hon. the Earl of
  Ackleton
  Bablockhythe
  Biddlecombe
  Blicester
  Blotsam
  Bodsham
  Brancaster

The Rt. Hon. the Earl of
  Hoddesdon
  Ickenham
  Ippleton
  Kidderminster
  Marshmoreton
  Oxted
  Powick
  Rowcester

Brangbolton
Bridgefield
Carricksteed
Choole
Datchet
Dawlish
Dreever
Drexdale
Droitwich
Emsworth
Havershot

Shortlands
Stableford
Sturridge
Tidmouth
Westbourne
Wetherby
Wickhammersley
Wivelscombe
Wivenhoe
Worplesdon
Yaxley

VISCOUNTS

The Rt. Hon. the Viscount
Binghampton
Heacham
Matchelow
Peebles
Tilbury

The Rt. Hon. the Viscount
Topham
Trevelyan
Uffenham
Wensleydale

BISHOPS

The Rt. Rev. the Lord Bishop of
Bognor
Bongo Bongo
Godalming
Poole

Rumtifoo
Stortford
Bishop Brimble
Bishop Fish

BARONS

The Rt. Hon. the Lord Allardyce
,,   ,,   ,,   Bittlesham
,,   ,,   ,,   Brangmarley
,,   ,,   ,,   Bridgeworth
,,   ,,   ,,   Bromborough
,,   ,,   ,,   Burper
,,   ,,   ,,   Burslem
,,   ,,   ,,   Carnaby
,,   ,,   ,,   Chuffnell
,,   ,,   ,,   Corstophine
,,   ,,   ,,   Gartridge

,,	,,	,,	Hemel of Hempstead
,,	,,	,,	Holbeton
,,	,,	,,	Knubble of Knopp
,,	,,	,,	Plumpton
,,	,,	,,	Roegate
,,	,,	,,	Rollo
,,	,,	,,	Rumbelow
,,	,,	,,	Seacliff
,,	,,	,,	Sidcup
,,	,,	,,	Slythe and Sale
,,	,,	,,	Snettisham
,,	,,	,,	Vosper
,,	,,	,,	Windhall
,,	,,	,,	Worlingham

PEERESSES IN THEIR OWN RIGHT

The Rt. Hon. the Countess of Goffin
The Rt. Hon. the Lady Bodbank

BARONETAGE

Sir Buckstone ABBOTT
Sir Alexander BASSINGER
Sir Herbert BASSINGER
Sir Cuthbert BEAZLEY-BEAZLEY
Sir Henry BOOLE
Sir Rupert BRACKENBURY
Sir Roderick CARMOYLE
Sir George COPSTONE
Sir Roger CREMORNE
Sir Quintin DEVERILL
Sir Ralph DILLINGWORTH
Sir Jasper ffINCH-ffARROWMERE
Sir Hercules FOLIOT-FOLJAMBE
Sir Stanley GERVASE-GERVASE
Sir Sutton HARTLEY-WESPING
Sir Claude LYNN
Sir Claude MOLESEY
Sir John MORRISON
Sir Herbert MUSKER
Sir Gregory PARSLOE-PARSLOE

Sir Gregory PEASMARCH
Sir Preston POTTER
Sir Mortimer PRENDERBY
Sir Murgatroyd SPROCKETT-SPROCKETT
Sir Percival STRETCHLEY-BUDD
Sir Derek UNDERHILL
Sir Cuthbert WICKHAM
Sir George WIDDRINGTON
Sir Mortimer WINGHAM
Sir Reginald WITHERSPOON
Sir George WOOSTER

KNIGHTAGE

Sir Jasper ADDLETON, O.B.E.
Sir Watkyn BASSETT, C.B.E., J.P.
Major General Sir Aylmer BASTABLE, C.B., K.B.E.
Sir Raymond BASTABLE, Q.C.
Sir Edward BAYLISS, O.B.E.
Sir Caradoc BELFRY
Admiral Sir G. J. BIFFEN, K.C.B., D.S.O., R.N.
Sir Hubert BLAKE-SOMERSET, K.C.M.G.
Sir Everard BLENNERHASSET
General Sir Hector BLOODENOUGH, V.C., K.C.I.E., M.V.O.
Sir Thomas BLUNT
Sir Joseph BODGER, K.C.
Sir Pharamond de BODKYN
Major General Sir Wilfred BOSHER, K.B.E.
Sir Aylmer BOSTOCK, K.B.E., C.M.G.
Lt. Col. Sir Redvers BRANKSOME, K.B.E.
Sir Eustace BRIGGS
Sir William BRUCE, M.P.
Sir Percy BUNT, K.B.E.
Sir Rackstraw CAMMARLEIGH, K.C.M.G.
Sir Hugo DRAKE, F.R.C.S., M.R.C.P.
Sir Everard EVERETT, K.C.M.G.
Major General Sir Miles FISH, K.C.V.O.
Sir Abercrombie FITCH-FITCH, F.R.C.S.
Lieut. General Sir Everard GARLAND, K.C.M.G.
Sir Roderick GLOSSOP, C.H., F.R.C.P.
Sir Leopold JELLABY, O.B.E.
Sir Rupert LAKENHEATH, K.C.M.G., M.V.O.
Sir Mallaby MARLOWE

Sir Sholto MULLINER, K.C.V.O.
Col. Sir Francis PASHLEY-DRAKE, K.B.E.
Major General Sir Masterman PETHERICK-SOAMES,
  K.B.E.
Sir Ramsworthy PINFOLD
Sir Wandesbury POTT
Major General Sir Everard SLURK, K.C.V.O.
Sir Godfrey STOOGE
Major General Sir Everard VENABLES, V.C., K.C.B.
Sir Alfred VENNER, M.P.
Sir George WIDDRINGTON, K.B.E.
Sir Oscar WOPPLE

A

Abbott, Sir Buckstone, Bart.: Lt. Col. (ret.) Territorial Battn. Royal Berkshire Regt.; s. his father Sir Wellington A., q.v.; m. Alice (Toots) Bulpitt; one dau.; res. Walsingford Hall, Berks, which under economic pressure he has converted to a country club. An engaging bart. with no illusions about his own limitations:

> Reconciled to the fact that I hadn't enough brains for the Diplomatic Service, I thought I could at least be a simple country gentleman. But Fate decreed otherwise. 'No, Buckstone,' said Fate, 'I have other views for you. You shall be the greasy proprietor of a blasted rural doss-house.' (SM)

Abbott, Lady: *née* Alice (Toots) Bulpitt, is of American birth and of a monumental placidity. If stoicism seems strange in one who earned her bread in the musical comedy chorus,

> it must be remembered that it is only in these restless modern days that the term 'chorus girl' has come to connote a small wiry person with india-rubber legs. In the era of Lady Abbott's professional career the personnel of the ensemble were tall, shapely creatures like hourglasses, who stood gazing dreamily at the audience, supporting themselves on long parasols. Sometimes they would emerge from the coma for an instant to bow slightly to a friend in the front row, but not often. And of all these statuesque standers, none had ever stood with a more completely statuesque immobility than the then Toots Bulpitt.

Such marmoreal anchylosis would seem ideal for holding the statue pose for the whole of Act V, Sc. 3 of *The Winter's Tale*. But Lady Abbott can provide the occasional sensation, as when she presents her husband with a bouncing new brother-in-law (SM)

Abbott, Imogen (Jane): o.c. (and C.O.) of Sir Buckstone, is virtually a blueprint for the nice Wodehouse girl with all the specifications for successful wife- and motherhood, and who is such an effective foil for the ebullient fishhooks-and-fireworks school. Yet they too have their own methods of enlivening the scene. Jane is small, slim and twenty, with a 'boyish jauntiness and eyes of cornflower blue', but those cornflower eyes can on occasion be suffused with that tender light which is noticeable in the eyes of women called upon to deal salutorily with a refractory child or parent. All the same, to Joe Vanringham, staring at her like a bear at a bun, she looks like a Fournier picture in *La Vie Parisienne* come to life (SM)

Abbott, the late Sir Wellington, Bart.: f. of the present baronet, nipped smartly from his blazing bedroom to watch the venerable Elizabethan pile of Walsingford Hall going up in flames. Having (like Sheridan at the burning of Drury Lane) warmed his hands at his own fireside, he set to work at once to indulge those architectural leanings which his best friends were at such pains to discourage, producing ultimately a new Walsingford in the Later Marzipan style, whose glorious technicolour causes the beholder to wink painfully (SM)

Abercrombie, George: lodestar of Lord Emsworth's niece Jane, through whose adroitness in snatching at a straw and converting it into a means of gentle blackmail George is appointed land agent to the Threepwood estates against fearful odds (LEO). (See also **All-England**)

Achilles Statue, the: Hyde Park, W.; that spirited if hybrid hound, William, has been observed to chivvy a Borzoi belonging to a baroness in her own right from, as far as the Marble Arch (MUN)

Ackleton, the Rt. Hon. the Earl of: faces a family crisis with sturdy Victorian resolution (see **Walls**). The Earl's title is interesting, as stemming from a village name in that relatively small strip of west midland England from which Wodehouse draws so many of his character names. On the forty-miles straight line from Bridgnorth to Tewkesbury (themselves both character names) one is never more than a mile or two from some village or town whose name carries overtones of good cheer for the aficionado. Some of them, like Beckford and Eckington, go back sixty years or more to the early school stories (DD)

Adams: head steward at the Senior Conservative Club, Northumberland Avenue, W.C.2. Among other talents he has the enviable one of remembering everyone's identity, even when two hundred or so Senior Conservatives are keeping body and soul together by means of the coffee-room luncheon. This omniscience even extends to the rarer category of country member, so that he can correctly name e.g. that infrequent and unhappy London visitor Lord Emsworth, who may well be unable to do as much for himself (SF)

Adams, Mrs: wife of the Senior Conservatives' best friend, relishes her husband's tales of their eccentricities (SF)

A DAMSEL IN DISTRESS: published 1919 (the first edition, is dated 1920) is not, in the purist sense, a Blandings novel, but is so close a parallel that, had anyone else written it, he could have been sued for plagiarism. Yet though Blandings, it is still very early Blandings, and the Marsh family of Belpher Castle and their titular head the Earl of Marshmoreton are palpably prototypes of what the contemporary American (and perhaps the English) reading public imagined them to be. Dramatised by Ian Hay, it was produced in 1928 with Ann Todd and Basil Foster in the cast (DD)

Addleton, Sir Jasper, O.B.E.: like Hermia, the beautiful Lady Millicent Shipton-Bellinger is ordered to fit her fancies to her father's will and to wed this elderly and moth-eaten millionaire, whose dubiously acquired riches beckon all too imperiously to the Earl of Brangbolton. A kindlier fate has other views (MUN)

Adelphi Hotel, Liverpool: Beefy Bingham's uncle, a wealthy shipping magnate, who breaks his bread at the, (BCE)

Aga Khan, H.H. the late: the impoverished Lord Rowcester's sudden acquisition of a domestic staff suggests to his surprised sister the home life of, (RJ)

Agincourt, Battle of: (Azincourt, 1415); notable rendezvous for noble ancestors, among them Lord Emsworth's and Lord Yaxley's (Sieur de Wocestre). A Belfry forebear of Bill Rowcester held the field there, but Bill (see **Moke Carmoyle**) forsakes it, while a Threepwood took cover at, and Clarence, Earl of Emsworth, prudently follows his example (*passim*)

Albert, H.R.H., the Prince Consort: prototype of firm disciplinary measures, would have had a word or two to say to a girl like Stiffy Byng, implementing his comments with a bedroom slipper (CW)

Albert: knives-and-boots boy in the below-stairs hierarchy at Belpher Castle, Hants., heads a school of thought which holds that every shilling paid in admission to that stately home sticks like glue to the grasping hands of Keggs the butler (DD)

Alcester, the Most Hon. the Marquess of: m. Lady Georgiana Threepwood, one of the eight daus. of the 8th Earl of Emsworth and a sister of the present peer. 1 s., 1 dau. *Heir*, Percival, Lord Stockheath, q.v. See also **Gertrude** (BCE)

Alcester, the Marchioness of: Georgiana, a sister of Clarence, 9th Earl of Emsworth and m. of the impressionable Gertrude. We picture her as a typical Threepwood of her generation, tall, fair, puissant, with a latent strain of resource and authority strangely missing in some of the male members of her family. Like her sisters Hermione, Julia and Connie, would be at her best in a Vesuvian eruption or a London air-raid while (one feels) in this weak piping time of peace they have no delight to pass away the time, save by imposing their ample talent on the over-organisation of households like Blandings or (in Georgiana's case) ensuring that Cruft's shall never lack for exhibits. Currently she maintains a matter of four Pekinese, two Pomeranians, a Yorkshire terrier, five Sealyhams, a Borzoi and an active Airedale, and is thus alone in being able to observe the dog fight in the amber drawing-room at Blandings in a relaxed and judicial manner, with an eye to the finer points of the contestants. She likewise represents a heaven-sent opportunity for a nephew such as Freddie Threepwood, deputed by an American tycoon to boost the sales of Donaldson's Dog-Joy. If the Alcesters' Warwickshire title carries with it a stately home in the west midlands we are not told of it, but Georgiana, when in town, ranches at Upper Brook St., W. (BCE)

Aldermaston: the peregrinations to/from; see **Ippleton** (PP)

Alfred: first footman at Blandings Castle (*passim*)

Allardyce: family name of Lord Allardyce, q.v.

Allardyce, the Rt. Hon. Lord: (SL)

Allardyce, the Lady: an efficient and unfailing unit in Lady Constance Keeble's private intelligence network (SL)

Allardyce, the Hon. Vernon: a sweet boy who tells mother everything (SL)

Allenby, Lady Jane: dinner guest of the Marshmoretons at Belpher Castle (DD)

All-England Lawn Tennis: the game never attains the prominence given to cricket or rugger, but George Abercrombie, q.v., wins through to a place in the last eight at Wimbledon (LEO), Dwight Messmore unwisely celebrates his selection for the Davis Cup, and the Drones Club (GBL) also acquire a Davis Club player in their new member, Austin Phelps

Allsop, Angela: orphaned dau. of Lord Emsworth's late sister Jane, her surname is nowhere chronicled but the facts (see **Wilfred A.**) seem indisputable. Nor is Angela called on to bear her maiden name for long. Like most orphan daus. she becomes the common concern of the whole female element in the family—a fate doubly certain in her case since she is, in the opinion of many young men well qualified to judge, one of the most winsome young prunes in Lord Emsworth's notable garden of nubile nieces. Her blue eyes remind all sorts of people of twin lagoons slumbering beneath a southern sky. The slumbering element is quite illusory, for Angela is discerning enough to spot the cracks in the Lord Heacham facade which have evaded her aunt's eyes, and she is resourceful enough to bring a tender form of blackmail to bear in favour of her sounder suitor, the Canadian-ranching James Belford (BCE)

Allsop, Wilfred: pint-sized and rather like the poet Shelley in appearance, he is an accomplished pianist in the modern genre. A late-comer to the Threepwood family tree, he shares a New York police-cell with Tipton Plimsoll after a Greenwich Village party and accompanies him to Blandings (his own ancestral home) where he wins the outsize hand and heart of Monica Simmons, the ex-Roedean hockey-knocker and ultimately becomes an executive of a music-publishing business which Tipton's late father was constrained to acquire (for a mere two million dollars) in order that his wife Betsy might find someone to publish her songs. It is just possible to pin-point Wilfred's (and Angela's) place in the family tree. As nephew of Clarence, Galahad and Hermione, he is a s. of one of the eight daus. of the 8th Earl. By deduction (for the married names of six are already known) his m. must be Lady Charlotte or Lady Jane Threepwood. Both m. and had issue, and facts seem to favour the last-named (GBL)

Ambrosia Chiffon Pie: see **night starvation**

Angela, the Lady: dau. of the present Earl of Biddlecombe q.v., of Berkeley Square, W. (MM)

aquatic impromptu, the: psychologists, in the exercise of their tricky craft, are said to set much store on the significance of the aqueous repertoire indulged in by the subject. In their interests, and with the object of overlooking no detail which may serve to clarify Clarence's hidden depths (if any) we must record that the only two songs known to have risen from his lips while bathing are 'I fee-eer naw faw in shee-ining armour', and 'Love me, and the wo-o-o-o-rld is ah—mi-yun'. It was the latter which occasioned his enforced rescue (BCE) from the park lake.

Ariosto, Ludovico: (1474–1533); to settle all disputes, wagers, club bets etc., regarding the precise wording of the telegram despatched from Paddington Station at 12.40, signed 'Clarence', the message which confronted the telephone operator was 'Ariosto totem with leprosy', with the proviso that the last word might equally have read 'lingfear' or 'landlady'. When Lord Emsworth composed telegrams two minutes before his train was due to leave his handwriting, never copperplate, degenerated into something which would have held interest for a professor of hieroglyphics (FM)

Arkwrights, the: of Bridgnorth; see **meanwhile**

Ascobaruch, Prince: dark and devious brother of the King of Oom, enters into treasonous league with the High Priest of Hec (CC)

ask Lock, or anyone . . . : nothing in the life of a great city is more complex than the rules that govern the selection of the correct headgear for use in the various divisions of that city. In Bond St. or Piccadilly a grey top-hat is *chic, de rigueur* and *le dernier cri*. In Valley Fields, less than seven miles distant, it is *outré* and, one might almost say, *farouche*. The Royal Enclosure at Ascot would have admired Lord Hoddesdon's hat. The cloth-capped man, in a muzzy, beery sort of way, took it almost as a personal affront. It was as if he felt that his manhood and self-respect had been outraged by this grey topper. Between Lord Hoddesdon and the cloth-capped man, therefore, there may be said to have existed an imperfect sympathy from the start.
'I want to go to Mulberry Grove,' said Lord Hoddesdon.
The man, without shifting his position, rolled an inflamed eye at him.
'Awright,' he said. 'Don't be long.'
'Can you—ah—direct me to Mulberry Grove?'
The eye rolled round once more. It travelled over Lord Hoddesdon's person searchingly, from head to foot and back again. Reaching the head, it paused.
'The way you City clurks get yourself up nowadays,' he said with evident disapproval, ' 's enough to make a man sick. They wouldn't 'ave none of that in Moscow. No, *nor* in Leningrad. The Burjoysy, that's what you are, for all your top-'ats. D'you know what would 'appen to you in Moscow? Somebody, as it might be Stayling, would come along and 'e'd look at that 'at and 'e'd say "What are you doing, you Burjoyse, swanking round in a 'at like that?" ' (BM)
The Hon. Galahad Threepwood holds other views. His brother, Clarence, he muses, has always been allergic to top-hats, but he likes them, especially when grey.
There were days in my youth when the mere sight of a bookie

whose account I had not settled would make me shake like a leaf, but slap a grey top-hat on my head and I could face him without a tremor (GBL)

a solemn warning: to temperance advocates; see **Buffy Struggles;** also **Freddie Potts**

Aspinalls, Ltd.: Bond St., W., the well-known purveyors of jewellery and *objets d'art*, is the scene of one of Lord Emsworth's more masterly misprisions (FM). The Countess of Worplesdon and her nephew Bertie Wooster are also among its clientèle (JM, JFS)

Astley, Sir John: see **Pink Un's and Pelicans**

as we were saying: Lord Emsworth, who had been scratching the Empress' back with the ferrule of his stick, an attention greatly appreciated by the silver medallist, turned with a start, much as the Lady of Shallot must have turned when the curse came upon her (SS)

Atlantic, the S.S.: moves in a slow and thoughtful way down the Solent, bearing the hopes and fears of many young hearts, not to mention a £20,000 diamond necklace:

> The Captain was on the bridge, pretty sure that he knew the way to New York but, just to be on the safe side, murmuring to himself 'Turn right at Cherbourg, and then straight on' (PP)

Attila the Hun: (fl. A.D. 445); is unlikely, we are assured, to have been capable of turning upon the redoubtable Lady Florence Craye like a tiger, even at the peak of his form (JM)

Attwater, J. B.: once butler to the Abbott line of baronets of Walsingford Hall, Berks, now landlord of the Goose and Gander inn at Walsingford Parva (SM)

Axminster, her Grace the Duchess of: transports the social climber, Eugenia Crocker, by inviting her to organise a stall for her charity bazaar. We are privileged to learn that her Grace is a superlative hand-waver (PJ)

B

Bablockhythe, Lady: sells the serial rights of her *Recollections of a Long Life* to Dahlia Travers, who anticipates a *succès de scandale* for *Milady's Boudoir* (COJ)

Bachelors Club, the: senior in foundation to the Drones. Freddie Threepwood surprises his fellow members by his inspiration when he parts his hair in the middle at a time when everyone else is brushing it straight back (LIP)

Bagshot, Berkeley (Boko): 'Interesting personality,' said Gally. 'He made a practice every year of kidding some insurance company that he wanted to insure his life for £100,000 or so, and after the doctors had examined him telling them he had changed his mind. He thus got an annual medical check-up for nothing' (GBL, HW, FM)

Bagshot, Samuel Galahad: s. of Gally's old sparring partner of Pelican Club days, devoted to Sandy Callender. It is the plain-lens spectacles, which she affects professionally, which rive their lute and cause him to pose at Blandings as the pig expert, Whipple. Sam inherits the imposing Sussex mansion Great Swifts, near Petworth, and sells it profitably to Oofy Prosser (GBL)

Bagshott: sorely-tried butler to the retired proconsul, Cammarleigh, q.v., has now endured his employer's story of old George Bates and the rhino eighty-six times (YMS)

Bailey, the Rev. Cuthbert (Bill): boxed three years for Oxford, going through the opposition like a dose of salts. His scruples about marrying Myra Schoonmaker, dau. of the Wolf of Wall Street, are finally straightened out by Fred Ickenham (SS)

Bal Bullier, the: Galahad remembers a sprightly do at, (GBL)

Ballindallochs of Portknockie, the: see WW for details of this Highland family, maternal ancestors of Lord Wivelscombe (YMS)

Banks, 'Cuckoo': a grinning young woman in fancy dress (FM)

Banks, Jno.: proud owner of Market Blandings' only modern emporium, the hairdressing saloon in the High Street (is he a 'hairstylist' nowadays?). Thither to get his grizzled locks shorn for the County Ball goes Joe Keeble, his thoughts so engrossed with his stepdaughter Phyllis's problems that he fails to stay Jno's overgenerous hand with the heliotrope-scented hairwash (a perfume he abominates) and subsequently emerges, niffing to high heaven (LIP)

Bannister, Ann: attractive ex-fiancée of Reggie Swithin (now a belted Earl) earns her bread the hard way, as nannie-governess to a juvenile film-star (LG)

Bannockburn, Battle of: (1314); not to mention Bruce, Wallace and other setaceous and blood-boltered heroes; see **Caledonia** (*passim*)

Barker, Robert: no-one can contemplate, without a modicum of sympathy, the lot of one called on to earn his living as second gardener at Blandings. In that paradisical garden the most superior birds forever hymn their madrigals, the sun forever beams, the lushest flowers forever bloom and cowbells lilt musically in the distance. Yet even the drone of the best bees must often suggest that of the warlike pibroch calling Clan McAllister to rise as one man, and an assistant gardener, mulch he never so mucilaginously, must approximate to false Edward on the field of Bannockburn. For Barker (we are told) is 'no substitute for the doughty McAllister' (BCE)

Barlow, Mrs: a stout party with a staircase of chins, nonetheless performs the intricate and uninhibited steps of the Ugubu tribal dances with the best of them at Shipley Hall (MB)

Barribault's Hotel: for twenty years or more we have been familiar with its majestic doors (guarded by an ex-monarch), its lobby frequented by maharajahs and American millionaires, its palatial dining room and the annexe where ev. dress is not oblig. In fact we knew practically everything—except its address. But, as observant Wodehouse readers are well aware, with patience all will be made known one day—even Whiffle's christian name—and Barribault's at last turns out (PP) to be (typically) located in Clarges St., W.—itself about the only Piccadilly tributary unrecorded elsewhere. Not surprisingly this exclusive spot can make the wrong sort of visitor feel like a piece of cheese, and cheap, yellow cheese at that. Even the former King of Ruritania who graces the frontage of its vasty facade has been selected primarily for his ability to curl the lip and to raise the eyebrows that extra quarter-inch which makes all the difference. Such niceties carry little weight, of course, with a high-stepping Earl bent on lushing up an attractive young protegée, and the ex-monarch has been known to unbend to the extent of a few friendly words with Bill Lister, and the exchange of civilities with Lord Uffenham on the incidence of elvers in southern rivers. The wealthy being almost uniformly repulsive, the lobby around the hour of one-thirty is full of human eyesores, and Terry Cobbold in her new hat (SFE) sitting at a table near two financiers with four chins, does a good deal to raise the tone. Freddie Threepwood, on the strength of a well-deserved

American expense-account, stays here for the sales drive which is to have so signal an effect on Beatle, Beatle and Beatle, of Liverpool:

> The directors, knowing how fastidious are the Duchesses, the Maharajahs and the Texas oil millionaires on whom they rely for patronage, spared no expense on the lobby. The result is something that would have satisfied Kubla Khan when passing the specifications for his stately pleasure dome . . . Joe had been sitting there about ten minutes when a burst of sunshine filled the lobby, harpsichords and sackbuts began to play soft music, and he saw Dinah coming through the swing door (PP) (*passim*)

Basham, Major Wilfred (Plug): 'One of my oldest friends,' said Gally. 'We've always been like Damon and what's-his-name. I once put a pig in his bedroom. It struck me as a good idea. It was the night of the Bachelors' Ball at Hammer's Easton. Old Wivenhoe's pig. I never learned what happened when he met it. No doubt they got together across a round table and threshed things out. Plug Basham, by Jove! I once saw Plug throw a side of beef at a fellow in Romano's. Laid him out cold, and all the undertakers present making bids for the body' (PHW *et al.*)

(See **Pink Un's and Pelicans** for a real life parallel—*Ed.*)

Bashford: porter at the block of flats where Sue Brown has her miniature abode, when retailing the facts to Ronnie Fish, is unaware that he is speaking to Othello's younger brother (SL)

Basil: of natural enemies, the Noblest of her Species has few, but certain small boys must be numbered among them. See e.g. the unspeakable **Huxley Winkworth**, and

> he would not readily forget the day when he had found her snapping feverishly at a potato on the end of a string, the vegetable constantly jerked from her lips by an uncouth little pip-squeak from Wolverhampton named Basil (GBL)

Bassett, Lady: explorer and big-game hunter and a woman of extraordinary formidableness, who reminds Cyril Mulliner of Wallace Beery. If, thinks her daughter Amelia, she were to elope with Cyril to Venice, sending her mother a postcard of their hotel marked with a cross and 'this is our room—wish you were with us', the wish would be fulfilled in no time; but to see her bridegroom laid across her mother's knee, being spanked with a hairbrush, would tend to spoil the honeymoon (MUN)

Bassett, Amelia: is the unknown occupant of the next stall to

Cyril Mulliner's at the St. James's Theatre, S.W., and is so enthralled by *The Grey Vampire* that she collects a fistful of Cyril's right thigh and twists it, so providing him with a good *point d'appui* (MUN)

Bassett, Sir Watkyn, C.B.E., J.P.: that pre-eminent pill, for so many years the stipendiary-sejant (he frequently contrives to be rampant as well) at Bosher St. Police Court, is chronicled fully in WW. Joins the landed gentry as a Gloucestershire squire. Res., Totleigh Towers, Totleigh-in-the-Wold (CW *et al.*)

Bassinger, Sir Alexander, Bart.: of the two Bassinger baronetcies listed, the present, of Bludleigh, Beds., is by far the senior, though both are held to stem from common stock. Bludleigh Court is as outstanding a shambles or abattoir as any country house in the land. Some claim for Sir Alexander the distinction of having cut off more assorted birds and beasts in their prime than any other shot in the midland counties. The galleries of his mansion vie with those of the Natural History Museum, South Kensington, in the rows of mournful, glassy-eyed heads of big game which gaze reproachfully from their walls. Readers of the shiny weeklies are familiar with photographs of the baronet, usually looking rather severely at a dying duck. Is m., with three s. Res., Bludleigh Court, Lesser Bludleigh, Goresby-on-the-Ouse, Beds (MMS)

Bassinger, Sir Herbert, Bart.: Mayfair host noted for the splendour of his parties, as, e.g., the one at which Berry Conway gatecrashes in pursuit of Ann Moon. A rubicund little man with walrus moustache and two chins, he m. a dau. of the 3rd Earl of Droitwich, and was guardian to the present peer, q.v., during his minority (BM, IWY)

Bassinger, Lady Lydia: society hostess, an aunt of the present Lord Droitwich, m. Sir Herbert Bassinger, Bart. (BM, IWY)

Bassinger, Lady: wife of Sir Alexander B., is given valuable advice by Col. Pashley-Drake on what to do with a dead gnu (MMS)

Bassinger, Aubrey Trefusis: second s. of the Baronet of Bludleigh, is the sole exception in a family dedicated to wreaking assorted havoc among the animal creation. Preferring town life, he produces Pastels in Prose, and becomes deeply attracted by Charlotte Mulliner, who creates Vignettes in Verse (MMS)

Bassinger, Reginald: e.s. and heir to Sir Alexander B., spreads general destruction throughout the animal kingdom (MMS)

Bassinger, Wilfred: y.s. of the Bludleigh Bart., though of tender years, prepares painstakingly for the slaughter of the larger fauna by practising on sparrows with his airgun (MMS)

Bastable, Major General Sir Aylmer: settling at Podraga Lodge, Arterio-Sclerosis Avenue, Droitgate Spa, is aggrieved to discover that a sufferer from gout rates a bare nod in the street from the really spectacular exponents, say, of telangiectasis or vesicular emphysema of the lung (EBC)

Bastable, Sir Raymond, Q.C.: there has been some deterioration in this outsize member of the Bar since the days when, as an Oxford rugger blue, he joyfully jumped on the faces of his opponents or suavely submitted to being thrown out of the old Empire on Boat Race night. There may be men in London who think more highly of Sir Raymond than Sir Raymond does, but they would be hard to find. His attitude to relatives and dependants is that of an arrogant tribal god who, should the burnt offering in any way fall short, is prepared to say it with thunderbolts. He qualifies plentifully, in fact, for Fate's brazil nut in the topper (CT)

Baxter, Rupert: in a letter (see WW) explaining why Rupert Psmith had to become Ronald Psmith, P. G. Wodehouse noted that 'Rupert Baxter seemed so right'. And so it is, provided one forgets all associations with Charles, King of England and Rupert of the Rhine, and that one foregoes the temptation to rechristen this austere young man with an appropriate name from the same historic period—say, O-Lord-Bind-Their-Nobles-In-Links-Of-Iron Baxter. A certain Duke, a brace of Earls, a breezy Honourable and a certain Yorkshire baronet would, in Baxter's view, seem to clamour for such treatment. A swarthy young man with flashing spectacles which tend to concentrate on the owner of any guilty conscience within a hundred yards radius, efficient of mind and habit, austere of outlook, impatient of half-measures, intolerant of all but perfection in others' duty as in his own, he is that most formidable of puritans, the type which loves power, knows how to seize it, to wield, maintain and extend it. Though discomfited, misunderstood, maltreated, humiliated, put to shame and ridicule and repeatedly cast into outer darkness, he bobs up again and again, determined as ever to court at Fate's hands worse ignominies than were reserved for Robertson Hare in the Aldwych farces. Both Usborne (WAW) and French (PGW) have amusingly searching sketches of this engaging character, and it was Martin Holmes (see WW) who called attention to Baxter's Malvolio image in *Shakespeare's Public* (1962). In a recent letter he notes:

Sir Toby Belch has a habit of cropping up here and there—not quite a Galahad Threepwood, but pretty near it . . . I don't think there was any conscious approximation on P.G.W.'s part; it was merely a recognition and delineation of a familiar type.

Perhaps so; but the Lady Olivia undoubtedly has her Lady Constance moments, while her cousin Maria is recognisable in Penny Donaldson and other gay young frippets roped in to encompass the discomfiture of Baxter. And students of the poignant moment may recollect the itching hand and toe of Sir Toby who, watching Malvolio's posturings in the garden, sums his feelings up with

O for a stone-bow, to hit him in the eye!

and may remember that Alaric, Duke of Dunstable, whatever his other shortcomings, did not neglect to lay in a stone-bow in the guise of a parcel of eggs when, for the last time on Blandings territory, Baxter tried to make 'Lomond' rhyme with 'afore ye' in the night watches. It remains only to record that Baxter, to his late employer's ineffable relief, is now 3,000 miles away in Pittsburg, U.S.A. (*passim*)

Bayard, the Chevalier: (Pierre du Terrail, Seigneur de Bayard, 1473–1524); in a dimmish light, several villagers mistake Beefy Bastable for, (CT)

Bayliss, Sir Edward, O.B.E.: a bird completely immersed in the jute industry. Res., Deeping Hall, Market Deeping, Sussex (EBC)

Beach, Mrs: aged mother of Blandings Castle's august butler, resides at Eastbourne, and would be delighted to see her son's name in a book of memoirs by the Hon. Galahad Threepwood (SL)

Beach, Maudie: colourful niece of the Blandings major-domo, becomes *seriatim* Maudie Montrose, Maudie Stubbs, Maudie Digby and finally Lady Parsloe-Parsloe; but see **Stubbs**

Beach, Sebastian: of the sixty-two varieties of the butlerine genus recorded in the opus and listed under **A Bulk of Butlers** (we exclude Sir Roderick Glossop's Swordfish because, almost certainly, he acted non-professionally; we include Lord Uffenham's impersonation of Cakebread for the opposite reason) Beach is our most familiar, most loved and (Jeeves's occasional buttling aside) our prototype. We have known, respected and liked him for over half-a-century (as against the eighteen or nineteen years he has served Lord Emsworth), watching him develop from the pompous crooked elbow ('Mrs Twemlow?') who spoke only in headlines, and headed, in SF, the dining hierarchy of the upper servants, into the warm, avuncular, dedicated family servant and friend who is ever ready to place his pantry (and port wine) at the disposal of direful conferences for the family's welfare, to play bears with the younger Threepwoods, and later to aid and abet their romantic yearnings in complex matters of the heart. The laws of their Guild forbid a butler to smile. Beach alone allows us to see one laugh aloud, exploding with a 'HA . . . HOR . . . HOO!' on reading the unpublished story of Tubby Parsloe and the prawns. The laws would likewise frown upon a butler's assumption of a pigman's duties, yet Beach is to be seen daily, without loss of dignity or prestige, fearfully treading the secret path through the Castle Park, food-pail in hand, to the Empress's temporary refuge. No-one else in all Wodehouse is dignified with the stark grandeur of 'a procession of one', nor as having 'a voice like old tawny port made audible'; nor, I think, does any character outdo the *preux chevalier* act by which he renounces his long reign after (allegedly) being shot in the seat of the pants by Connie (actually she missed him at point-blank range) because he had successfully pinked Baxter whom, long ago, he had Approved Of. If one may advance a personal opinion, I think we like him even more for his apparently constant friendship for that singularly lonely and dedicated figure, Angus McAllister. He is, incidentally, (and the fact ought not to be forgotten) possessed of two chins and a bow-window figure, a full-moon face, and has the appearance of imminent apoplexy. His proudest possession is the silver watch presented to him as victor in the annual darts competition at the Emsworth Arms. Both Usborne and French treat approvingly and percipiently of Beach, and French it is who in a peroration observes:

> How well in him appears the constant service of the antique world, where service sweat for duty, not for meed! He does not Disapprove. He loves and indulges his master. They have grown together over the years, and they will be together now through this life. Perhaps beyond it. When Lord Emsworth ends his happy life at last, may it not be that the first thing he hears as he settles himself on his cloud will be Beach's respectful 'Nectar or ambrosia, m'lord?' (PGW) (*passim*)

Bean, Elsie: a perceptive domestic; Lord Ickenham cheerfully subscribes to her view that Sir Raymond Bastable tops the category of overbearing dishpots (UD, CT)

Beatle, Beatle & Beatle: of Liverpool, order gratifying quantities of Dog Joy from Freddie Threepwood (PP)

Beaverbrook, the late the Rt. Hon. Viscount: not a solo trombonist (CT)

Beazley-Beazley, the late Sir Cuthbert, Bart.: see Lady Beazley-Beazley

Beazley-Beazley, Lady (Georgiana): relict of Sir Cuthbert, the old object lives at Wittleford-cum-Bagley-on-Sea where (more pertinently to her nephew Eustace Mulliner) she has the stuff in barrels (MUN)

Beckford: family name of the Marquess of Broxham

Beckford, Lord Augustus: y.s. of the Marquess of Broxham, has two claims to fame at his prep school; he can hold his breath longer than anyone else, and is always first to get hold of a piece of gossip, after which he holds it no longer (LN)

Beckford, Lady Sybil: dau. of the Marquess of Broxham and a sister of Earl Mountry, q.v. (LN)

Bée: putative Pyrenean village born rapidly in the fecund imagination of Gally Threepwood. (FM)

Beevor, Viscount: e.s. and heir of the Earl of Shortlands, lives (perhaps wisely) on his Kenya ranch (SFE)

Belford, the Rev. James: succeeds the venerable Canon Fosberry as Market Blandings' respected Rector (BCE)

Belford, James Bartholomew: a personable and likeable young man, this son of the Market Blandings Rector. He has made a success of ranching in Nebraska, and his devotion to Lord Emsworth's niece, Angela Allsop, is returned with ardour, though opposed by a formidable battery of aunts. Angela's talent for stonewalling tactics and (even more) James's proficiency in hog-calling techniques (see **bringing home**) win for them their heart's desire (BCE)

Belfry: family name of the Earl of Rowcester

Belfry, the Lady Agatha: conjectural consort of Sir Caradoc the Crusader, q.v., but still, after some 750 years, an active and most respected resident (see WW) at Rowcester Abbey. Herself the proto-martyr to the Abbey's congenital dampness, she makes sporadic appearances to warn guests of its rheumatoid-arthritic properties (RJ)

Belfry, Lady Barbara: coll. ancestress of Bill Rowcester, is claimed to have been 'the leading hussy at the court of King Charles II'. The claim is a little empirical, one feels, in view of the competition (RJ)

Belfry, Sir Caradoc: (fl. c. 1180); early ancestor of Lord Rowcester, did well at the Siege of Joppa (RJ)

Belinda: favourite doll of Hermione Threepwood who (a force to be reckoned with even in their mutual nursery days) converted it to an offensive weapon with which to lay out brother Galahad as flat as a Dover sole (GBL)

Bellamy, Barmy: shared the fancy of the Old Bold Mate of Henry Morgan in his addiction to rum—though Captain Stratton would not have approved the milk he added to it (SL)

Bellamy, the Hon. Edwin: succumbs to the delights of tobacco chewing in his school dormitory (LN)

Bellamy: demonstrably a tough baby, is lady's maid to the formidable Hermione Wedge (FM)

Bellamys Ltd.: of Piccadilly, W., exhibit in their windows, in midwinter, a platoon of anaemic strawberries which can be had, for a consideration, from the reduced duchesses who purvey goods at their fruit counters (MUN)

Bellamy-Johnstone, Jack: hero of a tattooing romance, which in the exigences of the moment remains unrelated by Gally Threepwood (HW)

Bellerophon, H.M.S.: Lord Tilbury appears to be mentally pacing its deck, en route for St. Helena, with vultures gnawing his breast (SS)

Belloc, Hilaire: see **Wilberforce Robinson.** The full passage appears as preface to WEW. Hugh Walpole's comic astonishment, with Wodehouse's tactful counterpoint, appear in PF

Belpher, Viscount: for analogies between the Threepwood and Marsh families see the entry on **A DAMSEL IN DISTRESS.** Even to-day small distinction can be made between this bovine young man and his Blandings counterpart, Lord Bosham. He is e.s. and heir of the Earl of Marshmoreton; ed. Eton and Christ Church, and extraordinarily obese. A second edition of his chin has already been published, he bulges opulently, affects a complaint rather than a moustache and is touched in the wind. His manners and habits are no more endearing. Altogether, a big piece of bad news (DD)

Belpher Castle: historic Hampshire home of the Marsh family (see **Earl of Marshmoreton**) who have occupied it since the 15th century. A symmetrical group of grey stone and green ivy, basically mediaeval but mainly early Tudor, it is open to the public (Thurs. only, 1/–) (DD)

Benedick: family name of Viscount Uffenham

Benedick, the Hon. Alice: a dau. of the 4th Viscount Uffenham and an aunt of the present peer, lives in a Shropshire village to which, in youth, the 6th Viscount was rusticated. As a result of ennui he found himself engaged in less than a week to the sister-in-law of a local cat-breeder named Postlethwaite (SFI)

Benedick, Anne: one of Lord Uffenham's bewitching brace of nieces, this y. dau. of the late Hon. Gregory B. Despite an innate intelligence Anne comes within an ace of marrying an interior decorator. Even the earthier of her beholders admit that Nature, in assembling her, has done a nice job of work. Her voice reminds some of spring winds sighing through pine trees; others opt for the muted lilting of sheep bells at sunset (MB)

Benedick, the Hon. Beatrice: sister of the Hon. Alice, is blessed with a period memory which records only the happenings of fifty years ago (SFI)

Benedick, the Hon. Gregory: y.s. of the 3rd Viscount, George Uffenham has lively memories of his great-uncle's active hunting-crop (SFI)

Benedick, the late Hon. Gregory: y.s. of the 5th Viscount, the present peer, frequently wishes he had a quid for every time he has seen his brother running like the wind down Piccadilly with a slavering bookie in hot pursuit (SFI)

Benedick, Jane: surpassingly lovely niece of Lord Uffenham, to whom her voice speaks even more eloquently than that of her sister Anne, reminding him of ice tinkling in a cocktail glass (SFI)

Benger, Puffy: constantly crops up over the years in Galahad Threepwood's reminiscences of that dedicated band whose mission it was to ensure that the West End of London (*temp.* 1890–1910) was painted not merely red but a pleasing vermilion. Surprisingly in GBL we learn he is still with us, though sadly changed:

'Poor Puffy . . . got himself hooked just because in a careless moment he allowed a girl to lure him into reading *Pale Hands I Loved* to her. But for that, he wouldn't to-day be the father of a son with adenoids and two daughters with braces on their teeth'

This was by no means the first occasion on which Puffy's impetuosity was instanced by Gally to point a moral:

'Did I ever tell you about Puffy and the thunderstorm? It was one time when Plug Basham and I and a couple of other fellows had gone to stay with him in a cottage he had down in Somersetshire. Puffy was always drawing the long bow. Charming man, but a shocking liar. He had a niece he was always bragging about. She was one of these business girls—must have been about the first of them. One day we'd been driven indoors by a thunderstorm and were sitting round yarning, and he happened to mention that she was the quickest typist in England. Well, we said "Oh, yes?" and "Fancy!" and so on—the fellow was our host—and there the thing would have ended, no doubt, only Puffy, who could never let anything alone, went on to say that this girl's proficiency as a typist had had a most remarkable effect on her piano-playing. It wasn't that it had improved it—it had always been perfect—but it had speeded it up quite a good deal. "In fact", said Puffy, "you won't believe this but it's true, she can now play Chopin's Funeral March in forty-eight seconds."

'This was a bit too much for us, of course. "Not forty-eight seconds?" said somebody. "Forty-eight seconds," said Puffy firmly. He said he had frequently timed her on his stop-watch. And then Plug Basham, who was always an outspoken sort of chap, took the licence of an old friend to tell Puffy he was the biggest liar in the country, not even excluding Dogface Weeks, the then champion of the Pelican Club. "It isn't safe sitting in the same house with you during a thunderstorm", said Plug, "because at any moment the Almighty is likely to strike it with lightning." "Listen," said Puffy, a good deal worked up, "if my niece Myrtle can't play Chopin's Funeral March in forty-eight seconds, I hope this house will be struck by lightning this very minute." And by what I have always thought rather an odd coincidence, it was. There was a sort of sheet of fire and a fearful crash, and the next thing I saw was Puffy crawling out from under the table. He seemed more aggrieved than frightened. He gave one reproachful look up at the ceiling, and

34

then said in a peevish sort of voice, "You do take a chap so dashed literally!" ' (HW *et al.*)

Benger, Scrubby: is inexplicably enthroned as headmaster of a famous school but, like his former schoolfellow the Bishop of Bognor, makes the best of things (MUN)

Bessemer: one-time valet to Ronald, last of the Fishes, and as ugly a devil as you'd expect to find outside the House of Commons (MN)

Bessemer: Lord Blicester's much-extended cook (LEO)

Bessemer, Beetles: a fundamentally loathsome young woman (FM)

Bevan, the late Aneurin, P.C., M.P.: Lord Uffenham is reminded by a Ruritanian ex-field marshal that, though born in the ermine, he is lower than the vermin (SFI)

Bickersteth: family name of the Duke of Chiswick

Bickersteth, Francis: s. of the late Lord Rollo B. and a nephew of the present Duke of Chiswick, q.v., and is an early beneficiary of Jeeves, who extracts him from the débacle ensuing on his accepting 150 dollars from 87 citizens of Birdsburg, Missouri, on consideration of their being privileged to shake hands with a live English duke (COJ)

Bickersteth, the late Lord Rollo: b. of the present Duke of Chiswick and f. of Bertie's friend Bicky (COJ)

Bickerton, the Rt. Rev. Percival (Boko) D.D.: see **Bishop of Stortford**

Bickerton, Priscilla: it was in Queen Victoria's heyday and at a dance in aid of the Distressed Daughters of Clergymen of the Church of England Relief Fund that the future Lady Bishopess first shook a demure foot with Boko Bickerton, then a curate. In those days she was no mean exponent of the schottische, the polka and the Sir Roger de Coverley. Her reign of terror dates from the point where Percy was enthroned as Lord Bishop of Stortford. It was then that the dreaded lorgnette swung into action and began its deadly work among the minor clergy of the diocese. Doubtless Priscilla's early ability to swing a shapely ankle aids her in skipping from a raided night-haunt at Walsingford-below-Chiveney-on-Thames and, after a midnight steeplechase in fancy dress, to beat the law by a short head (MM, MUN)

Biddle: family name of Lord Plumpton

Biddle, Conky: though his i.q. is negligible his outer crust is spectacular. He out-grants Cary and begins to peck where Gregory left off. Dependent on his uncle Lord Plumpton, he is the anti-hero of the outrageous affair at Lord's Cricket Ground (the only story featuring the national game since the early school stories) (NS)

Biddle, Dinah: what there is of this petite maiden is excellent, and to Joe Cardinal she looks like an angel of the better sort (PP)

Biddlecombe, the Rt. Hon. the Earl of: this Grecian-nosed old nobleman goes commercial, establishing, at his Berkeley Square home, an agency where he books orders for ties, scarf-pins, Clark's Corn Cure, Mouso-Penso (the combined mousetrap and pencil-sharpener) and *Our Tots*. He is f. of the fair Angela, whose charms captivate Lancelot Mulliner (MM)

Biffen, Admiral Sir George J. (Fruity), K.C.B., R.N.: outstanding member of that enterprising band of extroverts of which Gally Threepwood was a leading light, and the subject of some of his illuminating *contes*. Now a retired seadog, Fruity retains his famed foghorn voice, his repertoire of Western Ocean (and West End) yarns and his abiding love of London. Unable to sleep at Market Blandings because of the uproar caused by owls and nightingales, he returns to the peace and quiet of Piccadilly, and leaves his rented villa to be used as a temporary refuge for the Noblest of her Species (FM, PHW *et al.*)

Biggleswade: wristy butler to Sir Mortimer Prenderby, Bart., at Matcham Scratchings, Oxon (YMS)

Billing (Old): (pedigree, etc. unknown) is the potential alternative candidate for the by-election in the Bridgeford and Shipley parliamentary division of Shropshire (HW)

Bingham, the Rev. Rupert (Beefy): like Stinker Pinker, Boko Stortford and others in what Usborne rightly calls 'a succession of splendid men of God', Beefy is a prototype of muscular Christianity at its best:

> For sustained innocuous irreverence, without a hint of mockery towards a subject that popular humorists tend tastelessly to misuse or cravenly to avoid, see Wodehouse on the Church. Perhaps taking his original cue from W. S. Gilbert, but after that, out on his own, Wodehouse has given us . . . several superb church interiors and many most human predicaments

suffered by clergymen in pursuance of their saintly duties (WAW)

The excellent if hamhanded Beefy, devoted to Lord Emsworth's niece, Gertrude, is seen in strenuous action (as is his mongrel, Bottles) in the stories *Company for Gertrude* and *The Go-Getter*. One has the feeling that Lord Emsworth's motive misfires when he wishes Beefy upon his neighbour Tubby Parsloe as rector of Much Matchingham (BCE)

Binghampton, the Rt. Hon. Viscount: Theodore Phipps, 3rd V., is an uncle of that non-starter in any i.q. contest at the Drones, Barmy Fotheringay-Phipps. He m. Emerald, e. dau. and co-heiress of the late J. Middlemass Poskett, of whom he also was residuary legatee, thus neatly preserving intact one of the world's most notable collections of greenbacks. A well-known breeder of Siamese cats and a past president of the National Governing Council of the Cat Fancy, he is even better known as the Curse of the Southern Counties (BW)

Binstead, Arthur M.: see **Pink Un's**

Bird, Dr.: leading medical practitioner of Market Blandings. The euphoric air of that enchanted locality makes his job virtually a sinecure, but he is called in periodically for the extraction of lead pellets from residents at the Castle and the other *minutiae* inseparable from life in a baronial stronghold (SF)

Bird of the Difficult Eye, the: Lady Underhill, q. (if you must) v., is said to resemble. The Bird figures in the story of the same name in Lord Dunsany's *Tales of Wonder* (pub. 1916):

> On the shores of the risky seas of Shiroora Shan grows one tree only, so that upon its branches, if anywhere in the world, there must build its nest the Bird of the Difficult Eye

'Birmingham Post, The': earns deserved distinction as the only English provincial daily newspaper listed as being read daily by a character in the Wodehouse opus. It is delivered every morning to Lester Carmody, squire of Rudge Hall, Worcs (MN)

Biskerton, Viscount: Godfrey Edward Winstanley Brent, e.s. and heir of the Earl of Hoddesdon, a young man with red hair and the preliminary scenario for a moustache to match, confesses, over luncheon at the Drones with his friend Berry Conway, that he is so hard up that he only knows what money is by hearsay. He adds that his aunt, Vera Mace, is so broke that she has even tried to touch him, Lazarus in person:

'It all comes down to this,' said the Biscuit, 'if England wants a happy, well-fed aristocracy, she mustn't have wars. She can't have it both ways' (BM)

Bittlesham, the Rt. Hon. Lord: clambers to the Upper House with the aid of his product, Little's Liniment (It Limbers Up The Legs). See WW for the painful details. Res., 16 Pounceby Gardens, S.W. (IJ, FO *et al.*)

Bittlesham, the Very Rev. the Dean of: pronounces the decanal benediction at the fashionable wedding of Lady Millicent Shipton-Bellinger and Adrian Mulliner, but subsequently falls victim to the bridegroom's peculiar smile (MUN)

Black Shorts, the: (officially the Saviours of Britain); fascist organisation founded and led by Roderick Spode, now Lord Sidcup, q.v. (CW, JFS, FO)

Blake-Somerset, Lady: to the relict of Sir Hubert Blake-Somerset of Lower Basutoland and of The Cedars, Mafeking Rd., Cheltenham Spa, Glos. and a woman raised on *Trilby*, no girl living in Paris can have the slightest claim to respectability. Her attitude to her potential daughter-in-law resembles that of the mother in the music-hall song who looks meditatively at her son's fiancée and remarks 'Poor John, poor John!' (FA)

Blandings Castle: a note, at the start, on the name and its derivation may not be out of place. Castle, market town, and hamlet of Blandings Parva, all took their name originally from the Vale of Blandings, a pleasant region of well-watered meadows and bosky, undulating hills in south-eastern Shropshire through which, besides the parent Severn, two or three smaller rivers also meander. Etymologically, the name Blandings conforms to derivations observable of several other place-names. The first element is found in Blandford St. Mary and Blandford Forum (the latter indeed has a meaning almost identical with Market Blandings) in Dorset, and in Bland, Yorks, and is perh. originally a stream name from *Blanda* (which itself occurs as the name of a small river in Norway). The suffix *ings*, or *ing*, is a common ending of plural nouns, one very apposite source (v. *Concise Oxford Dictionary of English Place Names*) being a suffix esp. for names of streams, cf. Guiting (Glos), Wenning (Yorks) and Leeming (Ches). The suffix could also, however, be an Anglo-Saxon patronymic (cf. *Aethl-ing*) so that a second—and equally possible—alternative would mean 'the settlement of the sons of Blanda'. Separate entries will be found under **Market**

Blandings, Vale of Blandings and **Blandings Parva.**

It was an acute critic who observed of *Hamlet, Prince of Denmark* that the operative word in the title, as the dominant factor in the play, is not Hamlet, or Prince, but Denmark itself. I have always felt there is an echo of this truth in the Blandings saga, and have even wondered idly whether the early W. S. Gilbert influence has provided yet another antiphon (subconscious maybe) in Wodehouse's memory, summed up in that line from *The Yeomen:* 'But the grim old fortalice takes little heed of aught that comes not in the measure of its duty'. It may be fanciful, and is certainly not worth pursuing, yet it is the Castle, static and silent though it be, which perpetually plays a leading part. Gardeners, butlers, chatelaines, even Earls and their Countesses, all are expendable. It watches them come and go. Its ordered domestic routine is as smooth under a Hermione or Julia as under a Constance. It has watched its younger sons despatched to South Africa or North America with as much impassivity as it has observed an 18th-century Earl performing a neat gavotte, or a 16th-century one dealing adequately with a band of marauding Welsh caterans. It accepts, generation after generation, Tudor monarchs, Georgian statesmen or Texan millionaires as its guests, and has been nurse and guardian to all the members of a prolific family for many centuries. Far more than a mere setting, it has a dramatic role, and a puissant one, in its own right. The point needs to be made, that we may more fully appreciate that in the Wodehousian *ethos* such Variations on a Noble Theme in the Threepwood family key need, for their full expression, precisely such a setting as Blandings Castle provides.

On his own statement (though it is evident enough) this author's strongly developed stage sense impels the continual use of a series of scenes. Blandings can, and often does, make a long arm to embrace far distant places. The happenings in Kensington Gardens, or Mario's Restaurant, or Paddington Station, or Barribault's, or even Great Neck, N.Y., are just as hilarious, and as homogeneous, yet all the time we know them to be extensions, and that the master strings controlling them are in Shropshire, and will bring back the action to the epicentre which is that noble pile which stands immemorially at the head of the pleasant Vale of Blandings. As country houses go, it has a unique place in literature. It has the dominance and grandeur of the Tower of London without its grimness. To the Tower we turn our minds with a sense of history and romantic awe. To Blandings we would often be returning too, but with affection, delighted anticipation, and with an extraordinary sense of security.

Yet how little we actually know about the place. Incredible to think that half-a-century went by before we were told of what material it was built! Cover artists, unbriefed, had to improvise year after year, indulging their fancy in stone, brick or half-timbering. One of them, conceiving realistically enough that the west midlands suggested red sandstone, depicted it so, but added an Elizabethan-gabled silhouette. Eventually in GBL (1965) we learned that Blandings is built of grey stone. Nor is it old, as castles go. A little surprisingly (for the period was not an auspicious one for castellation) we learn that

> it came into existence towards the middle of the 15th century at a time when the landed gentry of England, who never knew when a besieging army might not be coming along, particularly if they lived close to the Welsh border, believed in building their little nests solid. Huge, grey and majestic, adorned with turrets and battlements in great profusion, it unquestionably takes the eye. The illustrated glossies often print articles about it, accompanied by photographs showing the park, the gardens, the yew alley and its other attractions. In these its proprietor sometimes appears, looking like an absent-minded member of the Jukes family, for he has always been a careless dresser and when in front of a camera is inclined to let his mouth hang open in rather a noticeable way.

Of these 'other attractions' we had in fact gathered something over the years. There is the famous rose garden, so often muttered about in young lovers' ears by a bribed and benevolent Beach; the imposing stone terrace with its urned balustrade overlooking the tennis courts, where a febrile secretary in citrous pyjamas wrought midnight havoc among the flower pots, and where later he was to lie weltering in his blood after being pinked neatly by his employer's airgun; the deer park described by Psmith to a wondering Eve Halliday; the fabled lake whence its seigneur was forcibly rescued while joyously swimming:

> 'Love me', sang Lord Emsworth, 'and the wo-o-o-o-rld is—ah mi-yun!'
> 'It's all right,' said a voice in his ear. 'Keep cool. Keep quite cool.' (BCE)

Undoubtedly the attractions would include the celebrated library with, among other treasures, the Mazarin Bible attributed to Johann Gutenberg, 1456—about the same age as the Castle; the picture gallery with its long series of Threepwood family portraits (one notably improved by Clarence's revolver) and, in the amber drawing room, that remarkably early landscape of Blandings by

Pourbus (Franz, the Younger?) which in view of its date must be worth a fortune. The amber drawing room has its own pregnant memories ('I have here a few simple rats'), so has Beach's pantry with its devoted bullfinch bursting into liquid song at the sound of a bulky butler's feet in the stone corridor. And there are the magnificent, tapestried bedrooms, last occupied by Tudor monarchs on their progresses and (even more fabled) that other bedroom in the corner of a buttercup meadow adjoining the kitchen-garden, in that bijou residence where dwells the Noblest of her Species.

We cannot pop down to Blandings as often as we could wish, but we see it, and its surroundings, very clearly on the ¼-inch Ordnance Survey map. To the south is the blue blur of the Wyre Forest; to the north, beyond Bridgnorth and the innumerable windings of the Severn, the Wrekin raises its solitary head. Eastwards towards Stourbridge is the champaign country forming the setting for Francis Brett Young's novels, and westwards the land rises to Clee, Wenlock Edge and the stormy hills of Wales. The view from the battlements of Blandings, therefore, is in its English way spectacular. We can remember it in three distinct moods. Standing there, alone with her sad thoughts on a sultry summer afternoon, the unhappy Sue Brown sees all Shropshire spread beneath her, but

> the lake was a grey smudge, and the river in the valley below a thread of sickly, tarnished silver. Gone was the friendly charm of the Scotch fir spinneys that dotted the park. They seemed now black and haunted and menacing, as if witches lived in crooked little cottages in the heart of them (HW)

More typically Lord Emsworth (had he not mislaid his pince-nez) might have seen

> up from the river, rolling park land, mounting and dipping, surged in a green wave almost to the Castle walls, breaking on the terraces in a many-coloured flurry of flowers, while away in the blue distance wooded hills ran down to where the Severn gleamed like an unsheathed sword (LIP)

Whilst equally spectacular, of course, was the view from the battlements which greeted the incensed nobleman when, giving his new telescope a first airing, he perceived his younger son engaged in pre-connubial fondlings and affectionate reciprocities with a totally strange young woman in the shrubbery (BCE)

Richard Usborne points to an observable kinship between the Blandings saga's author and the creator of the Iliad. He thinks, too, that the Castle owes a good deal to Wodehouse's early memories of the Methuens' stately home at Corsham in Wiltshire. What is certain is that the setting was chance-born. It is so easy to equate Wodehouse with a sense of relaxed, joyous loquacity and to forget that in fact he is one of the most reticent of men. Apart from the happy, stylised prefaces to SL and BCE, he has to my knowledge spoken only twice, and briefly, about Blandings. At the outset of the B.B.C.'s televised Blandings series in 1967, in a *Radio Times* introduction, he wrote significantly:

> I should like . . . to give a word of advice to any young fellow who may feel a Saga coming along, and that is to be very careful how in the early stages he commits himself to dates and what is known as locale. When I wrote *Something Fresh* I rashly placed Blandings Castle in Shropshire because my happiest days as a boy were spent near Bridgnorth, overlooking the fact that to get to the heart of Shropshire by train takes four hours (or did in my time). This meant that my characters were barred from popping up to town and popping back the same afternoon, which is so essential to characters in the sort of stories I write. Kent or Sussex would have served me better.

And there is that prescient sentence in BG, following a very lively description of a week-end at Knole, the famous Sackville seat in Kent:

> That was week-ending in England as still surviving in 1924. Not much left of that sort of thing to-day, my masters, save only at Blandings Castle.

And now, forty-five years later? At Windsor, Balmoral and where else? Only at Blandings the Blest where any of us, thank God, may still week-end when we will.

BLANDINGS CASTLE AND ELSEWHERE: published 1935, contains the only collection of Blandings short stories. Later ones appear singly. The six tales include the superlative *Company for Gertrude, Custody of the Pumpkin, The Go-Getter* and *Lord Emsworth and the Girl Friend*.

Blandings, Empress of: for some slight attempt to delineate the character, virtues and achievements of the Noblest of her Species, see **Empress of Blandings**

Blandings, Market: see **Market Blandings**

Blandings Parva Reveal'd: the little hamlet which nestles against the deer fence of Blandings Castle park never achieves the significance of its larger neighbour, Market Blandings, but holds our affections by that near proximity which permits us to see it clearly and see it whole. Here Lord Emsworth is still the feudal seigneur. He it is who looks forward pleasurably to judging the floral displays in the cottage gardens at the August Bank Holiday fête—his enthusiasm somewhat damped, to be sure, at the prospect of having to wear morning coat and a top hat which is sure to be the target for the biscuits of the tougher juvenile element. Here too he ponders the inscrutable fate which has accorded some of his tenantry such extraordinary surnames, and deplores the roundabouts, marquees, swings, balloons and paper bags which break out in a rash across his park. And here the villagers (e.g. Mrs Rossiter) give more noticeably at the knee as he passes down the village street, than in the more sophisticated market town:

> It consists of a few cottages, a church, a vicarage, a general store, a pond with ducks on it, a filling station (its only concession to modernity) and the Blue Boar Inn (GBL)

Amateurs of heraldry may care to ponder whether this tavern-name is too slight a theme on which to build an assumption. At no point in the saga are we given any hint or detail as to the Threepwood armorial achievement. Can this be one? Market Blandings has its Emsworth Arms (signboard unknown) and here, right under the Castle walls, the only tavern is the Blue Boar. May it be that the family crest is the not unknown one of a boar statant azure? It is out of the question that the nearest, and only, signboard should display anyone else's arms than those of the local landlord. Be that as it may, a conscientious editor must advise his readers to go, quickly and often, to Blandings Parva and its fellow-hamlets, dotted all too sparsely between Eddystone and Berwick Bounds. They will not be found much longer, and with their passing, the England of our youth will have lost the last, faint echoes of pre-Tudor days (BCE, GBL)

Blandings Stories, the: strictly a series rather than a saga, they began as long ago as 1915, and at a moment when both Britain and America were rather preoccupied. We, the masses, still hail the latest addition, in 1967, with gratitude and glee. The earliest were experimental and comprise the three novels **SOMETHING FRESH, A DAMSEL IN DISTRESS** and **LEAVE IT TO PSMITH.** The point may be made, without further labouring, that though set in another castle and county, with another earl and chatelaine, **A DAMSEL** has such a profuseness of parallels with Blandings that it is to all intents a Blandings novel. Wodehouse speaks eloquently of his surprise when **SOMETHING FRESH** was bought for serialisation. What really happened was that one of his own hunches had come off, and against the odds, for though he believed in the uninhibited comedy novel, he had been warned off it by conservative advisers. And he knew he could not only bring it off again, but improve on it, too. It was the next Blandings novel, **SUMMER LIGHTNING,** which ushered in the benign, long, midsummer period—exquisitely constructed and written, every word pulling its weight, each tale crowned by deft, dramatic dénouements. R. B. D. French calls it,

> the most solid and decorous . . . with family affairs treated seriously against a frivolous background, and Galahad Threepwood, the old bohemian, to bring the young lovers together (PGW)

Since then, things have hotted up somewhat and (short stories aside) Blandings novels have tended to come more or less alternately, taking their lively, hilarious and sunny course with Gally at the helm, or a more unpredictable one when Uncle Fred takes to dropping iron filings in the compass. One would not, perhaps, agree with those who think old Sureshot Ickenham makes the mixture too rich, but one would admit that his advent makes one grateful that the masons who built the mediaeval castle walls knew their job. But whichever it may be, it will be vintage stuff, superb of its kind. And, of its kind, there is no other.

The list of Blandings novels and short stories below is given in order of publication; but it should be remembered that though they cover (to the present) fifty-two years, their action accounts for no more than seven or eight. Less than a decade spans the life of a supreme champion sow; the same magic girdle binds the jet age with the horse-drawn cart in which Ashe Marson and Joan jolted from station to castle, more than half-a-century ago.

SOMETHING FRESH
A DAMSEL IN DISTRESS
LEAVE IT TO PSMITH
SUMMER LIGHTNING
HEAVY WEATHER
BLANDINGS CASTLE AND ELSEWHERE
LORD EMSWORTH AND OTHERS
UNCLE FRED IN THE SPRINGTIME
FULL MOON
NOTHING SERIOUS
PIGS HAVE WINGS
SERVICE WITH A SMILE
GALAHAD AT BLANDINGS
PLUM PIE

Blenkinsop-Bustard, Rupert: triflers with young ladies' affections seldom earn the full treatment, but Rupert, proto-martyr to the active horsewhip of Major General Sir Masterman Petherick-Soames, gets his on the steps of the Junior Bird Fanciers (MMS)

Blenkiron, Thomas (Rat-Face): shares top bracket as junior tough egg of Blandings Parva with Willie Drake (BCE)

Blennerhasset, Sir Everard and Lady: raise the *Clameur de Haro* at the onset of Bertie Wooster's banjolele phase (TJ)

Blicester, the Rt. Hon. the Earl of: Rodney Widgeon, 3rd of his line (for full dossier see WW). Prime exponent of the one-way pocket system and despite formidable competition, winner of the Drones Club's Fat Uncles' Sweepstake organised by his much-suffering nephew, Freddie Widgeon. Many have gasped incredulously on learning that even the House of Peers could hold a nobleman heavier on the hoof, but the superior adiposity of Lord Burslem, q.v., seems established. Res., Blicester Towers, Blicester Regis, Kent (LEO, YMS, FO *et al.*)

Blissac, Maurice, Vicomte de: o.s. and heir of the chatelaine of the Château Blissac; an engaging young man who, if he has any other ambition than to be in the forefront of those who believe in living it up, cherishes the fulfilment of a wish-complex to the effect that there is little point in wasting red paint if the town can possibly be embellished in a shade of luminous vermilion (HWA)

'Blobbs, Peter': see **Pink Un's**

Blood will tell: Chancing to glance floorwards, Lord Emsworth became immediately aware of what appeared at first sight to be a lady's muff. But, this being one of his bright afternoons, he realised in the next instant that it was no muff, but a toy dog of the kind which women are only too prone to leave lying about their sitting-rooms.
'God bless my soul!' exclaimed Lord Emsworth, piously commending his safety to heaven, as so many of his rugged ancestors had done on the battlefields of the Middle Ages. He opened the door and slipped through. Blood will tell. An Emsworth had taken cover at Agincourt (BCE)
'I discovered her in the summer-house,' said Lady Constance, 'with a young man. They were kissing one another.'
Lord Emsworth clicked his tongue. 'Ought to have been out in the sunshine,' he said disapprovingly.
Lady Constance raised her foot quickly, but instead of kicking

her brother on the shin merely tapped the carpet with it. Blood will tell (LEO)

Bloodenough, General Sir Hector, V.C.: after a distinguished Army career is put in charge of the Intelligence Service in West Africa, where his acumen wins from the natives the sobriquet *Wah-Nah-B'Gosh-B'Jingo* (lit. trans., 'Big Chief Who Can See Through The Hole In A Doughnut). When elected chairman of the governing body of Harchester College, therefore, Sir Hector is the last man whom the Bishop of Stortford would have wished to inquire officially into certain nocturnal ceremonies in the school grounds:

> The Bishop found his gaze far too piercing to be comfortable. 'Bad business, this,' he said. 'Bad business. Bad business.' 'O that I had wings like a dove, Psalm xlv. 6,' muttered the Bishop (MM)

Blotsam, the Rt. Hon. the Earl of: takes those sadly familiar steps characteristic of heavy uncles bent on curbing young men who wish to take the primrose path to the everlasting bonfire. Res., Blotsam Castle (miles from anywhere and an effective prison for nephews) and 66a Berkeley Square, W. (MUN)

Blunt, Lady Julia: dau. of the 10th Earl of Dreever and an aunt of Spennie, the present peer, Lady Julia Coombe-Crombie m. Sir Thomas Blunt, M.P. Res., Dreever Castle, Shropshire, and Eaton Square, S.W. (GL)

Blunt, Sir Thomas, M.P.: the ruler of Blunt's Stores Ltd. has a genius for trade, if for little else, and is an example of the came-over-Waterloo-Bridge-with-half-a-crown-in-my-pocket-and-look-at-me-now type of millionaire. Pink, fussy, obstinate, a great comfort to his party and a corresponding discomfort to the unfortunate young Earl whose menage he effectually controls (GL)

Boat Race Night: though universally regarded (except at Bosher St., Bow St., Marlborough St. and Vine St.) as an excuse for an outsize toot, is emphatically not one of the two annual occasions on which Jane Ickenham allows her lord off the leash in the Metrop. (*passim*)

Bodbank, the Rt. Hon. the Baroness: Constance Bodbank is a peeress in her own right. Readers with any pretence to *bon ton* and *comme il faut* will be acquainted with her standard work *Polite Behaviour* (MUN)

Bodger: Kent C.C.C. bowler, acquires a finger grip which makes the ball dip and turn late on a sticky wicket (NS)

Bodger, Colonel: committee member of Brown's Club, St. James's S.W., and member of an old Shropshire family, is prominent in the annual festivities of the Loyal Sons:

> as tight as an owl at the annual dinner (FM)

He may be identifiable with the 'tottery golfer of advanced years and a martyr to lumbago' (HG)

Bodger, Sir Joseph, K.C.: acting for the respondent in the test case Biggs v. Mulliner, establishes the inalienable right of a photographer to eject an unpleasing client from his studio at the tripod's point (MM)

Bodkin, Monty: amiable and moneyed Drone, prominent in LB, enters the Blandings scene as a nonchalant and cheerful unit in Clarence's long succession of secretaries, a position he achieves through being a nephew of Tubby Parsloe. Finding it imperative to hold a paid job for two years to qualify for the hand of J. G. Butterwick's daughter, he buys himself a contract in Percy Pilbeam's shady agency (HW *et al.*)

Bodkyn, Sieur Pharamond de, the: sweating (but literate) mediaeval forebear of Monty B., writes home feelingly to his wife of his experiences when unexpectedly unhorsed at the Siege of Joppa (LB)

Bognor, the Rt. Rev. the Bishop of (the late): of Theophilus Mulliner, D.D., it is recorded that the saintly prelate suffered a good deal from clergyman's throat. Signed+THEOPHILUS BOG: REG: (FO)

Bognor, the Rt. Rev. the Bishop of: disrobing in his bedroom at Branksome Towers, Leics (whither he has temporarily removed his *cathedra*) contentedly hums one of the song hits from the Psalms. The good man started his career as the Rev. J. G. Smethurst and was subsequently appointed headmaster of Harchester (founded c. 1595). He is consequently intrigued to find that one of his former alumni lies concealed beneath the episcopal bed. Signs+JONATHAN BOG: REG: (MUN)

bohunkus, a: though unknown to science as a zoological or ecological term, is defined to Lord Emsworth by one of his nieces (though he fails to take the point) as 'a very inferior species of worm' (BCE)

Boles, Boles, Wickett, Widgery & Boles: Lincoln's Inn Fields, W.C., men of affairs to Sir Buckstone Abbott, Bart., who has some hopes they may sanction the use of dynamite in the matter of removing Sam Bulpitt (SM)

Bolsover, the Very Rev. the Dean of: Theodore Mulliner, D.D., is enthroned as Bishop in the vacant see of Bongo Bongo, q.v. for the painful details (MUN)

bonanza: a run of luck, prosperity, good fortune; Amer. slang, (reports the *Shorter Oxford English Dictionary*) from Spanish term for good weather (FM *et al.*)

bones: iron men, rhino, blunt, oof, lolly, splosh, dibs, chink, dust, plunk, bucks, dough, tin, spondulicks, jack, the needful, brass, mazuma or, if you prefer it, greenbacks. Notable collectors include Oofy Simpson, Oofy Prosser, Lord Blicester and his Grace of Chiswick; on the other shore are Tipton Plimsoll, Donaldson and Rosie Spottsworth, at sight of whose signature even the blood-sucking leeches of the U.S. Internal Revenue raise their filthy hats with a reverent intake of breath

Bongo Bongo, the Rt. Rev. the Bishop of: Theodore Mulliner D.D., is Dean of Bolsover, Wilts. (*sic*) before his enthronement and, as uncle and former guardian of Lancelot Mulliner, is grieved to learn the young man has taken a studio in Chelsea to study art. As a prominent member of the Bolsover Watch Committee it has been the Dean's painful duty to attend a private showing of the super-film *Palettes of Passion*, and in a vibrant letter he speaks of his alarm on hearing that one of his flesh and blood should embark on a career which must inevitably lead to the painting of Russian princesses reclining on divans in the semi-nude with their arms round tame jaguars. He urges Lancelot to return and become a curate while there is yet time. Four years of estrangement follow, then, on his enthronement to the diocese of Bongo Bongo he hits on the expedient of sending Lancelot his pet cat:

> From both a moral and an educative standpoint (he writes) I am convinced that Webster's society will be a turning point in your life. Thrown, as you must be incessantly, among loose and immoral Bohemians, you will find in this cat an example of upright conduct which cannot but act as an antidote to the poison cup of temptation which is, no doubt, hourly pressed to your lips

For a time, the saintly divine's brightest hopes are fulfilled, but

Webster's moral fibre proves unequal to the beckoning finger of the back alleys of Chelsea, where he soon establishes a reign of terror. But when his former owner returns to England it is Webster who saves the unworldly prelate from the matrimonial trap which all but engulfs him. The good Bishop signs +THEODORE BONGO +BONGO or occasionally +THEODORE BONGO$_2$ (MUN)

Booker, p.c.: of the Walsingford-cum-Chiveney constabulary, Berks., is plugged in the eye by his Right Reverend quarry (MUN)

Boole, Sir Henry, Bart.: pedigree stock expert and suilline authority. One of three minds with but a single thought at the Shropshire Annual County Show (PHW)

Boole, Mr: of Mainprice, Mainprice & Boole, 3 Denison St., Strand, W.C., and the sole surviving partner (SF)

Bootle, the Most Noble the Duke of: his Grace moves a little fitfully over the scene. We learn casually that a wheezing woman would never have done for him; elsewhere he unwisely offers hospitality to the Bradbury Fishers, who repay him by stealing the ducal butler (HG)

Borstal, P. P.: member of the healing profession who messes in with four others in over-populated Harley St. (FM)

Bosham, Viscount: courtesy title of George Threepwood, e.s. and heir of Clarence, 9th Earl of Emsworth. Has made only two appearances over the years and, unlike most other members of the family, has not been developed as a character. The title is prcs. pronounced 'Bozzam' like the picturesque Sussex seaport. 'Pretty potty in his turn' is Usborne's succinct verdict, and it would be difficult to rebut it:

> he has had a breach of promise case in his day, he has bought a gold brick, he has lent Lord Ickenham his wallet and he talks almost total drivel (WAW)

The third premise alone would arouse the interest of, say, Sir Roderick Glossop. George has, however, achieved the main requirements of an heir to an ancient earldom. He has married one Cicely, of whom even Connie speaks highly and to whom he is devoted, and has produced two small sons, one at least of whom is both likeable and intelligent (LIP, UFS)

Bosham, Viscountess: Cicely Bosham m. George Threepwood, Viscount B., heir to Lord Emsworth, with whom and their two s. James and George she lives on the Threepwood estates in Sussex and Hants. She makes no personal appearances and data are few. We learn that she disapproves of card-playing as a hobby for husbands and is adequately equipped to apply the veto in this and other matters. Supposedly therefore she has acquired that grip on affairs (cf. Jane Ickenham) so necessary to the peace and solvency of noble households. From this and the deep regard in which her husband holds her views, we gather there will be no radical changes of policy when she becomes the reigning chatelaine at Blandings (UFS)

Bosher, Major General Sir Wilfred: victim of an unfortunate contretemps with his form-fitting trousers on the platform at a school prize-giving (RHJ)

Bosher St. Police Court, W.: where for so many years Sir Watkyn Bassett keeps open house for the unwary. Many of England's gilded youth see no point in waiting for the annual excuse provided by Boat Race Night. Ronnie Fish, e.g., makes an overwrought appearance there after the battle at Mario's (SL *et al.*)

Bostock, Sir Aylmer: is remembered at school, by Lord Ickenham, as a little tick, an opinion shared during his colonial governorships by the wiser native chiefs who called hurriedly on their most effective ju-ju before shinning up the nearest tree when he was sighted in the offing. He is a squatter on the grand scale. On his brother's death he comes barging over from Cheltenham to take over his sixteen-years-old nephew's hearth, home and estate at Ashendon Oakshott, Hants., bagging the best bed for himself and the best room in the house for his revolting African collection, and establishing himself and family on the estate for the next twelve years. Retribution arrives in the shape of Frederick, Earl of Ickenham. The pro-consular wits are no match (very few wits are) for that egregious conquistador when bent on the spreading of sweetness and light (UD)

Bostock, Lady: devoting half of her forty-five years to keeping her Colonial Made Gentleman in a reasonably equable frame of mind, not surprisingly has a face like an overworked cabhorse (UD)

Bostock, Bricky: impetuous companion of Fred Ickenham's nonage (UFS)

Bostock, Hermione: o.c. of Sir Aylmer, and a girl it does not do to cross. Places Pongo Twistleton on matrimonial probation briefly before casting him into outer darkness. Writes with some success under the pen name Gwynneth Gould. Her outer crust is spectacular:

Her father might look like a walrus and her mother like something starting at 100/8 at Catterick Bridge, but their offspring, tall and dark, with large eyes, a perfect profile and an equally perfect figure, was an oriental potentate's dream of what the harem needed (UD)

Brabazon-Plank, Major (Bimbo): explorer, leads an expedition to the upper Amazon basin. Judging a Bonny Babies competition in Peru, is spiked in the leg with a dagger by the Indian mother of one of the honourably mentioned, and learns about wimmen from 'er. A pear-shaped chap, the Major; rather narrow in the shoulders and very broad in the beam; in fact a callipygous gentleman (UD, SLJ)

Bracken: family name of the Earl of Stableford

Bracken, Lady Beatrice: dau. of the Earl of Stableford, raises the already high standard of looks at the Ascot Royal Enclosure, Lord's Cricket Ground, the Eton and Harrow match and the Biddlecombe Hunt Ball (HWA)

Bracken, Lady Gwendolen: outspoken sister of Lord Stableford, thinks Packy Franklin a flibbertigibbet, and has a case (HWA)

Brackenbury, Sir Rupert, Bart., M.F.H.: a descendant (we like to think) of that susceptive Lieutenant of the Tower who applied for leave of absence while certain dispositions were made. With the exception of ffinch Hall, Sir Rupert's home at Cogwych Hall, Cogwych-in-the-Marsh, Ches., represents the northernmost limit of the Wodehouse terrain for stately homes. As a M.F.H. he is astutely regarded by Freddie Threepwood as a likely candidate for Donaldson's Dog Joy (FM)

Bracy-Gascoigne, Ronald: receives timely warning from the Rev. Augustine Mulliner that the Bishop of Stortford (not to mention the Lady Bishopess with lorgnette at the ready) is at hand, and that the prudent man looketh well to his going, (Proverbs, 14, 15.) For the godly prelate, speaking *ex cathedra* on a matter of faith and morals, has infallibly iterated Ronald's inadequacy as an aspirant to his ward Hypatia's hand (MUN)

Bradbury-Eccleston, Jno.: gen. mgr., Sarawak and New Guinea Rubber Exploitation Co., Ltd., Strand, W.C. (SF)

Brancaster, the Rt. Hon. the Earl of: see WW for details of this well-known psittacophile and former employer of Jeeves. Besides parrots his lordship is much addicted to pontificating at school speech days (RHJ)

Brandon, Jane: superlative dau. of the Rev. Stanley B., Jane gives her heart to her f.'s pale (but highly potential) young curate Augustine Mulliner. Fate ensures that the couple are made to jump through hoops of fire before she can add her hand to her heart (MM)

Brandon, the Rev. Stanley (Pieface): cheerful, shrewd and extrovert Vicar of Lower Briskett-in-the-Midden, and an expert assessor of human goats and human kids. His rare reunions with his old schoolfellow, Boko Bickerton, now Bishop of Stortford, are as obvious a joy to them as to the reader. It is when rallied by the Bishop for wearing too many orphreys on his chasuble that the Vicar is tempted to put into practice those finer points which once contributed to his ringside reputation as heavyweight boxing champion of Cambridge University (MM)

Brangbolton, the Rt. Hon. the Earl of: is Reginald Alexander Montacute James Brampfylde Tregennis Shipton-Bellinger. (The list has an inspired West Country tang; the euphonious surname comes from the charming village of Shipton Bellinger, near Amesbury, Wilts.). The haughty peer is outspoken in his objections to Adrian Mulliner as a suitor for his dau. Millicent. Adrian is a gifted detective—a profession the Earl has disliked ever since his brother was sentenced to a salutary term in gaol. Hobbies; Persian Monarchs, Crown and Anchor, Blind Hookey, Find the Lady. Res., 16a Upper Brook St., W. (MUN)

Brangmarley, the Rt. Hon. Lord: of Brangmarley Hall, Little Seeping-in-the-Wold, Shropshire. Though exiled to an alien shore, butler Ferris keeps the standard of English chivalry majestically waving at Beverly Hills, Cal., where his nostalgic memories of his days spent in the service of the noble lord are frequently summed up in the words 'It never would have done at Brangmarley Hall' (OR)

Branksome, Lt. Col. Sir Redvers: as tough an egg as ever said Yoicks to a Leicestershire foxhound (MUN)

Breamworthy, Messmore: fellow vice-president, with Freddie Threepwood, of Donaldson's Dog Joy, Inc. (FM)

Brent: family name of the Earl of Hoddesdon

Brice, Colonel: one of an Empress's three best friends (PHW)

Bridgefield, the Rt. Hon. the Earl of: takes shrewd Victorian steps when his daughter, Lady Catherine Duseby, indulges in an infatuation with a social inferior (DD)

Bridgnorth, Lord: his is a courtesy title. He lives with his noble parents in Cadogan Square, S.W. (IWY) and there seems some ground for supposing they are the Duke and Duchess of Hampshire. Known as Tubby at the Drones, he turns an honest penny as a society gossip-writer (as the Duke in his time has also done) and follows the footsteps of the Iron Duke and others in patronising Price's, q.v., in Knightsbridge. Tubby finally achieves an engagement to marry Luella Beamish of New York City, whose father is not only crawling with the stuff but (what is *rem acu*) as bald as a coot (IWY *et al.*)

Bridgnorth, Shifnal and Albrighton Argus, with which is incorporated The Wheat Growers' Intelligencer and Stock Breeders' Gazetteer, The: is foremost in hymning (in imperishable verse) the third successive victory of Empress of Blandings at the Shropshire Agricultural Show:

> It isn't often, goodness knows, that we are urged to quit the prose with which we earn our daily bread and take to poetry instead. But great events come now and then which call for the poetic pen. So you will pardon us, we know, if, dealing with the Shropshire Show, we lisp in numbers to explain that Emp. of Blandings won again . . . (PHW, BCE *et al.*)

Bridgworth, the Rt. Hon. Lord: Digby Thistleton, cr. 1st Baron, is that resourceful financier who (as related by Jeeves) on the failure of a patent depilatory, re-markets it as a hair-restorer and makes a fortune:

> His favourite saying, sir, was that There Is Always A Way (COJ)

Briggs, Sir Eustace: opinionated Mayor of Wrykin, Shropshire, in the days when local political bigwigs collected knighthoods as easily as motorists now collect parking fines. Is a crabbed hater of all things Irish (GB)

Briggs, Lavender: Lord Emsworth is suffering from the stress of circumstances in thinking that not even the Efficient Baxter could compare with this secretary in the art of taking the joy out of life. Lavender thoroughly deserves the cheque which Fred Ickenham helps her to acquire, for the setting up of her typing agency, and earns her niche, too, for the part she plays in helping to deflate the Duke of Dunstable (SS)

brilliant critical emendation, the: by which (the classic example) Lewis Theobald, third editor of Shakespeare, inspired by the MS notes of 'an unknown gentleman now deceas'd', clarified the nonsensical 'table of Greenfield's' by substituting 'a babbled of green fields'. There are not wanting those Wodehouse admirers who (in an admittedly different kind of green field) advance the claim of 'hags' in *Macbeth*, IV. i (see **Caledonia**) the fine point of which is sharpened by the use of the Middle Scots plural suffix -*is* (OS)

Brimble, Hermione: a dau. of the late Bishop of Stortford, and a girl so divinely fair that when Augustus Mulliner first beholds her at a Wimbledon charity bazaar the top-hat rocks on his head and the thud, as he falls for her, is plainly heard at Putney Hill:

> as soon as he could get his limbs to function he hastened up and began buying everything in sight. And when a tea-cosy, two teddy-bears, a pen-wiper, a bowl of wax flowers and a fretwork pipe-rack had changed hands he felt that he was entitled to regard himself as a member of the club and get friendly (FO)

Brimbles, the inadequate: of Shrewsbury (FM)

'British Pigs': we are not told the name of the author of this obviously standard work on the suilline species, of which the noble owner of Blandings Castle possesses a well-thumbed copy. A sound work, but obviously not to be compared with the omniscient Whiffle (SL)

bringing home the bacon: even the noblest intellect can nod, and Whiffle himself has his *lacunae* in failing to treat fully of some of the more temperamental kinks in the porcine make-up. Breeders the world over are aware that the pig must be invited to drop in for a meal by means of an individual call, which may vary not only from state to state, but even from farm to farm. One noble owner, at least, has had cause for grave anxiety through this omission:

> 'Omit to call them,' said James Belford, 'and they'll starve rather than put on the nosebag. Call them right, and they'll follow you to the ends of the earth with their mouths watering.'
> 'God bless my soul! Fancy that!'
> 'These calls vary in different parts of America. In Wisconsin, for example, the words "Poig, Poig, Poig" bring home the bacon in both the literal and figurative sense. In Illinois I believe they call "Burp, Burp, Burp", while in Iowa the phrase "Kus, Kus, Kus" is preferred. Proceeding to Minnesota we find "Peega, Peega, Peega" or, alternatively, "Oink, Oink, Oink", whereas in Milwaukee, so largely inhabited by those of German descent, you will hear the good old Teuton "Komm

Schweine, Komm Schweine". Oh, yes, there are all sorts of pig-calls, from the Massachusetts "Phew, Phew, Phew" to the "Loo-ey, Loo-ey, Loo-ey" of Ohio . . .

Our many pig-breeding readers will be relieved to know that there is fortunately a master-call which is, to the pig world, what the masonic grip is to the human:

'Most people don't know it,' said James, 'but I had it straight from the lips of Fred Patzel, the hog-calling champion of the Western States. It is "PIG-HOO-O-O-O-EY!" You want to begin the "Hoo" in a low minor of two quarter-notes in four-four time. From this, build gradually to a higher note, until at last the voice is soaring in full crescendo, reaching F sharp on the natural scale and dwelling for two retarded half-notes, then breaking into a shower of accidental grace-notes. Like this!

'Pig-HOOOOO-OOO-OOO-O-O-ey!'

They looked at him, awed. Slowly, fading across hill and dale, the vast bellow died away. And suddenly, as it died, another, softer sound succeeded it. A sort of gulpy, gurgly, plobby, squishy, wofflesome sound, like a thousand eager men drinking soup in a foreign restaurant. The Empress was feeding (BCE)

Bromborough, the Rt. Hon. Lord: pardonably proud possessor of that outstanding moustache, Joyeuse, than which the eastern counties can boast no whicher save, perhaps, the equally outstanding moustache Love In Idleness of Sir Preston Potter, Bart. Lord Bromborough res. at Rumpling Hall, Lower Rumpling, Norfolk (LEO)

Brompton Register Office: Beaumont St., Brompton Rd., S.W.; a spot fraught with tense associations for various marital candidates Here, e.g., Bill Lister fails to find a bride, though Tipton Plimsoll, by way of compensation, finds a face which haunts his uneasy conscience (FM). It is also the *mise* for Flick Sheridan's marriage to Bill Paradene West. All in all, Bingo Little, Lord Bittlesham's nephew, is well advised to eschew the command to go west, young man, and to take his custom to the rival establishment at High Holborn (*passim*)

Brooks, R. S.: see **Pink Un's**

Brotherhood, the Rev. Aubrey: has a cure of souls at Ashendon Oakshott, Hants. A nice young man with pimples, he also acquires measles (UD)

Brown, Polly: small and shapely, with piquant features and eyes the colour of old sherry, this American manicurist pops out of the bushes in front of Lord Droitwich's sports car at a moment when his affairs are already at a critical point. Some such intervention by fate was badly needed, but this time fate nearly overdoes it (IWY)

Brown, Sue: stage name of Susan Cotterleigh, o.c. of the late Captain Jack Cotterleigh, Irish Guards, and of the late Dolly Henderson, celebrated music-hall star of the nineties and a reigning West End toast. Orphaned early and faced with the need to earn a living, she declines to capitalise either parent's name, and joins the musical comedy chorus. When we meet them, she and Ronnie Fish, q.v., are already that way, and Ronnie's uncle, Gally Threepwood, pierces the disguise of the daughter of Dolly, the one woman for whom his devotion provides the only serious moments in an otherwise irresponsible life. Clearly Sue is not only the apotheosis of a favourite type of Wodehouse girl, but is singled out also for special affection. She is 'a tiny thing, mostly large eyes and a wide, happy smile, with a dancer's figure and the zest of youth.' Her hard-won happiness with Ronnie is compound of mutual devotion and of her intuitive understanding of a possessive, prickly, modest and introvert young man to whom life hitherto has not been particularly kind (SL, HW, LB)

Broxham, the Most Hon. the Marquess and Marchioness of: parents of Earl Mountry and of Augustus and Sybil Beckford, q.v. (LN)

Bruce, Nannie: a tall, gangling light-heavyweight, her appearance suggests a Grenadier Guardsman dressed up to play Charley's Aunt. And difficult though it is now to imagine that she once had a girlish sliphood, it was factually as a slip of a girl that she joined the strength at Hammer Hall, where she is now as firm a fixture as the peculiar smell in the attic (CT)

Bruce, Sir William, M.P.: Old Wrykynian, now a school governor and donor of the Bruce Challenge Cup, successfully contests, in the Conservative interest, the parliamentary election for the Wrykyn division of Shropshire (WF)

Brutus, Lucius Junius: not since the days of, was there a father with so careless a regard for the comfort of a son. (The legendary First Consul put his two sons to death for conspiring to restore the Tarquins) (BCE)

Buckingham Big Boy: Lord Tilbury's considerable pig fades into the shadow of a shade as his lordship's astonished gaze first falls upon the majestic bulk of Empress of Blandings (HW)

Buckingham Palace, S.W.: Gally Threepwood faces up to a contretemps at a Royal Garden Party given at, by their Majesties King Edward VII and Queen Alexandra in 1906 (see **Mabel**) (PHW)

Buck-U-Uppo: the full list of case-reports on the famous Mulliner elixir lie off the present canvas. One teaspoonful, mixed well into ten or twelve bushels of provender, is guaranteed to make the most timid elephant trumpet loudly and charge the fiercest tiger without a qualm. Under its influence the Rev. Augustine settles firmly the dispute over the orpheys between his Bishop and his Vicar; and it is after an overdose that the Bishop and the Lady Bishopess visit the dubious nightclub on the Thames in fancy dress (MM *et al.*)

Budge Street, S.W.3: Wodehouse readers who have lived in or near the King's Road, or who even know their Chelsea, have their own identification for this rather narrow, rather plebeian and (let's admit it) rather insalubrious thoroughfare. For them it spells the nostalgia associated with the character-change undergone by this most homologous London borough—now not even a borough in its own right. Since the Old Master himself, in the *Globe* period of his career, lived at the Sloane Square end of the King's Road, those of us whose memories do not go back to the turn of the century are given a first-hand picture of a Chelsea we shall not see again. No everyday duchesses, countesses or Almanach de Gotha princesses in those days picked their way through the litter of cabbage leaves, banana skins and fish-and-chips paper in the Budge Street visited by Lord Ickenham. Princes and Dukes did not inscribe their names, with those of film stars and group singers and advertising tycoons, in neat slots beside parti-coloured front doors whose desirability has soared with their rateable values. Debrett's most exclusive names were not then seen over the dingy but lively and virile shops which are now boutiques, restaurants, antique establishments and day-and-night grocery stores. A hardy breed of alley cats reigned on the roofs and walls by night and would have made short work of the Abyssinian and Burmese immigrants of to-day. As for the dogs, we are told that the best fights in London were to be seen in the Sloane Square district, where the pampered stray from Eaton Square or Belgravia occasionally encountered those scraggy nondescripts, reared sedulously on gin and old iron in the famous pubs of the artists' quarter. Miniature poodles and King Charles spaniels (despite the royal origins of the King's Private Road) were not to be found then, though Fred Ickenham's Aunt Brenda (see **Lorg-nettes**) would doubtless welcome the reappearance of the pug species. Even the artists and sculptors are now dispersed and scattered to the back streets of Fulham and bowery Islington. The door of No. 11 Budge Street, from which Mrs Keating never stirred further in her life than to the King's Road itself (save once, when Keating was laid to rest at Kensal Green) is now painted pale lilac, and the good lady, if still with us, probably lives in style in Eaton Square on the proceeds of the sale of her bijou residence. There may be, in the side streets of the World's End and the New King's Road, some slight echoes of the old, robust way of life still discernible, though not for much longer. However, there are compensations which life, in its inscrutable way, has seen fit to bestow. Recollecting the immeasurable improvement of Budge Street when Sally Painter, slim, trim and pretty, tripped round the corner to lunch with Uncle Fred at Barribault's, we can reflect with advantage on that hour of the day, between 8.45 and 9.45 a.m., at Sloane Square and South Kensington stations, when to-day's male beholder may well go goggle-eyed at the sight of the plenitude of pulchritudinous, nubile, Olympian goddesses taking train for the model agencies of Mayfair; a sight that Caesar never knew, and one of those totally unexpected compensations with which nature confounds art. One other Chelsea event in the opus should not be forgotten. The Stamford Bridge ground of the Chelsea Football Club makes the headlines in MT (published 1917). It is a great day by any standards when two famous American baseball teams, New York Giants and Chicago White Sox, line up there before George the Fifth of England, Scotland, Ireland and the British Dominions Beyond the Seas King, Defender of the Faith, Emperor of India, to give him and 60,000 other spectators an exhibition game lacking nothing of the quality of a home match. For three American exiles, meeting there by chance, it is a poignant occasion. One of them, father-in-law of an English earl, has not seen a ball-game in two years. Another is watching his first for five years and is a fugitive from justice. And the third? That is quite a story (*passim*)

Bulstrode, Mr, M.P.S.: Market Blandings' popular and courteous Chymist may be found in the High Street. Here Sir Gregory Parsloe's butler, Binstead, purchases the Slimmo tablets which are to have disastrous results in the Much Matchingham pigsties (PHW, UFS)

Bunt, Sir Percy: senior civil servant with an austere outlook (FL)

Bunting, Mr: senior partner in the law firm Bunting and Satterthwaite, contemplates with gloomy satisfaction the pre-marital trials of Judson Phipps. Normally looking like an amiable vulture, at mention of Phipps he resembles a vulture dissatisfied with its breakfast corpse (PP)

Bunyan, Roscoe: there is rather a lot of this offspring of the U.S. tycoon, J. J. Bunyan, who leases Shipley Hall, Kent, from Lord Uffenham. Most of his acquaintance would have opted for far less, but he insists on giving full measure, bulging freely in all directions. Young as he is, a second edition of his chin has already been published. Possesses twenty million dollars and loves each one of them individually (SFI)

Burns, Robert: (1759–96); did not spell very well (see **moments**)

Burper, the Rt. Hon. Lord: that young Tubby Parsloe pawned his false teeth seems unquestioned, since Galahad's evidence is borne out by Clarence who remembers seeing them wrapped in cotton wool in a cigar box. That the future Bart. later pawned them in the Edgware Road remains unproven (SL)

Burslem, the Rt. Hon. Lord: his adiposity even exceeds that of the Empress who, according to Gally, is 'the fattest pig in Shropshire except for Lord Burslem, who lives over Bridgnorth way' (FM)

Butlers do not smile. The rules of their Guild do not permit it (OR)

A BULK OF BUTLERS

Sixty-two varieties of the butlerine genus have so far been noted in the opus, not including one honorary member of the profession, Sir Roderick Glossop (Swordfish) who, like Jeeves, can buttle with the best on occasion, but only for his own inscrutable purposes. It may be pointed out, too, that the Junior Ganymede, of which Jeeves is a highly respected member, draws a sharp distinction between gentlemen's personal gentlemen and the lower orders (butlers, footmen, chauffeurs etc.) who are admitted only on a quota basis. Nor, one imagines, would some of the younger, scruffier and more modern elements, who creep in below, be allowed within the club's Curzon Street portals, even on a country-member basis. Alphabetically the sixty-two (employers' names bracketed) are:

Bagshaw (Richard Little), Bagshott (Sir R. Cammarleigh), Barlow (Headmaster of Sedleigh), Barter (Julia Ukridge), Bayliss (B. Crocker), Beach (Lord Emsworth), Bewstridge (J. Briggs), Biggles- wade (Sir M. Prenderby), Binstead (Sir G. Parsloe), Blizzard (B. Fisher), Brookfield (Rev. Heppenstall), Brookfield (Lord Wickhammersley), Bulstrode (C. H. Brimble), Bulstrode (Col. Wyvern), Butterfield (Sir W. Bassett), Cakebread (Mrs W. Cork), Chaffinch (T. P. Brinkmeyer), Chibnall (Mrs Steptoe), Coggs (Lord Ickenham), Dobson (Sir R. Glossop), Fotheringay (Lord Biddlecombe), Ferris (S. Waddington), Gascoigne (Lord Wivels- combe), Keggs (J. Bannister), Keggs (Lord Marshmoreton), Keggs (J. J. Bunyan), Maple (Lord Worplesdon), Merridew (Lord Emsworth), Mulready (Sir R. Witherspoon), Murgatroyd (Sir J. ffinch-ffarrowmere), Oakshott (W. Wooster), Oakshott (Julia Ukridge), Parker (Headmaster of St. Austin's), Parker (Mrs Drassilis), Peasemarch (Sir R. Bastable), Phipps (Lord Brom- borough), Phipps (Lord Powick), Pollen (Sir B. Abbott), Pomeroy (T. P. Travers), Purvis (S. Gregson), Riggs (Lady D. Garland), Roberts (C. Paradene), Saunders (Lord Dreever), Seppings (T. P. Travers), Silversmith (E. Haddock), Simmons (Lady Wickham), Skidmore (R. Bunyan), Skinner (P. Pett), Sleddon (W. Braddock), Slingsby (Lord Droitwich), Spenser (S. Gregson), Spink (Lord Shortlands), Staniforth (Mrs Gudgeon), Stout (Julia Ukridge), Sturgis (L. Carmody), Vosper (Duke of Bootle), Wace (S. Ham- mond), Weeks (Nigger's noble master), Wilberforce (Mrs Been- stock), Williams (Mr Merevale), Willoughby (Lord Tilbury), Wrench (Duchess of Waveney).

'I have been in service from a very early age, madam. Domestic service is a tradition in my family. I started my career as what is known as a hall boy in a large establishment in Worcestershire.'
'Where the sauce comes from?'
'I believe the condiment to which you allude is manufactured in that locality, madam.'
Phipps stood silent for a moment, his thoughts back in those happy days. Apart from having to carry logs of wood upstairs and deposit them in bedrooms, hall boys in English country houses have it pretty soft (OR)

He found Albert Peasmarch in his pantry, having his elevenses, two hard-boiled eggs and a bottle of beer. Butlers always like to keep their strength up with a little something in the middle of the morning (CT)

Everything in Mrs Adela Cork's domain spoke eloquently of wealth and luxury, but nothing more eloquently than Phipps, her English butler. In Beverley Hills, as a general thing, the householder employs a 'couple' who prove totally incompetent and leave the following week, to be succeeded by another couple, equally sub-human. A Filipino butler indicates a certain degree of modest stepping-out. An English butler means magnificence. Nobody can go higher than that (OR)

If there is one class of the community that has reduced knocking on doors to a fine art, it is butlers (BC)

'I sometimes think', said Bagshott the butler, 'that gentlemen do not realise how distressing it is for a butler to have to listen to their after-dinner stories. His official position, involving as it does the necessity of standing with his back against the sideboard, makes a butler's life very wearing.' (YMS)

'The man's an ass,' said Lord Emsworth.
To such an observation the well-trained butler, however sympathetic, does not reply 'Whoopee!' or 'You said it, pal!' Beach merely allowed his upper lip to twitch slightly by way of indication that his heart was in the right place (PHW)

In stating that there is no anguish so acute as that experienced by a hostess who mistakes a member of her staff for a scion of the nobility we were guilty of an error. It is equalled, if not surpassed, by that of a butler of haughty spirit who finds that he has been calling a fellow-toiler 'Sir' (OR)

In the golden age before the social revolution, a gaping, pimpled tripper-over-rugs like this Bulstrode would have been a lowly hall-boy, if that. It revolted a Tory of the old school's finer feelings to have to regard such a blot on the scene in the sacred light of a butler (RJ)

'What would Phipps be doing, strewing five hundred and fifty-seven bottles about the room?'
'Butlers do put bottles all over the place,' urged Smedley.
Lord Topham endorsed this dictum. His had been a life into which butlers entered rather largely, and he knew their habits.
'Absolutely. Quite. He's right. They do, I mean, what? They're noted for it. Bottles, bottles everywhere, in case you want a drink.' (OR)

The butler gave the dog an austere look, as if he had found him using a fish fork for the entrée (MS)

A shadow flitted across Keggs's ample face. He was able to bear up bravely at the thought of Lord Uffenham, his circumstances reduced by post-war conditions, economising by living in lodgings in a London suburb, but he had never been able to reconcile himself to the fact of his lordship's niece soiling her hands in the kitchen. Though so much of his butlerhood had been passed in the United States, Augustus Keggs had never lost his ingrained reverence for the aristocracy of his native land (OR)

He took me right back to the days when I was starting out as a flaneur and man-about town, and used to tremble beneath butlers' eyes and generally feel very young and bulbous. Older now and tougher, I am able to take most of these fauna in my stride. When they open doors to me I shoot my cuffs nonchalantly. 'Aha, there, butler,' I say, 'how's tricks?'. But Jeeves's Uncle, Charlie Silversmith, was something special. He looked like one of those steel engravings of nineteenth century statesmen. He had a large, bald head and pale, protruding, gooseberry eyes, and those eyes, resting on mine, enhanced the Dark Tower feeling considerably. The thought crossed my mind that if something like this had popped out at Childe Roland, he would have clapped spurs to his charger and been off like a jack-rabbit (MS)

Beach possessed a rather attractive singing voice. It was a mellow baritone, in timbre not unlike that which might have proceeded from a cask of very old, dry sherry, had it had vocal cords; and we cannot advance a more striking proof of his lightness of heart than by mentioning that, as he walked home through the wood, he broke his rigid rule and definitely warbled.
'There's a light in thy bow-er,' sang Beach. 'A light in thy BOW-er.' He felt more like a gay young second footman than a butler of many years standing (SL)

Dunsany told me a story about the Troubles in Ireland which amused me considerably. Lord Whoever-it-was had a big house near Cork or somewhere, and one day a gang of Sinn Feiners rolled up and battered down the front door with axes. Inside they found a very English butler, a sort of Beach of Blandings Castle. He looked at them austerely and said coldly 'His lordship is not at home.' They paid no attention to him and went in and wrecked the place from basement to attic, finally setting fire to it. On leaving, they found the butler still in the hall. Flames were darting all over the place and ceilings coming down with a bang, but Fotheringay, or whatever his name was, was quite unperturbed. 'Who shall I say called, sir?' he asked (PF)

As a rule, at four in the afternoon he could count on having the hall to himself, and being able to scrounge his customary half-dozen cigarettes from the silver box on the centre table (SFE)

Like all proprietors of furnished apartments in the south-western district of London, he was an ex-butler, and about him, as about all ex-butlers, there clung like a garment an aura of dignified superiority. He was a man of portly aspect and prominent eyes. 'H'm,' they seemed to say, 'young—very young. And not at all what I have been accustomed to in the best places.' (U)

He thought nostalgically of his young manhood in London at the turn of the century and of the butlers he had been wont to encounter in those brave days. Vintage butlers who weighed two hundred and fifty pounds on the hoof, butlers with three chins and bulging abdomens, butlers with that austere, supercilious butlerine manner which has passed away so completely. Butlers had been butlers then, in the deepest and holiest sense of the word (RJ)

'Phoebe's marrying a butler!'
'Somebody's got to, or the race of butlers would die out.' (CT)

Outside, there had become audible the booming sound of a bulky butler making good time along a stone-flagged corridor, and the bullfinch, recognising the tread of loved feet, burst into liquid song (PHW)

Byng, Lady Caroline: nee Lady Caroline Marsh, dau. of the 6th Earl of Marshmoreton, m. the late Clifford Byng. Now chatelaine to her widowed brother, Lord Marshmoreton, q.v., at Belpher Castle, Hants (DD)

Byng, the late Clifford: wealthy colliery owner, m. *en secondes noces* Lady Caroline Marsh. 1 s., Reginald, q.v. (DD)

Byng, Reggie: s. of Clifford Byng by a first marriage, elopes with Alice Faraday to Paris (DD)

Byng-Brown-Byng: Terry Cobbold, Lord Shortlands' attractive dau., is related to this otherwise unspecified family through her mother (SFE)

Byron, Lord: (George Gordon, 6th Baron, 1788–1824); the holograph MS of his *Don Juan*, Canto 9, is acquired for a mere song. Collectors able to ignore the green goddess running up their legs and biting them may consult the same source for equally well-attested bargains in the matter of rare Burns and Browning items (BC) (*passim*)

C

C 231, P.c.: (old London City's favourite son); 'What means this conduct? Prithee stop!' exclaimed this admirable cop, with which he placed a warning hand upon the brawler's collar-band. Let us be brief; some demon sent stark madness on the well-dressed gent. He gave the constable a punch just where the latter kept his lunch. The constable said 'Well, well, well!' and marched him to a dungeon cell . . . (Newspaper readers of these dull and degenerate days may reflect that when an Earl's e.s. and h. was pinched for assault in those more colourful times, you got your full ha'pennyworth from the evening newspaper— *Ed.*) (DD)

Caesar, Caius Julius: (102?–44 B.C.); Shakespeare's tragedy of, is one of the three Sh. plays most often quarried for images and quotations. There is an exquisite example in OR of the point-counterpoint of Wodehouse prose and Shakespearian verse (the purple passage on the sheeted dead). Elsewhere readers are grateful for the reminder that, on Shakespeare's authority, Caesar habitually went swimming with all his clothes on (*passim*)

Caine & Cooper Ltd.: those (we imagine there are many) wishing to regain admission to Paradise (it now passes under the name of Market Blandings, Shropshire) will do well to approach this excellent firm of house and estate agents in the High Street. They will find its junior partner, Lancelot Cooper (is he a godson of Lord Emsworth's late brother?), a courteous and helpful, if somewhat dressy, ally (PHW)

Cakebread: name assumed by Viscount Uffenham as butler. His disguise is penetrated by that farsighted moll, Fainting Dolly Molloy, when she finds him burrowing under her bedroom dressing-table, his rear end sticking up like Pyke's Peak (MB)

It is never difficult to distinguish between a Scotsman with a grievance and a ray of sunshine (BCE)

CALEDONIA, STERN AND WILD

The fact that I am not a haggis addict is probably due to my having read Shakespeare. It is the same with many Englishmen. We come across that bit in *Macbeth* in our formative years and it establishes a complex. You remember the passage to which I refer? Macbeth happens upon the three witches while they are preparing the evening meal. They are dropping things into the cauldron and chanting 'Eye of newt and toe of frog, wool of bat and tongue of dog', and so on, and he immediately recognises the recipe. 'How now, you secret, black and midnight haggis,' he cries shuddering . . . (WEW) (No editorial commentary can do justice to an inspired passage quoted gleefully by Shakespearian scholars, but see **brilliant emendation**)

Do you remember McPherson at that dorm. feed? His food ran out, so he spread brown boot-polish on bread and ate that. Got through a slice, too. Wonderful chap (MW)

Scottish by birth, she had an eye that looked as if it was forever searching for astral bodies wrapped in winding-sheets—this being, I believe, a favourite indoor sport among certain sets in North Britain.
'Sir,' she said, 'there's a body in your sitting-room.'
'A body?' This Phillips Oppenheim introduction gave me something of a shock. Then I remembered her nationality. 'Oh, you mean a man?'
'A woman,' corrected Mrs Bowles. 'A body in a pink hat.' (U)

'McAllister,' said his lordship, 'that girl. You must send her away.'
A look of bewilderment clouded such of Mr McAllister's features as were not concealed behind his beard and eyebrows.
'Gurrul?'
'That girl who is staying with you. She must go!'
'Gae whaur?'
Lord Emsworth was not in the mood to be finicky about details.
'Anywhere,' he said. 'I won't have her here a day longer.'
Mr McAllister mentioned an insuperable objection.
'She's payin' me twa poon a week,' he said simply.
Lord Emsworth did not grind his teeth, for he was not given to displaying that form of emotion; but he leaped some ten inches into the air and dropped his pince-nez. And, though normally a reasonable and fair-minded man, well aware that modern earls must think twice before pulling the feudal stuff on their employees, he took on the forthright truculence of a large landowner of the early Norman period ticking off a serf.
'Listen, McAllister! Listen to me! Either you send that girl away to-day or you can go yourself. I mean it!'

A curious expression came into Angus McAllister's face—always excepting the occupied territories. It was the look of a man who has not forgotten Bannockburn, a man conscious of belonging to the country of William Wallace and Robert the Bruce. He made Scotch noises at the back of his throat.

'Y'r lorrudsheep wull accept ma notiss,' he said with dignity (BCE)

'I've just discovered the great secret of golf. You can't play a really hot game unless you're so miserable that you don't worry over your shots. You don't care where the ball is going so you don't raise your head to see. Grief automatically prevents over-swinging and pressing. Look at the top-notchers. Have you ever seen a happy pro?'
'But pro.s are all Scotchmen,' argued Barbara (HG)

'Are you sure it was his ghost?'
'Of course I'm sure,' said Lord Wivelscombe. 'Do you think I don't know a ghost when I see one? I've been psychic all my life. All my family have been psychic. My mother was a Ballindalloch of Portknockie and used to see her friends in winding-sheets. It got her disliked in the county' (YMS)

As the King stood sombrely surveying the garden, his attention was attracted by a small, bearded man with bushy eyebrows and a face like a walnut. Apparently unconscious of the royal scrutiny, he had placed a rounded stone on the gravel and was standing beside it, making curious passes over it with his hoe. The King had a curious feeling that there was a deep, even a holy, meaning behind the action.
'Who', he inquired, 'is that?'
The Vizier was a kind-hearted man, and he hesitated for a moment. 'It seems a hard thing to say of anyone, your Majesty,' he replied, 'but he is a Scotsman' (CC)

Tough eggs, these Scottish forwards. I don't know why it is, but education at Merchiston, Loretto, Fettes and such establishments seems to bring out all that a man has of boniness of knee and the ability to kick cavities in the rib structure of the opposition talent (MW)

'McAllister . . . I wonder . . . I wish . . . What I want to say,' faltered Lord Emsworth humbly, 'is, have you accepted another situation yet?'
'I am conseederin' twa.'
'Come back to me!' pleaded his lordship, his voice breaking. 'Robert Barker is worse than useless. Come back to me!'
Angus McAllister gazed woodenly at the tulips.

'A' weel—' he said at length.

'You will?' cried Lord Emsworth joyfully. 'Splendid! Capital! Excellent.'

'A' didna say A' wud.'

'I thought you said "I will," said his lordship, dashed.

'A' didna say "A' weel"; A' said "Ah weel," said Mr McAllister stiffly. 'Meaning mebbe A' mecht, mebbe no.'

Lord Emsworth laid a trembling hand upon his shoulder.

'McAllister, I will raise your salary.'

The beard twitched.

'Dash it, I'll double it!'

The eyebrows flickered.

'McAllister . . . Angus . . .' said Lord Emsworth in a low voice, 'Come back! The pumpkin needs you.' (BCE)

The Squashy Hollow golf course is one of the most difficult in the country. It was constructed by an exiled Scot who, probably from some deep-seated grudge against the human race, has modelled the eighteen holes on the nastiest and most repellent of his native land, so that, after negotiating—say—the Alps at Prestwick the pleasure-seeker finds himself confronted by the Schoolmaster's Garden at St. Andrews, with the Eden and the Redan just round the corner (PP)

My meditations were broken in upon by an odd, gargling sort of noise, something like static and something like distant thunder, and this proved to proceed from the larynx of the Aberdeen terrier Bartholomew. He hopped from the bed, took a seat, breathed through the nose with a curious whistling sound and looked at us from under his eyebrows like a Scottish elder rebuking sin from the pulpit (CW)

Across the threshold of this Eden the ginger whiskers of Angus McAllister lay like a flaming sword . . . Lord Emsworth wrestled with his tremors. 'Certainly, certainly, certainly,' he said, though not without a qualm. 'Take as many as you want.'

And so it came about that Angus McAllister, crouched in his potting-shed like some dangerous beast in its den, beheld a sight which first froze his blood and then sent it boiling through his veins. Flitting to and fro through his sacred gardens, picking his sacred flowers, was a small girl in a velveteen frock. And—which brought apoplexy a step nearer—it was the same girl who two days before had copped him on the shin with a stone. The stillness of the summer evening was shattered by a roar that sounded like boilers exploding, and Angus McAllister came out of the potting-shed at forty-five miles per hour. Gladys did not linger . . . With a horrified yelp she scuttled to where Lord Emsworth stood and, hiding behind him, clutched the tails of his morning-coat.

Lord Emsworth was not feeling so frightfully good himself. The spectacle of the man charging so vengefully down on him with gleaming eyes and bristling whiskers made him feel like a nervous English infantryman at the Battle of Bannockburn. His knees shook and the soul within him quivered. And then something happened, and the whole aspect of the situation changed. It was, in itself, quite a trivial thing, but it had an astoundingly stimulating effect on Lord Emsworth's morale. What happened was that Gladys, seeking further protection, slipped at this moment a small, hot hand into his. It was a mute vote of confidence, and Lord Emsworth intended to be worthy of it.

'Well, McAllister?' said Lord Emsworth coldly. He removed his top-hat and brushed it against his sleeve. 'What is the matter, McAllister?' He replaced his top-hat. 'You appear agitated, McAllister.' He jerked his head militantly. The hat fell off. He let it lie. Freed from its loathsome weight he felt more masterful than ever. It had needed just that to bring him to the top of his form.

'This young lady,' said Lord Emsworth, 'has my full permission to pick all the flowers she wants, McAllister. If you do not see eye to eye with me in this matter, McAllister, say so and we will discuss what you are going to do about it, McAllister. These gardens, McAllister, belong to me, and if you do not—er—appreciate that fact, you will, no doubt, be able to find another employer—ah—more in tune with your views. I value your services highly, McAllister, but I will not be dictated to in my own garden, McAllister. Er—dash it,' added his lordship, spoiling the whole effect.

A long moment followed in which Nature stood still, breathless. The Achillea stood still. So did the Bignonia Radicans. So did the Campanula, the Digitalis, the Euphorbia, the Funkia, the Gypsophila, the Helianthus, the Iris, the Liatris, the Monarda, the Phlox drummondii, the Salvia, the Thalictrum, the Vinca and the Yucca. The evening breeze had died away.

Angus McAllister stood glowering. His attitude was that of one sorely perplexed. So might the early bird have looked if the worm earmarked for its breakfast had suddenly turned and snapped at it. Blandings Castle was in his bones. Elsewhere, he would feel an exile. He fingered his whiskers, but they gave him no comfort. Better to cease to be a Napoleon than be a Napoleon in exile.

'Mphm,' said Angus McAllister (BCE)

The golden stillness of a perfect summer morning brooded over Blandings Castle and its adjacent pleasure-grounds . . . Gay cries arose from the tennis-courts behind the shrubbery. Birds, bees and butterflies went about their business with a new energy and zip, and even head gardener Angus McAllister was as happy as a Scotsman can ever be (LIP)

Callender, Alexandra (Sandy): this last, and attractive, secretary to Lord Emsworth has red hair and the low boiling point that goes with it. The hard-tried peer leaps at the suggestion by Gally that by supplying her fiancé with a small loan he can lose her services painlessly (GBL)

Cammarleigh, Sir Rackstraw: retired proconsul, barks at butlers, snubs his wife and tells the same after-dinner story four nights in succession before being permanently deflated. Res., 36a Park St., W. (YMS)

Cammarleigh, Lady: with good reason a pale, worn, little person (YMS)

Cammarleigh, Aurelia: dau. of Sir Rackstraw C., goes for a Mulliner's impression of a hen in a big way (YMS)

Canterbury, his Grace the Archbishop of: usu. in instances of the unlikely, but Connie's threat to retire Beach on pension would be, in Gally's view, equivalent to sacking the Primate (PP) and elsewhere we learn (GOB) that by getting the good man out of bed, or by going to Doctors Commons or the Court of Arches, you can obtain a special licence and be married before lunch (*passim*)

Cape Cod: Jimmy and Lady Connie Schoonmaker elect to honeymoon at:

> 'I know it well,' said Gally. 'Cape Cod, the Forbidden City' (GBL)

Cardinal, Joe: Cupid lays down his dart and uses the stuffed eelskin when Joe first sets eyes on Dinah Biddle. Their first conversation consists of twenty-two words, of which he speaks four (PP)

'Care of the Pig, On The': see the omniscient Whiffle

Carmody, Amyas: (fl. 1570); is given a silver salt cellar by the Virgin Queen for services rendered (MN)

Carmody, the late Eustace: his brother Lester regrets bitterly that Eustace did not live and die a bachelor (MN)

Carmody, Hugo: cheerful young extrovert with no secrets from his fellow-men, looks like a clean-shaven Laughing Cavalier. Son of the late Eustace C. and nephew to the present owner of Rudge Hall; ed. Eton and Trinity Coll., Cambridge. Partners his fellow Drone, Ronnie Fish, in the ill-fated Hot Spot nightclub venture. Appointed secretary to Lord Emsworth, steers clear of trouble by his masterly inactivity, and wins the hand of Millicent, orphan dau. of Clarence's late b. Lancelot, despite family opposition (MN, SL, PHW)

> Hugo squeezed her fondly and with the sort of relief that comes to men who find themselves squeezing where they had not thought to squeeze. No need for that snappy bit of talking now. No need for arguments and explanations, for pleadings and entreaties. No need for anything but a good biceps (SL)

Carmody, Lester: head of the Worcestershire family with roots going back 400 years at Rudge Hall, Rudge-in-the-Vale. All his life Lester has been saving up to be a miser, and ought in decency to subsist like an American millionaire on a diet of hot milk and triturated sawdust. That Fate should have endowed him with a complete recklessness as to the pleasures of the table is both ironic and indecent. An obvious candidate for Healthward Ho!, the nature-cure resort conducted by Chimp Twist (MN *et al.*)

Carmody, Nigel: holds Rudge Hall for Charles I against the wolves of the Commonwealth (MN)

Carmoyle, Sir Roderick, Bart.: see WW for full dossier. Rory m. Monica (the Moke) Carmoyle, sis. of Lord Rowcester, q.v. (RJ)

Carmoyle, Lady: Lady Monica Belfry, dau. of the late Earl of Rowcester, m. a premier ornament of Harridge's Stores, W. (see WW) (RJ)

Carnaby, Lady: makes a good thing out of her book of memoirs. So do Riggs & Ballinger (COJ)

Carricksteed, the Rt. Hon. the Earl of: when Hugo Percy de Wynter Framlinghame, 6th Earl, marries Mae Elinor, o.c. of J. Wilmot Birdsey of East Seventy-Third Street, New York City, the U.S. loses one of its foremost baseball fans, for scarcely has the marriage knot been tied than J. Wilmot is scooped out of his Morris chair by his wife and transported to England and exile, where he suffers the tortures of the damned at Lord's, the Oval and similar establishments (MT)

Carricksteed, the Countess of: see **Earl of C.** (MT)

Carroway, Lady: m. of the superlative April and (by natural compensation) of the catalyst Prudence (see WW). Res., Tudsleigh Court, Worcs. (YMS)

Carroll, John: the only Old Rugbeian in the opus, this beefy and likeable young man is a nephew of Lester Carmody (a fact most of his friends have agreed to forget) and cousin to Hugo C. An Oxford rugger blue, has been capped for England (MN)

Chalk-Marshall: family name of the Earl of Droitwich. For a theory on the name's deriv. see **Long Sword** (IWY)

Chalk-Marshall, the Hon. Frederick: a character of whom one instinctively feels that most of his music is still within him. Of this percipient Drone his b. Lord Droitwich, though titular head of the family, has often felt that when Freddie is around he himself is a babe in the presence of a veteran man of the world:

> 'Are you trying', asked Lord Droitwich, 'to tell me that a girl like Violet would run after a man like me?'
> 'Does a mousetrap,' asked his brother, 'run after a mouse?' (IWY)

Chalmers: family name of the Earl of Dawlish

Charles: most men who have not been christened Charles acquire the name on becoming footmen. We meet them wearing Lord Emsworth's livery at Blandings, Lord Wickhammersley's at Twing Hall, Glos., and (among others) in Mrs Steptoe's service at Claines Manor, Loose Chippings, Sussex (FM, IJ, QS *et al.*)

chasubles and the orphreys thereon: are the cause of the painful scene between two old school friends, Boko, Bishop of Stortford and Pieface Brandon, Vicar of Lower Briskett-in-the-Midden:

> 'Whoever told you you were an authority on chasubles?'
> 'That's all right who told me,' rejoined the Bishop.
> 'I don't believe you know what a chasuble is.'
> 'Is that so?'
> 'Well, what is it, then?'
> 'It's a circular cloak hanging from the shoulders, embroidered with a pattern and with orphreys. And you can argue as much as you like, young Pieface, but you can't get away from the fact that there are too many orphreys on yours. And what I'm telling you is that you've jolly well got to switch off a few of these orphreys or you'll get it in the neck' (MM)

check without mate: she proceeded to the butler's pantry and found its occupant seated at the table, playing chess with himself. From the contented expression on his face, he appeared to be winning (MB)

Cheever, Julia: sister of Judson Phipps and co-heiress to the Phipps suspender-braces millions (PP)

Chelsea, S.W.3: see **Budge Street**

Chester: an awesome, statuesque lady, personal maid to Lord Emsworth's elusive sister Ann (SF)

Chesterton, Gilbert Keith: (1874–1936) gen. in contexts of avoirdupois, but see **Sir Jasper ffinch-ffarrowmere.** Incidentally no writer (not even Wodehouse) has championed the pig species in more winning or eloquent prose than G.K.C. See his 'On Pigs As Pets' in *A Gleaming Cohort* (1926)

Chinnery, Elmer: American guest at Walsingford Hall, contrives to keep the fortune he has made from the fish-glue business, despite inroads by the platoon of ex-wives to whom he pays alimony. Elmer it is who provokes what we have always thought one of the neatest ripostes by a Wodehouse girl:

> Like so many substantial citizens of his native country, he married early and has kept on marrying, springing from blonde to blonde like the chamois of the Alps leaping from crag to crag. A large and spreading man, this Elmer, for next to wives he loved eating waffles.
> 'No ordinary purse', said Sir Buckstone, 'could stand the drain of what he pays out to ex-wives.'
> 'Not to mention ex-waffles, I expect,' rejoined Jane (SM)

Chiswick, the Most Noble the Duke of: the northern associations of the ducal family name of Bickersteth are apposite, since his Grace, we learn, owns 'half London and about five counties up north'. He also possesses the virtues proper and (who knows) causal to great wealth:

> 'A terrible country! Nearly eight shillings for a short cab drive! Iniquitous! Have you any idea what my nephew pays for this flat? What? Forty pounds a month?' (MJ, COJ)

Choole, the Rt. Hon. the Earl of: 7th of his line, is f. of the misguided Lady Chloe Downblotton, q.v. (MMS)

Chuffnell: family name of Lord Chuffnell

Chuffnell, the Rt. Hon. Lord: Bertie Wooster's old schoolfellow, his aggrieved stepmother and forebears are documented in WW. Res., Chuffnell Regis, Som. (RJ)

Church Hesitant, the: 'No chance of Bill Bailey becoming an earl?'
    'Not unless he murders about fifty-seven uncles and cousins.'
    'Which a curate, of course, would hesitate to do.' (SS)

Churchill, the late Sir Winston, K.G.: even that great man, in Lord Ickenham's view, might have been nonplussed if anyone came to him and said 'Jelly this eel' (YMS). Elsewhere we are reminded that there were things up with which he would not put (OR)

Clarkson, Ada: motherly person, once Eve Halliday's schoolmistress, owns an employment agency in Shaftesbury Avenue which secures Psmith as a client (LIP)

Cobbold: family name of the Earl of Shortlands

Cobbold, Lady Clara: prototype of what Aunt Dahlia would designate as that menacing type, a dog-girl, i.e. one who perambulates the countryside in brogues and tweeds with an assortment of dogs, meddling so vigorously in the lives of the peasantry that it is a wonder England escapes a Reign of Terror (SFE)

Cobbold, Lady Teresa: y. dau. of the Earl of Shortlands, Terry is considerably more worth looking at than her sisters, Adela and Clara. Slim, blue-eyed, fair-haired and bearing youth like a banner, she is the sort of girl at sight of whom strong men quiver and finger their ties (SFE)

COCKTAIL TIME: first published 1958. In it Lord Ickenham becomes Inspector Jarvis of New Scotland Yard, employing strong arm methods when impersonation fails:
    'It is madness to come to country houses without one's bottle of Mickey Finns' (CT)

Coggs: Lord Ickenham's formidable butler at Bishop's Ickenham is one of the only two beings for whom the effervescent nobleman entertains a wholesome respect. Has a full moon face and the eye of a discriminating codfish (UD)

Cohen Bros.: of Covent Garden, W.C. (see WW); Chloe Downblotton drags Claude to, to buy some civilised clothes. Another client finds himself unexpectedly the purchaser of a smoking cap, three boxes of poker chips, a fishing-rod, some polo sticks, a concertina, a ukelele and a bowl of goldfish (*passim*)

A good many dukes and earls drop in on the Cohen brothers when they need ermine-fringed robes to wear at the opening of Parliament or raiment suitable for the royal enclosure at Ascot, and some of the polish of these aristocratic clients rubs off on the staff of attendants. So much had rubbed off on their Mr Scarborough that he might have been the son of a marquis in good standing or of a particularly respectable baronet. He was a blond young man with a small moustache which would have interested Percy Pilbeam, that moustache aficionado, and his diction was pure B.B.C. (FA)

Coleman, Fatty: real-life brother-in-arms of Gally Threepwood. See **Pink Un's**

College of Arms, the: London E.C.; Heralds trace the ancestry of G. Ellery Cobbold (SFE). See also **Tan-Tantara : Whiffle**

Colman, Ronald: it wasn't; it was Oofy Prosser (MUN)

Connaught and Strathearn, H.R.H. the Duke of: y.s. of Queen Victoria, is alleged by the school sergeant of Sedleigh to have remarked ' 'Ere comes Sergeant Collard—'e's feeflee good at spott'n'.' (MP)

Coombe-Crombie: family name of the Earl of Dreever

Copstone, Sir George, Bart.: innocent cause of Horace Bewstridge's being instructed to play 'customer's golf' in the President's Cup. A tall and bony Englishman with no nerves, is affectionately known on American courses as the Frozen Horror (NS)

Corbett-Fitzsimmons Fight, the: the finer points of this historic contest delay Gally Threepwood's departure from a roadside inn when journeying from London to Blandings (FM)

Corstophine, Lady: adulated by overseas tufthunters as an exclusive hostess who is also a sister of the Duke of Devizes (PJ). Dines at Mario's with that other snob, Lady Vera Mace (BM)

Cortez, Stout: (Hernando C., 1485–1547); many, in the matter of breadth of vision rather than obesity, prefer Balboa (SFI)

Cotterleigh, Dolly: see **Dolly Henderson**

Cotterleigh, Capt. Jack: Irish Guards, see **Sue Brown**

Cotterleigh, Susan: see **Sue Brown**

Courier-Intelligencer, the: of Mangusset, Maine, goes to town in florid emphatics in its comments on the romantic engagement of Ann Moon and Godfrey, Lord Biskerton (BM)

Craye: family name of the Earl of Worplesdon

Craye, the Hon. Edwin: s. of Lord Worplesdon, a compulsive boy scout devoted to his daily good deed, sparing neither age nor sex (COJ)

Craye, Lady Florence: dau. of Lord Worplesdon. For the dossier of this intellectual platinum blonde see WW (COJ, JFS, MS)

Cremorne, Sir Roger: writes a book called *America From Within* after a residence of two weeks in that country (COJ)

Cricklewood, the Most Hon. the Marquess of: no-one under 85 is eligible to preside at a British electoral rally. As well as adenoids, he seems to have a potato of maximum size and candescence wedged in his mouth.

> I caught his first sentence, which was that he would only detain us for a moment, but for fifteen minutes after that he baffled me completely (U)

Cripps, the late Sir Stafford, P.C.: seldom given to impersonating a hen laying an egg (YMS)

Curates Open Heavyweight Championship: is won two years in succession by the future Bishop of Stortford (MM)

Cyril: knives-and-boots boy at Blandings Castle (LEO)

D

Dante: (Dante Alighieri, 1265–1321); had Montague Grayson been a, he would have written a new *Inferno* in which George Pyke, future Lord Tilbury, would occupy a position in the centre of the middlemost of the seven hells (BC)

Datchet, the Rt. Hon. the Earl of: thrown out of the old Empire every Boat Race night in his Oxford days (PJ); marries happily into the chorus (HW); writes gossip column for the *Daily Post* (YMS); heir, Viscount (Dogface) Rainsby (IJ)

Dawlish, 3rd Earl of: was Beau Dawlish of Regency days, under whose liberal auspices the family coffers first showed signs of cracking with the strain (UM)

Dawlish, 7th Earl of: performs the last obsequies at the dispersal of the Chalmers family doubloons (UM)

Dawlish, the Rt. Hon. the Earl of: the financial affairs of William Fitzwilliam Delamere Chalmers, 8th of his line, are in even worse case than those of his friend Spennie Dreever, and for the same historic reasons. With the exception of his other friend, Lord Wetherby, he is probably England's most indigent earl. Engaged to marry Claire Fenwick, he is, through the intervention of friends, appointed secretary of Brown's Club, S.W. (UM)

'Debrett's Peerage': first edn. 1790; Lord Ickenham occasionally reads, to get a laugh out of the names (UFS); a Mulliner's constant bedside book (MM); society beauties, listed in collateral family branches of, are eclipsed by the surpassing pulchritude of Vee Wedge (FM); Jeeves on the desirability of being in large print in, (RJ); (see **Tan-Tantara**)

> Reluctant though one may be to admit it (said Mr Mulliner) the entire British aristocracy is seamed and honeycombed with immorality. If you took a pin and jabbed it down anywhere in the pages of 'Debrett's Peerage' you would find it piercing the name of someone with a conscience as tender as a sunburned neck (MUN)

Dempsey, Jack: butler Keggs casually avers that 'there are no nippy welterweights to-day like,' and wins fifteen and sixpence when challenged on his facts (SFI)

d'Escrignon, M. le Comte: is Jefferson, e.s. and heir of M. le Marquis de Maufringneuse et Valerie-Moberanne, q.v. Working with moderate success as a writer of popular fiction, Jeff maintains a modest bedsitter in the Rue de Jacob, Paris (FL)

Devenish, Valerie: scintillating cinema star, as a modest offering to the great god Publicity acquires a puma which seems totally devoid of any news sense. Weeks go by of masterly inactivity. Then the animal suddenly strikes mid-season form. Having clawed the lift-boy, it bites a postman, holds up the traffic and is finally despatched in glory by a policeman (UM)

Deverill, the late Sir Quintin, Bart.: donates a village hall to King's Deverill, Hants., which does much to promote the steady drift to the towns (MS)

Devizes, the Most Noble the Duke of: for the apparent confusion over his Grace's family name (both Whipple and Stokeshaye have been listed) see **Augustus Whiffle** (now Whipple); according to Eugenia Crocker, is the Prime Minister's oldest friend (PJ); in Arnold Abney's less reliable opinion, is a most able man (LN); Res., Cleveland Row, S.W.

Digby, Mrs: Mrs Twemlow's opposite number, is the kindly housekeeper at Belpher Castle, Hants. (DD)

Dillingworth, Sir Ralph, Bart.: head of an ancient Yorkshire family which evinces those cracks incidental to the strain of the centuries, Sir Ralph's behaviour is odd. On his acquiring the Efficient Baxter as secretary it not unnaturally becomes bizarre. His ultimate exploit is a mouse-hunt in the drawing-room with an elephant gun. We are visited with the strange conviction of the ensuing sad scene—Sir Roderick Glossop seated firmly on the Bart.'s head as he calls for the strait-jacket (UFS)

'Diseases In Pigs': one of the battery of standard works conducing to the pre-eminence of the Empress before the take-over by the superlative Whiffle (SL)

Distressed Daughters of Clergymen of the Church of England Relief Fund: at a dance in aid of, occurred the momentous meeting at which that armoured fighting vehicle the future Lady Bishopess first perceived (hull down) her lifelong mate, Boko Bickerton (MUN)

Donaldson: the absence of christian names is significant, and shared only by the elect. Lesser forces of unbridled Nature (volcanic eruptions, earthquakes, hurricanes) are given names by which to distinguish their relatively modest achievements; a Donaldson needs none. We have the fixed impression that in the United States there is but one Donaldson, the casual mention of whose name sounds alarm bells in Wall Street, as once did the cry 'an Donnelach' on the Braes of Lochaber. Like other sons of Somerled (e.g. Angus McAllister) he is prone to react on the meanest intelligence (under-gardeners, and even English Earls) like a sudden sight of the Fiery Cross. Nor is it surprising that Donaldson and McAllister, despite their different status, are closely related and old Glaswegian buddies. Like Alexander the Great or Attila the Hun (in whom the prefix 'Mr' would be equally misplaced and with whom he has much in common) Donaldson is the founder of his own fortunes and destiny, and is First President of Donaldsons Inc. of Long Island City, N.Y. manufacturers of Donaldsons Dog Joy. It is through his kinsman, Angus, that he first meets Lord Emsworth in the Flower Walk at

Kensington Gardens, at a moment when that misty nobleman's affairs are entering a phase of peril and poignancy. For many, his outstanding achievement is the conversion of Freddie Threepwood into a solid and successful citizen. Of his consort we have (beyond their place of honeymoon) no knowledge, but evidence of her sterling character is latent in the attractive characters of his two charming daughters Niagara and Penny. After years of silence it was pleasant to hear (PP) that while staying at Westhampton Beach, Long Island, he is likely to perform the dance of the Seven Veils on hearing of Freddie's latest successes on the English market. The great man is still temperamental however, and liable to bark like a seal surprised when bathing

looks like a Roman emperor: has an aloof and wary attitude towards the impecunious suitor (PHW); has a habit of hammering on the conference table and shouting 'Come on! Come on! I'm waiting for suggestions!' (FM); is not a wealthy man; doubts if he has as much as ten million dollars in the world (BCE)

Donaldson, Niagara: e. dau. of the Dog Joy king, Aggie owes her first name to her parents' honeymoon at Niagara Falls. Weds the Hon. Freddie Threepwood, y.s. of the Earl of Emsworth, helping him to become an asset to commerce and the family. Foregathers with Freddie in the lakeside undergrowth (BCE); gets the idea at the age of six that her word is law, and never loses it; throws her weight about on occasion, but always in a fairly static manner; is the light of her husband's life and the moon of his delight (FM); now lives in connubial bliss and a bijou residence at Great Neck, N.Y., in a menage which includes the Cockney cook, Lana Tuttle (PP);

> 'Who', asked Lord Emsworth, 'is Aggie?'
> 'Come, come, Guv'nor. This is not the old form. My wife.'
> 'I thought your wife's name was Frances.'
> 'Well it isn't. It's Niagara.'
> 'What a peculiar name.'
> 'Her parents spent their honeymoon at the Niagara Falls Hotel.'
> 'Niagara is a town in America, is it not?'
> 'Not so much a town as a heavy downpour.' (FM)

Donaldson, Penelope: y. daughter of Donaldson, is described as 'a saffron-haired midget' She has her sister's strength of character, but this emerges only when strictly necessary. The picture is one compound of the warm sparkle and gaiety of an early spring day— as brief but as memorable. One could wish to have seen more of this complete and lovable young woman, but must cherish the vignette in which she joins Gally, Beach and the pet bullfinch in the butler's pantry on a summer's morning, rivalling the glittering sunshine with a glory of golden hair

has kept off fortune-hunting deadbeats ever since ripening into womanhood: is the divinest of her species: walks on the light feet of love: yearns to do a swan-dive into a bimbo's arms (PHW)

Donaldson's Dog Joy: it was President Roosevelt's New Deal that helped materially to consolidate the product's reputation. All over America, reported Donaldson—and England too, thanks to Freddie Threepwood's sales talents—dogs were now Thinking the Donaldson Way (PHW, FM, NS, BCE, PP)

Doolin of Mayence: (subj. of a Fr. *geste* of the 13th cent.); Merveilleuse the fav. sword of, (LEO)

Dore, Billie: chorus girl in the successful *Follow the Girl* at the Regal Theatre, W., is dau. of an Indiana nursery gardener. The genuineness of her blonde hair is equalled by that of her heart. Becomes successively secretary and Countess to the Earl of Marshmoreton (DD)

Downblotton: family name of the Earl of Choole

Downblotton, Lady Chloe: that sycophantic snob, Cedric Mulliner, makes it his business to discover that she is related through her mother not only to the Somerset Meophams but to the Branmarleys of Bucks., the Widringtons of Wilts. and the Hilsbury-Hepworths of Hants; moreover that her second cousin, Adelaide, is none other than the Lady Slythe and Sale, and that among other alliances of her family are those to the Sussex Booles and the ffrench-ffarmiloes—not the Kent ffrench-ffarmiloes but the Dorsetshire lot. Cedric therefore feels it an affront that Chloe should be seen abroad with one who wears tan shoes with morning dress in the Park. For all that, Chloe is a sweetie, and Cedric condignly gets his (MMS)

Doxology, the: unable to sleep, the venerable Headmaster of St. Austin's beguiles the small hours with the composition of a thoughtful article on. This is subsequently declined by a leading review, thus demonstrating that Providence is not incapable of a kindly intervention in human affairs. (The passage comes from Wodehouse's first book, published 1902, and may have raised the discriminating eyebrows of those who hailed an author of a different and refreshing kind of school story) (TP)

Drake, Sir Francis: had he been playing golf instead of bowls, would have ignored the Armada altogether (HG)

Drake, Sir Hugo: the eminent Harley St. specialist prefers golf to bowls (DS)

Drake, Willie: shows early promise of his namesake's pugnacity (see **Rat Face Blenkiron**) (BCE)

Drassilis: family name of the Earl of Westbourne

Drassilis, Cynthia: handsome and aspiring, with expressive grey eyes in whose wake the inexperienced swimmer, such as Lord Mountry, is apt to flounder helplessly (LN)

Drassilis, the Hon. Hugo: is considered by the family to have married beneath him (LN)

Drassilis, Mrs Hugo: querulous and snobbish, this indigent widow is surrounded by relatives with money, but can herself obtain it only in rare and minute quantities. Res., Marlow Square, S.W. (LN)

Dreever, the Rt. Hon. the Earl of: Hildebrand Spencer Poyns de Burgh John Hannasyde Coombe-Crombie, 12th Earl. At no point in its long history has the noble family of Coombe-Crombie been remotely guilty of parsimony. If a chance of losing money in the grand manner presented itself, the Dreever of the period invariably sprang at it with all the vim and éclat with which his Norman ancestors engaged Welsh marauders from beyond Offa's Dyke. The South Sea Bubble alone absorbed some £200,000 of good Dreever cash and the balance was dissipated to the last farthing by the insouciant peer of Regency days. When Spennie succeeded his father, therefore, he found about eightpence in the old oak chest, and even this under the fussy domination of an uncle by marriage. Res., Dreever Castle, Shropshire (GL)

Drexdale, the Rt. Hon. the Earl of: the American Bingley Crockers, by purchasing Drexdale House, Grosvenor Square, W., from this peer forty years ago, seem to qualify as pioneers among their many fellow-countrymen who have set Old Glory waving on all sides of the famous Square (PJ)

Droitwich, the Rt. Hon. the Earl of: the pivotal character of the novel **IF I WERE YOU** is Anthony Claude Wilbraham Bryce Chalk-Marshall, 5th of his line; a massive young man of thirty who, if not handsome, is at least clean and attractive. He finds himself the central figure in what (had it come to court) would have been without shadow of doubt the cause célèbre of all time in the matter of peerage claimants. Is a J.P. for Worcestershire and M.F.H. of the Maltbury. The principal family seat has long been at Langley End, Worcs. (Tel. Langley 330). London res., Arlington St., W. (see also **Long Sword**) (IWY)

Drones Club, the: Dover St., W. Since the list of fifty-three known members was assembled in WW we have been notified of the election of four new ones. All have separate entries here. They are Sam Bagshot, Austin Phelps, the international lawn tennis player, Judson Phipps and Tipton Plimsoll. We also include here those many Drones (e.g. Rupert Psmith, Freddie Threepwood, Hugo Carmody, Pongo Twistleon, Monty Bodkin, Ronnie Fish) who make sunny entrances on the Blandings summer scene. (It would be a rewarding exercise if some devoted pen were to give us a comparative study of the close relationship and subtle distinctions between the Drones and the old Pelican Club) (*passim*)

Drummond, Hughie: see **Pink Un's and Pelicans** (SL)

Dr Wilberforce's Golden Gargle: is swept shatteringly to the floor of the Bishop of Bognor's bedroom with a series of other bottles which include Scalpo (It Fertilises the Follicles) (MUN)

ducks: these agreeable birds act as a sedative in times of mental stress, soothing the soul and bringing new life and courage. Whatever earthquakes and upheavals may be affecting the general public, the duck stands aloof from them and just goes on being a duck (FM)

Duff & Trotter Ltd.: the West End's most eminent provision store occupies 'an island site near Regent St., W.' and connotes 'those human benefactors at mention of whose name every discriminating Londoner raises a reverent hat'. Entering the swing doors, the patron finds himself in a sort of cathedral of food, in which the Paramount Ham (the firm's most famous product) has a special shrine to itself. Most of the business being conducted over the telephone, one finds here none of the squash and bustle of baser establishments—only a sprinkling of duchesses with watering mouths and a few earls licking their lips (QS *et al.*)

Dunsany, the late Lord: see **Bird of,** also **Butlers:**
I am re-reading Dunsany. I never get tired of his stories. I can always let them cool off for a month or two and then come back to them (P.G.W. to W. Townend, 1928) (PF)

Dunstable, 4th Duke of: while lunching at his club in St. James's, rubs the nose of a committee member in an unsatisfactory omelette (UFS)

Dunstable, 5th Duke of: twice cuts the barbed wire fence separating his garden on the Côte d'Azur from the local golf links (UFS)

Dunstable, the Most Noble the Duke of: Alaric Pendlebury-Davenport, 6th Duke, s. his f. the 5th D, q.v. In youth conceived a tender if temporary regard for the then Lady Constance Threepwood—a friendship that still subsists somewhat fitfully. His Grace res. principally in Wiltshire, where he has a permanent lair, but inheriting in full measure the mercurial disposition of all the Pendlebury-Davenports and the impetuosity and hot blood of that ancestress (founder of the ducal fortunes) who could not say No to King Charles II, he is much given to billeting himself (no notice given) on a wide circle of acquaintances. His Grace asks little of life, save that it gives whatever he asks unstintingly, immediately and often. A convinced believer in direct action, can say it indifferently with either eggs or pokers. Is held erroneously to be even fatter than Lord Blicester, but few coots could have less hair than, and any walrus would be proud of the moustache through which he strains his soup. In short, an outstanding candidate for the attentions of Lord Ickenham when in Spring form. Educ. (extent unverified) at Eton and Cambridge, his Grace's opinion that 'all Harrovians are the scum of the earth and Oxonians are even worse' (SS) coming from such a source will be taken as a compliment by all concerned. Recreations: pokerwork, omelette (human var.) making, training racing pigs, and discerning signs of pottiness in most of his friends and relatives. Antipathies: nephews, male secretaries, Robert Burns. His Grace is unm. Heir, nephew, Horace Pendlebury-Davenport, Bloxham Mansions, Park Lane, W., q.v. (UFS, FM, SS)

Duseby: family name of the Earl of Bridgefield

Duseby, Lady Catherine: dau. of the Earl of Bridgefield, undergoes an injudicious infatuation for a roller-skating instructor (DD)

Dwornitzchek, H.S.H. the Princess Héloise von und zu: there is a certain melancholy interest in the character. If any writer can fairly be said to be incapable of disliking even the meanest of his fellow beings, it is Wodehouse. Sixty-five years' productivity is more than a long enough span on which to base the pronouncement that here, if anywhere, is a bad hater and one of the most tolerant of men.

His two principal biographers are agreed that even the unsavoury Wodehouse characters (of whom there are many) never undergo the stigma of obvious dislike or any more condign retribution than indignity. For me at least the Princess approaches—even achieves—an odium reserved for no other character in the opus. For once, the gloves are off:

'Why did you really leave home?'
The smile faded out of his eyes. There was a short silence.
'Oh, there were reasons . . . I left because I have a constitutional dislike for seeing murder done—especially slow, cold-blooded murder.'
'What do you mean?'
'My father. He was alive then—just. She didn't actually succeed in killing him till about a year later . . . Oh, I don't mean little-known Asiatic poisons. A resourceful woman with a sensitive subject to work on can make out quite well without the help of strychnine in the soup. Her method was just to make life hell for him. If you want to know her better, see that play of mine. I've put her in it, hide, heels and hair, with every pet phrase and mannerism she's got and all her gigolos and everything. Thank goodness she is—or was when I knew her—a regular playgoer, and she's sure to see it. It'll take the skin off her.' (SM)

E

Ebbsmith, Sarah Ursula: a supposititious, hurriedly conjured up, young lady, she occurs to the lively wits of a lover faced with the need for explaining why the initials S U E are found tattooed on his chest, following his warm attachment to Sue Brown (HW)

Edgelow, Mary: early friend of Phyllis Jackson whose home at Much Middlefold neighbours that of Psmith's parents (LIP)

Editha of the Swan Neck: heroine of a historic romance with the ill-fated Harold II of England. Like Editha after the Battle of Hastings, Otis is anxious to know what goes (UD, SM *et al.*)

Emerson, George: square-chinned, resolute in his devotion to Aline Peters despite her current engagement to Freddie Threepwood, this second-in-command of the Hong Kong police force announces his plans for her future over luncheon with her at Simpsons in the Strand, and carries them out in a matter of a month (SF)

Emmelines and Ermyntrudes: the, of the 'nineties, thinks Gala- had Threepwood, compare unfavourably in most ways with that golden-haired honey, Penny Donaldson (PHW)

Emperor, his Most Apostolic Majesty the Holy Roman: despatches his spotted and inconstant friend, Gessler, to govern the heart-whole inhabitants of Switzerland (WT)

Emperor Caligula, the: has a visit from the boys (OR)

Emperor Charlemagne, the: Flamberge the favourite offensive weapon of (LEO)

Emperor Galba, the: has ominous visitors (OR)

Emperor Marcus Aurelius, the: would have a hard time selling the idea that nothing happens which one is not fitted by nature to bear (OR); a primitive Bob Hope or Groucho Marx, given to throwing off wisecracks (RJ); some of his best stuff swiped by the unprincipled Professor Orlando Rollitt for his book *Are You Your Own Master?*, the Emperor's copyright having run out some time ago (CC)

Emperor Napoleon, the: might, in Mr Kay's eyes, have been adequate to be head of his house at Eckleton College (HK)

Emperor Tiberius, the: there is that about Uncle Donald which would cast a sobering influence even over the orgies of, at Capri (AS)

Emperor Vitellius, the: has unpleasant premonitions (OR)

Emperor Wilhelm, the: see **Kaiser Wilhelm II**

Empress Catherine of Russia, the: not everybody's girl (SFE, DS, SB)

Empress of Blandings, the: the lot of a conscientious editor who seeks to summarise the perfections, achievements and adventures of so superlative a being as Lord Emsworth's champion sow is indeed a hard one. Whiffle, doubtless, would advise one to begin with her breed. Let it be stated therefore that the Empress is a Berkshire, not (as depicted by some cover artists) a Welsh White or a Large White, nor (as shown by the B.B.C.) a Wessex Saddleback. There is no need to specify 'Black Berkshire', since Berkshires *are* black. Discussing the points of the breed, the *Encyclopaedia Britannica* states (a little unkindly) that 'the face is dish-shaped'. One may interpret this as meaning that the rather short head and retroussé nose combine to give the Empress an impression of mild and kindly interest—qualities in no way belied on closer acquaintance. To them one may add that outstanding characteristic of hers, an open and philosophical contentment with her lot and an entire willingness to endure what vicissitudes Fate may visit upon her. She may or may not be conversant with Shakespeare's works, but she obviously endorses his ob. dic. to the effect that 'travellers must be content'. She has endured kidnapping and recapture, imprisonment in a gamekeeper's cottage, in a rival's sty, in an admiral's kitchen, in a duke's bathroom, in a secretary's caravan; she has been conveyed, stealthily by night, in half-a-dozen types of vehicle, menaced by quantities of Slimmo, threatened with dieting and early morning gallops, even (by mistake) once almost entered for the Grand National Steeplechase. Once only in her long career has she caused anguish to her noble owner by going off her feed. This was when her mentor and guide, who had already previously deserted her basely for another, was deservedly gaoled without the option by the local Bench. And the only recorded occasion when her normally benign and equable nature suffered a temporary setback was on the morning after she had consumed the contents of a whisky flask carelessly dropped on her dining-room floor. Yet, mark the signal consequences: Lord Emsworth was on the point of sinking for the last time in the dark matrimonial sea when the obnoxious Huxley Winkworth tried to eject her from her bijou residence. Under the influence of a sharp hangover, she bit him. As a result the boy's outraged mother overheard the Earl telephoning the vet for re-assurance that the Empress was in no danger of infection. The immediate consequence was a complete clearing of the clouds. At one bite, the Empress achieved a rescue operation which had even baffled the resources of a Galahad.

Visitors to Blandings on open days will like to be reminded that the Empress's abode is reached by way of the drive which skirts the lawn outside the garden suite of the Castle. It passes a thick shrubbery and then curves past a flowery meadow adjoining the kitchen-garden. In the meadow is the Empress's modest home, adorned with the triple crown of three red rosettes, commemorating her three consecutive triumphs as winner of the Silver Medal in the 87th, 88th and 89th Annual Shows of the Shropshire County Agricultural Society. Her four successive attendants (Percy Pirbright, Edwin Pott, Monica Simmons and George Cyril Wellbeloved) not to mention her honorary mentor, the great Whiffle himself, are listed separately. A selection from her heavy Press follows:

is no razorback; tucks her meals away with all the old abandon; shape of—dubious question whether she has any; hoists in a spot of lunch and wiggles her tail with *joie-de-vivre*; schoolgirl slimness, undesirability of; familiar and penetrating odour of; attractive and amiable face of; room, her, empty and bed, her, unslept in; like favourite daughter kidnapped from ancestral home; speaks to Millicent in German; returns to the agenda (SL)

within liberal radius of her headquarters, other scents cannot compete; Lord Emsworth, draped bonelessly over sty wall, sniffs sensuously; watching her tuck into hash of bran, acorns, linseed and swill, her owner feels his heart leap like that of poet Wordsworth; requests a Fleet St. peer to pass the potato; resembles in the moonlight an outsize silver medal (HW)

mild and inquiring face of; is not singing or reciting *Dangerous Dan M'Grew*; utters low, soft, hollow sound on trying to reach potato which has passed beyond reach (FM)

turns ascetic and declines all nourishment after imprisonment of her keeper; still far from ill-nourished, resembles captive balloon poised for its flight; as nearly globular as pig can be without bursting; responds happily to master-call as advocated by hog-calling champion of Western states of America (BCE)

is engaged in hoisting into her vast interior the daily 57,800 calories laid down by Wolff-Lehmann; thanks Hon. Galahad with grateful snuffle; is not on the telephone; is solitary jewel in Lord Emsworth's crown; does not care for hurried journeys; bosoms of her friends, inspires brightest confidence in the; triple crown, her, unanimously awarded by three expert judges; is hymned in verse by Press; in a newspaper interview, attributes her victory to clean living; silence falls on sty of, so far as silence can fall near trough where she is dining (PHW)

is slandered by a Duke who calls her a bulbous mass of lard and snuffle; is offered for ransom to her owner for £3,000 (SS)

is libelled by Huxley Winkworth who avers that Beach is fatter; is ready to pose for photography by Whiffle; defended by her noble owner, armed with hunting-crop and hot with his ancestral Crusader blood; is nominated for Alcoholics Anonymous; is edgy and inclined to take offence at trifles; bites aggressor but escapes tetanus; lowers her noble head and gets hers (GBL)

Emsworth, 2nd Earl of: beard, a principal feature of, (HW)

Emsworth, 5th Earl of: a notable exponent of the minuet and gavotte in his day, looks down approvingly, from his portrait, on the complicated sidesteppings of the 9th Earl and butler Beach in the night watches (HW)

Emsworth, 7th Earl of: erects a little sort of Greek temple on a knoll overlooking the lake, in the days when landowners went in for little sorts of Greek temples in their grounds (SS)

Emsworth, Emilia Jane, 7th Countess of: closely resembled George Robey. Painted in the heavy classical manner of the period in the character of Venus (suitably draped) rising from the Cyprian waves, her portrait is immeasurably improved when the fifth of Clarence's six revolver shots is drilled through it in the portrait gallery in Blandings Castle (SF)

Emsworth, 8th Earl of: though seen only in the mirror of his family's memories, we have a surprisingly lively image of Clarence's father. A family man in the fullest sense, he devoted his energies to his estates in Shropshire, Sussex and Hampshire, to county affairs and to the upbringing of his eleven children. They in turn, if not outstanding in intellectual, professional or political attainments, are yet in their various ways a memorial to those traditional attributes of which he himself was a capable and (it seems) energetic exponent. He had issue: Ann; Clarence, Viscount Bosham (the present peer); Galahad; Georgiana; Jane; Constance; Charlotte; Julia; Hermione; Lancelot; Dora. The late Earl met an early and untimely death at the age of 77 in the hunting field
beats Clarence with walking-stick, consequent on paint episode: settles debts of £1,000 owed by Galahad when the latter's club venture fails; thumps table energetically with fist, preparatory to shipping Galahad off to South Africa for loving not wisely but too well (SF, SL, BCE)

Emsworth, 8th Countess of: direct allusions are scanty. Galahad, with better reasons than Beatrice in *Much Ado*, tells us that his mother wept when his father banged the table on exiling him. But if her records are few, her progeny are not. The bearing and upbringing of a family of eleven, and those including such extroverts as Georgiana, Julia, Hermione, Constance and Galahad himself, must have represented something of a feat, even for a Victorian mamma. For there were occasions, we learn, in that recalcitrant and perilous nursery era, when even governesses had cause to be grateful that fashion dictated the wearing of bustles (BCE *et al.*)

Emsworth, the Rt. Hon. the Earl of: Clarence Threepwood, 9th of the present line, s. his f. the 8th E., q.v. Ed. Eton. Lieut.

(ret.) Shropshire Yeomanry. A widower for many years, has issue 2 s., 1 dau. Heir, George, Viscount Bosham, q.v. An extensive landowner in Shropshire, Hampshire and Sussex and patron of many benefices. Is D.L. and J.P. for Shropshire. Principal interests, agriculture, gardening, pig-breeding. Has had several successes at the larger flower shows, incl. first prizes for roses at the Shrewsbury where he has also been successful in the pumpkin class. Even more successful at the Shropshire Agricultural Society's annual shows where his prize Berkshire sow, Empress of Blandings, has broken standing record by winning Silver Medals in Fat Pigs Class in three successive seasons. A past president of the Shropshire, Herefordshire and South Wales Pig Breeders Association. Club, Senior Conservatives, W.C.

So much for the biographical data. The character is more complex (inevitably so, with men who become a legend in their own lifetime) and should be approached with circumspection. It is significant that his christian name is unappropriated by any other Wodehouse character, and evident for many years that, for a worldwide public (solid in its preferences and acuity, however lacking in judgment or even accuracy) Clarence is one of the small handful of names marked out to perpetuate and immortalise the name of Wodehouse. Those who associate him only with a sense of vague and vacillating vapidity are deceiving themselves. Those who see him only as a fluffy-minded old gentleman do him, and themselves, a grave injustice. To establish first his physical appearance: like most of the Threepwoods (Galahad and Hermione are exceptions) he is tall. He is also lean and gangling and somewhat round of shoulder through leaning over sty walls, bending over flower beds and waffling over Whiffle of an evening. He is also myopic and pretty helpless without his pince-nez. And (an unmistakable trait) he 'allows his lower jaw to sag restfully'. His voice is high in register and somewhat querulous when he is harried. His shanks are long, thin and cumbersome, and are always an encumbrance to him in getting in and out of cars—even the imposing and antique Hispano-Suiza that Blandings maintains. On a railway journey they extend in all directions like the tentacles of an octopus. But those long legs can be stirred to speedy and decisive action when required. He is cleanshaven (save for the beard experiment which causes such anguish to Beach) and is fresh of countenance. He is a practised swimmer and (for he entertains frequent shooting parties) a competent shot, though not, it seems, so good with a revolver.

But though dim of sight, Clarence must not be thought of as dim of wit. Just as his son Frederick gave early evidence of a latent spirit of enterprise, so (for those with eyes to see) did his noble sire. There is nothing lack-lustre or apathetic in those who elect to take a dead rabbit to bed with them or who invoke paternal walking-sticks consequent on red paint episodes, or who are mentally equipped to think and act quickly on hearing parental footsteps approaching the stable in which one is enjoying, at sixteen, one's first purloined cigar. Clarence is no craven; nor, save by dissimulation, is he a nitwit. His is no penetrative intellect, however. His cerebration is not equal to producing a consciously reasoned judgment on his fellow beings. Yet for all that he can, and as often as not does, arrive at surprisingly accurate conclusions on them. He belongs, I think, to a group of mortals upon whom nature, in her bounty, has bestowed a kind of compensatory mechanism. To employ a homely metaphor (as Jeeves would say) there was a popular song emanating from the southern American states some years ago, one of whose verses ran:

> The butterfly has wings of gold,
> The firefly wings of flame ;
> The bedbug has no wings at all
> But he gets there just the same.

If one pictures Gally Threepwood as the butterfly and Rupert Baxter as the firefly, it may with justice be said that the 9th Earl's judgment, though pedestrian, is fully equal to the first and generally a good deal sounder than the second. He does not consciously arrive at a conclusion; his perception of the picture is hazy, but once formed, it is usually uncannily and demonstrably sound. Take for instance his encounter with 'the Girl Friend'. The kindly Gally would have chatted to her about her Drury Lane home, with many animadversions to nearby Romano's and Covent Garden, and strongly warned her to abjure tea. The firefly Baxter, like Connie, would have shooed her imperiously away. Clarence is much more discerning. They are virtually unable to converse, so divergent are their backgrounds, yet each recognises in the other a similarity of mental outlook, a bond of wariness towards a strange and unpredictable world, and within minutes they are friends. Clarence's eclectic ear ignores the Cockney accent—indeed he finds himself adopting it—and his astigmatic eye perceives in her no child, no waif, but a full-fledged, active, reliable, adult intellect with 'a face of wizened motherliness which in some odd way caused his lordship from the first to look on her as belonging to his own generation'. As indeed, through force of home circumstances, she does. A mother-figure therefore, who has not only just rescued him from a savage dog with one brief 'Hoy!' but who, it transpires later, has copped the tyrannous McAllister neatly on the shin with a flint, and whose admirable brother has bitten his overweening sister, Constance, in the leg while playing puppies. Such allies swim but rarely within Lord Emsworth's orbit, and are to be grappled with hoops of steel. Their signal, subsequent, joint victory over McAllister in the matter of the yew alley could patently have been foretold.

The fact is that Lord Emsworth can always rise coolly to an occasion. He does so with a revolver in the small hours; with a shotgun while hunting the supposedly crazed Baxter under a bed; with an air rifle twice discharged unerringly at the seat of Baxter's trousers; even (with some luck) in the triumphant sale of several sets of encyclopaedias to aid yet another girl friend. At such times he is capable of emulating the cool resolution of his noble ancestors on many a bloody field. But though not lacking in willpower he is by nature an escapist. He is also essentially a modest man with an ingrained sense of his own strict limitations. He can, and does, under rigorous pressure, occasionally perform public duties—sitting on a magisterial bench, opening a flower show, addressing a meeting of pig breeders, even attending the opening of Parliament. His reluctance to do these things is logical and born of the constant reminder that there are thousands of men far better equipped to carry out these duties and that the time thus wasted would be far more happily employed in the rose garden or at the pigsty. Of course he is right, but this is not the light in which the world regards an earl and a landowner. Yet, considering his background—a childhood dominated by a Victorian father in a family filled with a regiment of despotic sisters—it says much for Clarence that his personality has survived, and little wonder that his real qualities lie hidden and fallow.

Emsworth, the late Countess of: poring meticulously (as the conscientious biographer must) over the few references to Clarence's late consort, one is grateful (and not for the first time) for the comparative clarity with which a Wodehouse character can emerge, despite the few data. Our researches led us first to the office of the *Bridgnorth, Shifnal and Albrighton Argus* in whose pages (we were informed at Market Blandings) a considerable obituary notice had appeared at the time of Lady Emsworth's death. Alas, this eminent, influential and widely respected organ had itself succumbed, it appeared, to a takeover bid by the *Much Middlefold Visiter with which are incorporated the Rudge Recorder, Ilsworth Indicator and the Agriculturists' Advocate*, and its files lost. The setback, however, was a little compensated for by the reflection that factual details of birth and blood are minor matters compared with incidents which throw light on character. Vague the impressions must inevitably be. How vague, will be apparent when it transpires that the only references to the deceased lady come from her lord, the present Earl. From him we learn that, at the time of the birth of her second son Frederick, she complained freely about the rising costs incidental to childbirth:

'Oh dear,' she said. 'Oh dear, oh dear.'

It is deducible that she was as economical in her habits of speech as in her household affairs, never using three expressions if the same one would serve three times over, and that she was accustomed to express herself in a restrained and civilised fashion, without recourse to the current vulgarisms of the day. On another occasion Lord Emsworth states (not without a sense of wonder) that 'she got ideas into her head'. This is not without significance, despite its ambiguity, for students of the Threepwood *gens*. It will be salutary, though, to take a conservative view of the phrase, as coming from one who, in course of a long lifetime, is not known to have undergone the experience of having had an idea come into his own head. However, Lord Emsworth goes further, in stating that 'she imagined things'. Highly interesting, for the ability to form ideas and the imagination to cope with them are rare qualities in the Threepwoods. Perhaps we need seek no further for the fount of that business acumen which has helped the Hon. Frederick to become a high-pressure American salesman. Lastly we learn from the Earl:

'My wife, I recollect, used to speak of my niece Veronica as Freddie's little sweetheart, when they were both children';

and, careful to make it clear that this was no voice from the tomb, he explained: 'My wife was alive at the time.'

To us she seems as assuredly among those present as does, e.g., her lord (FM, NS)

Emsworth earldom, the: see **Threepwoods, the**

Erbert: potboy at the Emsworth Arms, is an advocate of *liberté* and *egalité*, though not so hot on *fraternité* (FM)

Ern: of Drury Lane, W.C., shares that spirit and hardihood evinced by his sister Gladys which is so necessary to the survival of Cockney waifs in Nell Gwynn's manor. Their *ésprit* pushes up Lord Emsworth's resolution to a point at which he is able to withstand a Highland charge and assert his own authority—er—dash it! As a result, Ern (who has no gouty tendency) is consulted on the quality of a sample consignment of port wine (BCE)

escrow: Freddie Threepwood holds the Pinkney necklace in, (PP)

Estapore, H.H. the Maharajah of: owner of the talisman stone brought to England for safe keeping by Col. Stewart (LS)

Euclid: (Eucleides, fl. 290 B.C.); nudges a friend and points to an example of length without breadth (UFS)

Evans, P.c.: of Market Blandings, like most rural constables, suffers from a lack of spirit and initiative in the local criminal classes:

> a man like New York's Officer Garroway has always more dope pushers and heist guys and Fiends With Hatchet Slaying Six than he knows what to do with, but in Market Blandings you were lucky if you got an occasional dog without a collar or a Saturday night drunk and disorderly (GBL)

Nevertheless the constable achieves the hat trick by catching out three successive generations of Wellbeloveds (BCE)

experto crede: So I strongly urge you, Clarence, old man (said Gally earnestly) to be alert and on your guard. Only ceaseless vigilance can save you. Don't let her get you alone in the rose garden or on the terrace by moonlight. If she starts talking about the dear old days, change the subject. On no account pat little Huxley on the head and take him for walks. And above all be wary if she asks you to read extracts from *The Indian Love Lyrics*. The advice I would give to every young man starting out in life, and that includes you, though of course it's some time since you started, is to avoid the *Indian Love Lyrics* like poison (GBL)

If your allusion is to the American poet John Howard Payne, sir, he compared it to its advantage with pleasures and palaces. He called it sweet and said there was no place like it (PP)

EVEN STATELIER

This brief survey of English country homes covers the entire Wodehouse corpus. It is of passing interest to note that their distribution by counties does not accurately reflect the author's own predilections for settings. Until his middle period the choice almost always fell on the 'Wodehouse Country' shires—Shropshire, Worcestershire, Gloucestershire and Hampshire. These necessarily still hold their place, but the inconvenience of having characters barred from being able to pop up to London and back the same day has for some years prompted him to choose settings in the home counties (and especially in Sussex) for many of the later stories. The pertinent fact remains that Wodehouse England is highly selective. The great concentration is in the Welsh Marcher counties and in Hampshire. Scotland and Wales are not represented; Eire has but one entrant, as has France. Yorkshire marks the northern limit and Somerset the western. Hants leads the list with 15 stately homes, followed by Shropshire (12), Worcs and Sussex (9 each), Kent (4), Glos, Herts and Norfolk (3 each), Berks and 'Southmoltonshire' (2 each), Beds, Ches, Dorset, Essex, Leics, Oxon, Somerset, Wilts and Yorks (1 each), with Co. Clare (1), Brittany (1) and anon (1), a total of 74.

Ashenden Manor, Ashenden Oakshott, Hants	William Oakshott	its incarnate spectre is exorcised by Lord Ickenham
Badgwick Hall, Glos	Sir A. Venner	
Barkley Towers, Sussex	Sir Mortimer Wingham, Bart.	
Beechwood	Augustus Mannering-Phipps	
Beevor Castle, Kent	Earl of Shortlands	one wing (now disused) built in 1259
Belpher Castle, Hants	Earl of Marshmoreton	held by the same family since the 15th cent. but mainly early Tudor. Open to public Thurs. only.
Biddleford Castle, Norfolk	Earl of Havershot	legendarily haunted by a Wailing Lady
Binghampton Hall, Sussex	Viscount Binghampton	haunted by the Curse of the Southern Counties and a clowder of Siamese cats
Bittleton Manor, Sussex	Col. Sir F. Pashley-Drake	haunted by the glassy glare of rows of stuffed gnus

Blandings Castle, Market Blandings, Shropshire	Earl of Emsworth	(see separate entry)
Bleaching Court, Upper Bleaching, Hants	Sir Reginald Witherspoon, Bart.	haunted at Christmas by a Giant Squirt and a Luminous Rabbit
Blicester Towers, Blicester Regis, Kent	Earl of Blicester	any other Curse would seem superfluous
Blissac, the Chateau St. Rocque, Brittany	Vicomtesse de Blissac	
Blotsam Castle, Shropshire	Earl of Blotsam	5 miles from anywhere, haunted periodically by errant nephews
Bludleigh Court, Goresby-on-the-Ouse, Beds	Sir Alexander Bassinger, Bart.	haunted by the death-rattle of pheasants, partridge, snipe, pigeons and sparrows and by the reproachful gaze of glassy-eyed big game in serried rows
Brangmarley Hall, Little Seeping-in-the-Wold, Shropshire	—	though exiled to the U.S. butler Ferris never forgets that he was once its major domo
Branksome Towers, Leics	Sir Redvers Branksome	
Branstead Towers, Sussex	Miss Cammarleigh	haunted by the indistinguishable spectres of Shakespeare and Bacon
Brinkley Court, Market Snodsbury, Worcs	Thomas Portarlington Travers	its ghost can always be dispelled by giving it a cold look and then walking through it
Bumpleigh Hall, Steeple Bumpleigh, Hants	Earl of Worplesdon	its chatelaine conducts human sacrifices at time of full moon

Castle Taterfields, Co. Clare, Eire	Donough O'Hara	
Chuffnell Hall, Chuffnell Regis, Som	Viscount Chuffnell	suffers a visitation by the devil in person (but see WW for details of attendant imps)
Claines Hall, Loose Chippings, Sussex	Miss Leila Yorke	
Claines Manor, Loose Chippings, Sussex	Mrs Howard Steptoe	tel. Loose Chippings 803
Cogwych Hall, Cogwych-in-the-Marsh, Ches	Sir Rupert Brackenbury, Bart.	
Corfby Hall, Much Middlefold, Shropshire	R. E. Smith	
Deeping Hall, Market Deeping, Sussex	Sir Edward Bayliss	
Deverill Hall, King's Deverill, Hants	Esmond Haddock	is awash with a surging sea of aunts
Ditteredge Hall, Hants	Sir Roderick Glossop	
Dreever Castle, Shropshire	Earl of Dreever	one of England's oldest inhabited houses. Early Norman, embodying some Saxon features, it is famous alike for its history and its ghost, whose details are passed from heir to heir on coming of age
Easeby Hall, Shropshire	Willoughby Wooster, Earl of Yaxley (?)	see *Yaxley*

Edgeling Hall, Tonbridge, Kent	Earl of Hoddesdon	
ffinch Hall, ffinch, Yorks	Sir Jasper ffinch-ffarrow-mere, Bart.	see separate entry
Graveney Court, Lowick, Worcs	Alexander Twist	suffers a sea-change into Healthward Ho!
Great Swifts, Petworth, Sussex	Samuel Galahad Bagshot	sold to Oofy Prosser, the unhappy mansion now houses England's premier collection of pimples
Hammer Lodge, Dovetail Hammer, Berks	Jonathan Pearce	
Hammer's Easton, Essex	Earl of Wivenhoe	haunted by a luminous pig
Heron's Hill, Sussex	Viscount Matchelow	
Hollrock Manor, Herts	Dr Hailsham	
Ickenham Hall, Bishop's Ickenham, Hants	Earl of Ickenham	houses a record collection of nude Venuses and looks like a Turkish bath on ladies night
Ilsworth Hall, Shropshire	R. E. Smith	
Kingham Manor, Pershore, Worcs	Sir Percival Stretchley-Budd, Bart.	
Knubble Hall, Knopp, Worcs	Lord Knubble of Knopp	
Langley End, Worcs	Earl of Droitwich	tel. Langley 330
Marling Hall, Shropshire	Col. Fanshawe	has a hot line to Blandings

Marsham Manor, Marsham-in-the-Vale, Hants	Miss Cornelia Fothergill	houses the Fothergill Venus
Matcham Scratchings, Oxon	Sir Mortimer Prenderby, Bart.	infested by a clowder of cats, a kindle of kittens, a Donnybrook of dogs and an anthropoid ape
Matchingham Hall, Much Matchingham, Shropshire	Sir Gregory Parsloe-Parsloe, Bart.	scene of the reunion of two faithful if fatty-degenerate hearts. Tel. Matchingham 83
Middlefold Hall, Much Middlefold, Shropshire	Marquess of Malvern	
Midways, Wilts	Eustace Derrick	
Milbourne Hall, Milbourne Bay, Hants	Col. Milvery	
Monks Crofton, Much Middlefold, Shropshire	Bruce Carmyle	is demonstrably not haunted
Rising Manor, Rising Mattock, Hants	Sir Leopold Jellaby	
Rowcester Abbey, Southmoltonshire	Earl of Rowcester	haunted by mildew, mice and the wraith of the Lady Agatha, proto-martyr of its dampness
Rudge Hall, Rudge-in-the-Vale, Worcs	Lester Carmody	its mellow Elizabethan brick walls have sheltered the same family for 400 years in the valley of the River Skirme
Rumpling Hall, Lower Rumpling, Norfolk	Lord Bromborough	beatified by the presence of the great moustache Joyeuse

Sanstead House, Hants	orig. Col. Boon; now Arnold Abney	declines into a private school
Shipley Hall, Tonbridge, Kent	Viscount Uffenham	its spectre is implicit: 'Roscoe Bunyan started as though the Shipley Hall ghost had confronted him'
Skeldings Hall, Herts	Lady Wickham	periodically haunted by a red-haired Jezebel
Smattering Hall, Lower Smattering-on-the-Wissel, Worcs	orig. Reginald Watson: now Sir Murgatroyd Sprockett-Sprockett, Bart.	
Sudbury Grange, Shropshire	Col. R. B. Finch	
Totleigh Towers, Totleigh-in-the-Wold, Glos	Sir Watkyn Bassett	with Aberdeen terriers in the bedrooms and newts in the bath, little better than a lazar house
Tudsleigh Court, Worcs	Lady Carroway	
Twing Hall, Twing, Glos	Earl of Wickhammersley	
Walsingford Hall, Walsingford Parva, Berks	Sir Buckstone Abbott, Bart.	rebuilt to the designs of the late Bart. in the Later Marzipan style, now gleams in glorious technicolour
Wapleigh Towers, Norfolk	Sir Preston Potter, Bart.	is dignified by that transcendent moustache Love-In-Idleness

Wapshott Castle, Wapshott-on-the-Wap, Hants	Capt. John Fosdyke	an ephemeral edifice, visible only to the eye of faith—apparently of the same architectural order as those in Spain
Weatherley Court, Hants	Matthew Burgess	
Widdrington Manor, Bottleby-in-the-Vale, Hants	Lady Widdrington	
Wivelscombe Court, Upton Snodsbury, Worcs	Earl of Wivelscombe	is haunted by a White Lady and a pink secretary
Woollam Chersey Manor, Hants	William Bannister	
Woollam Chersey Place, Herts	Spenser Gregson	its chatelaine reputedly wears barbed wire next the skin and kills rats with her teeth
Worbles, Dorset	Earl of Stableford	resounds to an ever-flowing torrent of verbiage
Wyvern Hall, Southmoltonshire	Col. Aubrey Wyvern	haunted by an adolescent butler and a pigtailed cook

F

Family Curse, the: years before, when a boy, and romantic as most boys are, Lord Emsworth had sometimes regretted that the Threepwoods, though an ancient clan, did not possess a Family Curse. How little had he suspected that he would one day become the father of it (BCE)

Fanshawe, Col., M.F.H.: speaking on the hot line connecting Marling Hall with Blandings Castle, adjures Beach to request Lord Emsworth, in his capacity as J.P., to come over and sentence a prowling marauder now immured in his coal cellar. So far it has been overlooked that the prowling m. is Clarence himself (PP)

Fanshawe, Valerie: dau. of the M.F.H.; Gally finds he had forgotten some of her finer points. In the best and deepest sense of the words she was a dish and a pippin—in short the very last type of girl to whom a young husband should have given his wife's Alsatian (PP)

Fanshawe-Chadwicks, the: Worcs. family converted to the Donaldson Way (BCE)

Faraday, Alice: Lord Marshmoreton's competent but ambitious secretary (DD)

Farmers & Merchants Bank Ltd.: Keggs, the Marshmoretons' butler, caches his not inconsiderable savings at the Belpher branch in the High Street (next to the Oddfellows Hall) (DD)

Farren, Nellie: vividly remembered at the Old Gaiety (DD)

Fauntleroy, Gladys (Toots): chorus lady who has no objection to letting the sun go down on her wrath when Lord Topham remarks that her new hat makes her look like a famous film star. It would have been tactful had he refrained from adding that the star he has in mind is Boris Karloff (OR)

Fawkes, Guido, e.g.: gloomily he took one last, lingering look at the Empress and pottered off, thinking, as so many others had thought before him, that the ideal way of opening Parliament would be to put a bomb under it and press the button (SS)

Fenwick, Claire: decorative but congenitally dissatisfied actress engaged to Lord Dawlish (UM)

Fenwick, Percy: ten-years-old bro. of Claire F. (UM)

Ferguson, the Rev. Cyril: has a cure of souls at Little Weeting, Hants., where he performs prodigies of valour on behalf of a damsel in distress (DD)

Ferraro: one does not turn the corner from Piccadilly, round the stately premises of the Berkeley Grill, without registering mild wonderment at the L.C.C.'s lack of imagination in failing to set up one of the familiar blue plaques to commemorate so many happy and romantic meetings in this room facing the Green Park. Ferraro, the Berkeley's celebrated head waiter, who was present at all of them, feels much the same (BM, Y.M.S. *et al.*)

Ferris, Capt.: assists at the ennui felt by Lord Belpher during the boring ordeal of his coming-of-age ball (DD)

ffinch-ffarrowmere, Sir Jasper, Bart.: All Baronets Are Bad, and some are worse than others. Sir Jasper, of ffinch Hall, ffinch,

Yorks, is a rarity—a Bart. who is not only not in the least bad, but does his best to appear very bad indeed. See e.g. **ffinch Hall.** See (if you can bear it) butler **Murgatroyd.** Yet we are left with the conviction that Sir Jasper, if called on to propose a motion that Things Are Not What They Seem, would carry it as conclusively as G. K. Chesterton did at a celebrated Oxford Union debate:

> 'Sir Jasper Finch-Farrowmere?' asked Wilfred courteously.
> 'ffinch-ffarrowmere,' corrected the visitor, his sensitive ear detecting the capital letters.
> 'Ah, yes, you spell it with two small f's.'
> 'Four small f's.'
> 'You little thought, Sir Jasper ffinch-ffarrowmere, when you launched your dastardly scheme, that I guessed your plans from the start. Give me that key, you Fiend!'
> 'ffiend,' corrected Sir Jasper automatically (MM)

ffinch Hall: ffinch, Yorks, as befitting the lair of such a Bart. as Sir Jasper ffinch-ffarrowmere, seems one of those gloomy, sombre houses that exist only for the purpose of having horrid crimes perpetrated in them. In one brief tour of the grounds one may note fully half-a-dozen places which seem incomplete without cross indicating spot where police found body. The sort of house where ravens croak before the death of the heir and shrieks ring out from barred windows in the night. As for the domestic personnel, it is even less exhilarating. Besides Murgatroyd, there is an aged cook who, bending over her cauldrons, looks like something out of a travelling company of *Macbeth* touring the smaller northern towns (MM)

Field, Sally: the hard-up chorus girl for whom Sue Brown sacrifices her job at the Regal Theatre (SL)

Finch, Lady Emily: friend of Connie Keeble and, not unexpectedly, a strong-minded type (FM)

Finch, Major R. B.: of Sudbury Grange, Shropshire, a friend of the Threepwoods (FM)

Fish, the Rt. Rev. Bishop: f. of George F. and uncle of the Last of the Fishes, performs George's nuptials. The prelate, bro. to that late ornament of the Brigade of Guards, Gen. Miles Fish, has evidently retired from diocesan duties, and signs (perhaps)+PISC. EPIS: (HW)

Fish, George: s. of Bishop Fish and a cousin of Ronald Overbury F. who is best man at George's wedding (HW)

Fish, Lady Julia: a dau. of the 8th Earl of Emsworth and a daunting member of Clarence's regiment of sisters, m. the late Gen. Miles Fish, C.V.O., Brigade of Guards, q.v. Although she is part of the general Blandings fun and games, students of the opus should re-read the passage (Ch. 6, HW) between Julia and her son Ronnie regarding the young man's matrimonial plans, where both characters are displayed rather more than semi-seriously and in marked contrast to the farcical note which, in fact, has already taken over in SL (HW, *passim*)

Fish, the late Major General Miles (Fishy), C.V.O.: Bde. of Guards, m. Lady Julia Threepwood, q.v. Issue, one s., Ronald Overbury, q.v.:

> Lady Julia took up her paper. 'Well, if you have no further observations of interest to make' . . .
>
> 'I have something to say', said the Hon. Galahad, 'which I fancy will interest you very much.
>
> 'That will make a nice change. It isn't, by any chance, that if this marriage of Ronnie's is stopped you will publish those Reminiscences of yours, is it?'
>
> 'It is.'
>
> Lady Julia gave another of her jolly laughs. 'It will be nice to think of you making some money at last, and as for the writhings of the nobility and gentry—'
>
> 'Julia, one moment. You are the relict of Major General Miles Fish, late of the Brigade of Guards.'
>
> 'I have never denied it.'
>
> 'Let us speak for a while', said Galahad gently, 'of the late Miles Fish.'
>
> Slowly a look of horror crept into Lady Julia's blue eyes. Slowly she rose from the chair. A hideous suspicion had come into her mind.
>
> 'When Miles Fish married you he was a respectable—even a stodgily respectable—colonel. I remember your saying the first time that you met him you thought him slow. Believe me, Julia, when I knew dear old Fishy Fish as a young subaltern, while you were still poisoning governesses' lives at Blandings, he was the reverse of slow. His jolly rapidity was the talk of London.'
>
> She stared at him, aghast. Her attitude towards the famous Reminiscences had been airy, detached, academic. The thought of the consternation they would cause among her friends had amused her. But she had naturally supposed that

this man would exercise a decent reticence about the pasts of his own flesh and blood.

'Galahad! You haven't—?'

The historian was pointing at her a finger of doom.

'Who rode a bicycle down Piccadilly in sky-blue underclothing in the late summer of '97?'

'Galahad!'

'Who, returning to his rooms in the early morning of New Year's Day, 1902, mistook the coal scuttle for a mad dog and tried to shoot it with the fire tongs?'

'Galahad!'

'Who . . .?' He broke off. Lady Constance had come into the room. 'Ah, Connie,' he said genially, 'I've just been having a chat with Julia. Get her to tell you about it.' He paused at the door. 'Supplementary material', he said, focusing his monocle on Lady Julia, 'will be found in chapters 3, 11, 16, 17 and 21. Especially 21.' (HW)

Fish, Ronald Overbury: there are specially likeable traits in this slightly-built nephew of Lord Emsworth, offspring of the late 'Fishy' and of Julia Fish. Ed. Eton and Cambridge, he may (in Uncle Gally's view—but it coincides with his own) look like a minor jockey with scarlatina; he may too be a somewhat tongue-tied lover; but he undoubtedly realises that in winning Sue Brown he has beaten the field and is about the luckiest man of his generation, and he is prepared (even to the point of really hard work) to go through hell and high water to keep her. He is that Wodehouse *rara avis*, a real-life character, compound of modesty, pugnacity, jealousy and enterprise, and on these and other issues is probably the best value among the younger Blandings set (SL, HW, MN)

Fisher, Mrs Bradbury: has never nursed a dear gazelle but (had she done so) her attitude to the animal would have approximated to that towards the butler Blizzard whom she purloins from an English duke and maintains at her palatial home at Goldenville, Long Island, N.Y. (HG)

Fitch-Fitch, Sir Abercrombie: member of the healing profession, shares a space of two-by-two with four other practitioners about half-way down Harley St., W. (FM)

Fitzgerald, Ronnie: is to be discouraged from giggling at a wedding (DD)

Flaming Youth Group Centre, the: after dining with a group of earnest friends at the Crushed Pansy (the Restaurant With A Soul) Lavender Briggs goes on to, with them, to see

the opening performance of one of those *avant-garde* plays which bring the scent of boiling cabbage across the footlights and in which the little man in the bowler hat turns out to be God (SS)

Flamme, la: continental dancer of Jerry Vail's (literary) acquaintance is discovered with a dagger of Oriental design doing its stuff between her fourth and fifth ribs (PHW)

Flapton, Ebenezer & Sons, Ltd.: printers at Worcester and London, Ebenezer and the boys are exhorted by wire to drop everything and rush another large edition of Sir Raymond Bastable's sensational success *Cocktail Time* (CT)

Flynn, Eddie: redoubtable pugilist, goes twenty rounds with Porky Jones at the National Sporting Club (SF)

Foliot-Foljambe, Sir Hercules, Bart.: a man so vast, so like a captive balloon, that Bingo Little feels even a woman so globular as his Aunt Myrtle, before linking her lot with him, would do well to consult her legal adviser to ensure that she was not committing bigamy (PP)

'Follow The Girl': George Bevan's new musical scores immediate success both in London and Broadway (DD)

Forsyth, Freddie: agreeable, if solemn, escort for Billie Dore (DD)

Forth: family name of the Duke of Lochlane

Forth, Lord Leonard: scion of the noble and ducal house of Lochlane, adds lustre to the family escutcheon at a period when a woman's reputation was perhaps at no greater a premium than now (see **Leonard's Leap**) (DD)

Fosberry, the Rev. Canon: respected Rector of Market Blandings, Shropshire, until his retirement when he is succeeded by the Rev. James Belford, q.v. (HW)

Foul Fiend, re-enter the: it was most unfortunate that he should have caught his foot in an unseen root, for this caused him to come out at a staggering run, clutching the air with waving hands, the last thing calculated to restore Veronica's already shaken morale. If he had practised for weeks he couldn't have given a more convincing impersonation of a Fiend starting out to Dismember A Beautiful Girl.

BLANDINGS CASTLE HORROR, thought Veronica, paling beneath her Blush of Roses make-up. MANGLED BEYOND RECOGNITION. HEADLESS BODY DISCOVERED IN RHODODENDRONS (FM)

Fowles, Lady Patricia: dinner guest at Belpher (DD)

Framlinghame: family name of the Earl of Carricksteed

Frampton, Mr, M.P.: representing the Bottleton, E. Division, does not intend to stand again, and who shall blame him (CT)

Frankenstein: almost certainly an Old Harrovian (LG)

Fraser, Brian: stars in the film **Love or Mammon** (LIP)

frozen gastric juices: as a schoolboy, Sir Raymond Bastable suffered from, as a result (it is said) of the too rapid consumption of seven large vanilla ice-creams at a sitting. Researches show the condition to be a rare one, few cases having been diagnosed with certainty in modern medicine. However Sir Raymond's case may be identifiable with a celebrated 15th cent. instance in which the patient (one Jack Falstaff) after compulsively imbibing some gallons of Thames water at Datchet Mead, Windsor, complained 'My belly's as cold as if I had swallowed snowballs' (CT)

FULL MOON: though not published until 1947, its first third had been written in the inauspicious surroundings of a concentration camp

> disturbed only by the sound of musical gentlemen practising trombones next door, or somebody else lecturing on Chaucer or Beowulf . . . All that I know of Beowulf to-day I owe to these lectures (PF)

Yet **FULL MOON**, with the Galahad-Plimsoll-Beach contingent engaging the Wedge coterie, is one of the blithest and deftest of the whole Blandings saga (FM)

G

Gaiety Theatre, the old: is remembered and chronicled nostalgically in many Wodehouse stories. Lord Marshmoreton e.g. says he never missed a first night there:

> Those were the days of Nellie Farren and Kate Vaughan. Florence St. John too. How excellent she was in *Faust Up To Date*. Meyer Lutz was the Gaiety composer then . . . Don't suppose you've ever heard of Meyer Lutz? Johnny Toole was

playing a piece called *Partners*. Not a good play. And *The Yeomen of the Guard* had just been produced at the Savoy (DD)

At the Gaiety, too, Wilfred Slingsby gives Prudence Stryker the elbow, receiving in return the flat of the hand (BC)

GALAHAD AT BLANDINGS: published in 1965 (precisely half-a-century after the first Blandings book) is as deft and polished as any earlier story, with the Pride of the Pelican Club back at the old stand as master tactician (GBL)

Gardenia, the old: Galahad, his mind ranging over far off happy things and battles long ago, recalls that the commissionaires there used to fight for the privilege of throwing him out of, and grows indignant at the suggestion of a modern parallel:

> What! That boy like me? Ronald, like me? Why, I was twice the man he is. How many policemen do you think it used to take to shift me from the Alhambra to Vine St. when I was in my prime? Two! Sometimes three! And one walking behind carrying my hat! How many commissionaires do you think . . . (SL)

Gally, nonetheless, is not recorded as having excelled Ronnie's exploit in taking on the entire waiting staff of Mario's (SL)

Garland, the late Sir Everard, K.C.B.: m. Lady Dora Threepwood, dau. of the 8th Earl of Emsworth; 1 dau., Prudence, q.v. (FM)

Garland, Lady Dora: of Wiltshire House, Grosvenor Square, W., is described by her nephew Freddie as 'not such a hellhound as Aunt Hermione'. But the difference, as we see it, is comparable to that between a tigress who is always ready to make an hors d'oeuvre course of an unwary traveller and a tigress who, having tasted human blood, will now eat no other. However, tigresses make model mothers, and when a strange young man rings up and addresses Dora as his dream rabbit, she knows precisely what to do, as he subsequently learns:

> 'Then where was Prudence?'
> 'Bowling along in a cab on her way to Paddington.'
> 'Why on earth did she want to go to Paddington?'
> 'She didn't. She was sent there, with gyves upon her wrists, in the custody of a stern-faced butler, who had instructions to bung her into the 12.42 for Market Blandings. Aunt Hermione advised Aunt Dora to wait till Prue had popped out with the dumb chums and then go through her effects for possible

compromising correspondence, and it wasn't long before she struck a rich lode—a bundle of about fifty letters from you, each fruitier than the last. Prue, grilled on her return, was forced to admit that you and she were that way, and confessed that you were a bird short alike on Norman blood and cash. Ten minutes later her packing had begun, Aunt Dora supervising, she weeping bitterly (FM)

Garland, Prudence: the relative specifications of pipterinos and dream-rabbits being, confessedly, obscure to us, it is perhaps enough to note that, before Grosvenor Square became an Occupied Zone, with Old Glory rampant on all sides, its appearance must have been immeasurably enhanced by the vision of this blue-eyed half-pint giving the dumb chums their morning airing. Prue's loyalty and resolution, too, place her in the forefront of the bevy of attractive nieces with whom nature in her bounty (perhaps by way of compensation for his sisters) has endowed Clarence Emsworth:

> The hands of those of London's clocks which happened to be seeing eye to eye with Greenwich Observatory were pointing to twenty past nine when the ornate front door of Wiltshire House flew open and there came pouring forth in close formation an old spaniel, a young spaniel and a middle-aged Irish setter, followed by a girl in blue. She crossed the road to the railed in gardens and unlocked the gate, and her associates streamed through; first the junior spaniel, then the senior spaniel, and finally the Irish setter, who had been detained for a moment by a passing smell (FM)

Garroway, Officer: of the New York City Police, is indulgent to two young men who are sharing one of New York's popular police cells; he is even more memorable for a three-word summing up of the peerage:

> 'The Plaza Hotel? And your buddy's name is Clarence?'
> 'Ask for the Earl of Emsworth. He's a lord.'
> 'Oh, one of those? Right.' (GBL) (CH)

Gartridge, the Rt. Hon. the Lord: deleterious effects of the mastication of tobacco in a school dormitory, on the delicate interior of, (LN)

Gascoigne: his stern attitude towards a defaulting nobleman (his employer, Lord Wivelscombe) seems to suggest his descent from that Lord Chief Justice Gascoigne who dealt condignly with a Prince of Wales. Gascoigne must figure prominently, too, in the annals of the

107

Psychical Research Society as one of the few who is tipped a five pound note by a ghost, and a moment later a second one (MM)

Gervase-Gervase, Sir Stanley, Bart.: see **Rosherville**

Gilpin, Alaric: between Horace Davenport and his cousin Alaric Gilpin there was nothing in the nature of a family resemblance. Each had inherited his physique from his father, and the father of Ricky Gilpin had been an outsize gentleman with a chest like an all-in wrestler's. Looking at Ricky, you might be a little surprised that he wrote poetry, but you had no difficulty in understanding how he was able to clean up costermongers in Covent Garden

Cast therefore in the heroic mould, Ricky, under the powerful stimulus of his love for Polly Pott, attempts the Herculean labour of prising money from his uncle, the Duke of Dunstable—a feat incidentally which only Uncle Fred, and he on one of his best days, is recorded as having achieved:

> the cosy glow which had been enveloping the Duke became shot through by a sudden chill.
> 'My cheque? What do you mean, my cheque?'
> 'For two hundred and fifty pounds.'
> The Duke shot back in his chair, and his moustache, foaming upwards as if a gale had struck it, broke like a wave on the stern and rockbound coast of the Dunstable nose (UFS)

Gilpin, Archibald: y.bro. of Alaric G. and nephew of the Duke of Dunstable (SS)

Gimblett, Lady: yet another tenacious tendril in the grapevine sedulously nurtured by Connie Keeble (UFS)

girlish sliphood: see **Nannie Bruce** (CT)

Gladys: Drury Lane waif; a visitor to Blandings Castle under the auspices of a charity organisation. One could call her a Dickens character and do her less than justice, for it was not in Dickens to portray a child who could stiffen the sinews of a vacillating earl, sharing modestly his victory over his own weaknesses, yet emerging lightheartedly free from any sentimentalising taint whatever. The result is surprisingly and tenderly humanistic, and as economical as it is effective:

> a combination of London fogs and early cares had given her face a sort of wizened motherliness. The type of girl you see in back streets carrying a baby nearly as large as herself and still

retaining sufficient energy to lead one little brother by the hand and shout recriminations at another in the distance. Her cheeks shone from recent soaping and she wore a velveteen frock which was obviously the pick of her wardrobe. Her hair, in defiance of the prevailing mode, she wore drawn tightly back into a short pigtail (BCE)

Feudal strongholds in the Welsh Marches have a full complement of heroes and heroines whose exploits through the centuries have enriched the pages of history. None in their way have excelled the shining courage and example of Gladys, who at thirteen inspires a noble Earl to assert his authority in the face of a Highland charge, and win the day against the odds (BCE)

Glossop, Sir Roderick: the eminent neurologist (6b Harley St., W., if you feel like calling) makes only one appearance on the present scene. This is on the Market Blandings train between Paddington and Oxford, where he is prevailed on by Lord Ickenham to carry out an examination of the keen-eyed, swarthy young man in the next compartment, under the implanted belief that this is that noble screwball the Duke of Dunstable. Sir Roderick m. (1) a Miss Blatherwick and (2) the Dowager Lady Chuffnell (UFS *et al.*)

Godalming, the Rt. Rev. the Bishop of: family connection of the Threepwoods and a guest at Blandings (SF)

Godiva, the Lady: trad. Countess of Mercia and the orig. strip-tease artist, m. the Earl Leofric. Of modern emulators see e.g. Prudence Carroway under Tennysonian influence, whose steed kicked her clothes into the river (YMS)

Goffin, the Rt. Hon. the Countess of: peeress in her own right; arrives on the Riviera (EBC)

Goldberg, William Farm: see **Pink Un's and Pelicans**

Gorbals and Strathbungo, the Most Noble the Duke of: details of the present holder of this ancient Sc. title are scanty. See, however, **Lord Ronald Spofforth** (DD)

Graustark, T.S.H. the Prince and Princess von: arrive at the Hotel Magnifique, Nice (EBC)

Great Neck, N.Y.: genned up as he is on his screen idol, Pauline Petite, Freddie Threepwood can assert authoritatively that she has taken a house at, (BCE); not surprisingly, he makes it his own future home (PP); Kitchie Valentine arrives from (BM)

Gusset & Mainprice: Tailors to the Nobility and Gentry, Cork St., W., keep the better half of *Debrett* up to scratch sartorially (MM)

Gussie, Lady: in the audience at the Palace Theatre, W. (TS)

H

H.M.S. Blotto: neither *Jane's Fighting Ships* nor (on inquiry) the Information Division of the Defence Ministry divulge any details of this evidently top secret vessel's existence. We have it nonetheless on a prelate's evidence that its name appeared on the headgear worn by him (in the guise of a Naval Chaplain?) at a fancy-dress ball at that dubious night resort near Walsingford-cum-Chiveney-on-Thames, Berks. (That the Lord Bishop of Stortford assumed the role from motives of the highest churchmanship we are in as little doubt as we are regarding that old priest of Dun Laoghaire

> Who stood on his head for the Kaoghaire;
>> When his people asked why
>> He explained it all by
> The latest liturgical thaoghaire—*Ed.*)

Hale, Mrs Jack: collateral of the Threepwoods, stays at Blandings (SF)

Halliday, Eve: dau. of an excellent (and therefore indigent) literary man, is singled out by the egregious Psmith for a lifetime's devotion. Tall, fair, 'valiantly gay' and intelligent, she is advised to marry 'someone eccentric', and does so. She seems endowed with those qualities necessary to one who must be prepared to assimilate the innocent effronteries (proffered always with courteous sincerity) which pop like champagne corks from the *arbiter elegantiae*, but does there, in effect, exist the flesh and blood that can face up to a lifetime of it? (LIP)

Hamlet, Prince of Denmark: the royal dramatist's sensational success '*The Mousetrap*', unlike its modern namesake, is withdrawn from production after its first night (UD)

'Came off last night,' said Burb., 'How long do you expect these charades to run?' (OS)

Hampshire, the Most Noble the Duke of: titular head of the Southbourne family, writes the gossip feature for the *Daily Tribune*. Putatively his Grace's heir is his e.s. Lord Bridgnorth, q.v., and the London ducal res. Cadogan Square, S.W. (YMS)

Hampshire Hogs, the: county pride in Hampshire swells in a crescendo, perhaps excelling even that in Shropshire and Worcestershire, q.v. The roots may lie in that homogeneity imposed on a county once virtually covered by the Queen's New Forest. Many fanciful if specious explanations, with apparent if erroneous etymological bases, have been advanced for the term 'Hog'. Few would accept the 'castrated male pig' though some offer the county's original wealth in wild boar as the explanation. Others (even less generous) derive it from an English perversion of the Dutch *Hogen Mogen* (their High Mightinesses) and still others (unkindest of all) prefer the dictionary version: 'a coarse, gluttonous, self-indulgent or filthy person'. The plain fact is that 'hog' is the historic Saxon term for an unshorn sheep (tup-hog, chilver-hog, ewe-hog etc.) dating back to mediaeval times or beyond and referring to the famous Hampshire Down breed.

As indicated in WW, Wodehouse has a personal affection for Hampshire as a variant setting for the Marcher counties, and it heads the county list in the Stately Homes section. Of the older families we have the Oakshotts of Ashenden Oakshott, the Marsh family (Earls of Marshmoreton) of Belpher Castle, the Threepwoods of Shropshire but with estates (and perh. origins) in Hants., the Milverys of Milbourne, the Twistletons of Bishop's Ickenham, the Hignetts of Windles (near Windlesham, and one of the county's finest mansions) and the Witherspoon line of baronets of Bleaching Court. The direct male line of Deverills of King's Deverill came to an end in the last generation but survives in the female line on an estate they have held since the Middle Ages. The Boons of Sanstead have also departed. The Bannisters of Woollam Chersey and the Fothergills of Marsham Manor are old-established, as are the Burgess line of Wetherly Court. Later comers (honorary Hogs in course of adoption) are the Crayes (Worplesdon) of Steeple Bumpleigh, the Glossops at Ditteridge and the Jellabys at Rising Mattock. But of particular interest to readers with a feeling for the English countryside are those incidental rural characters who crop up sporadically, and who are as indigenous to the county as Hampshire oak or Hampshire chalk

Harchester College: founded from motives of piety (and/or conscience) by Henry VII, c. 1495. That it might one day produce such by-products as the Bishop of Stortford, the Rev. Trevor (Catsmeat) Entwistle or Lord Hemel of Hempstead might have given the royal founder profoundly to think. It is when the school's governing body decide to give Fatty Hemel a statue that those temptations are presented to which greater churchmen have yielded than Boko Stortford and the Vicar of Lower Briskett-in-the-Midden (MM)

Harley St., W.: (where every door has burst out into a sort of eczema of brass plates) numbers, among its medicine men, e.g., E. Jimpson Murgatroyd (qualified to banish pink patches from the chests of young Americans), Sir Abercrombie Fitch-Fitch and his four merry messmates, and at No. 6b the beetling figure of that eminent witch-doctor Sir Roderick Glossop. All may be consulted herein under their own brass plates (the last with caution—clients are advised to take their own strait-jackets) (*passim*)

Hartley-Wesping, Sir Sutton, Bart.: had had a pretty good afternoon. Like all baronets who attend society wedding receptions he had been going round the various tables since his arrival, pocketing here a fish-slice, there a jewelled egg-boiler, until now he had taken on about all the cargo his tonnage could warrant, and was thinking of strolling off to the pawn-broker's in the Euston Road, with whom he did most of his business (MUN)

Harvest, Geoffrey: once fleetingly engaged to Terry Cobbold q.v., is that ultimate in tickdom, *pediculus oleacus, var. Hollywoodensis*. Terry's final disillusionment is 'like being skinned alive in front of an amused audience' (SFE)

Hastings, Macdonald: last Editor of *The Strand*: See **Pink Un's**

Havant, her Grace the Duchess of: the slight chagrin of, on disappearance of the ducal diamonds (GL)

Havershot, the Rt. Hon. the Earl of: Reginald John Peter Swithin finds himself unexpectedly the 3rd Earl (see **Tan-Tantara**). Despatched to Hollywood to rescue a cousin from a romantic entanglement, Reggie himself becomes involved in a psychical one. Res., Biddleford Castle, Norfolk (LG)

Hayling, Lord Arthur: better known to many as Assiduous Willie, aspires to the hand of Betty Silver (PB)

Heacham, the Rt. Hon. the Viscount: eligible if haughty neighbour of the Threepwoods of Blandings, has no advice to offer on pining pigs and little sympathy for their owner—shortcomings which prove costly in his approaches to Lord Emsworth's niece, Angela (BCE)

HEAVY WEATHER: published 1933, is the sequel to SL. The story flows like an iridescent spring; yet mark the understatements in the author's own comments:

> I have been sweating at **HEAVY WEATHER,** and must be getting a little stale . . . It's a curious thing about this novel, and probably means that it's going to be good, but I must have written at least 200,000 words so far. I kept getting dissatisfied with the first 30,000 words and starting again. All up to page 254 now looks all right. It really reads as if I'd written it straight off without a pause (PF)

hedgehog poisoning: medical case-history records; see **Freddie Potts**

Hemel of Hempstead, the Rt. Hon. Lord: the decision to honour, with a statue in the grounds of his old school, surprises those who recollect his former proficiency with inky darts and his glue-like laugh, and causes certain of them to take steps to palliate the threat (MM)

Henderson, Dolly: we never meet in the flesh the girl who married Jack Cotterleigh of the Irish Guards and who became the mother of the nice Sue Brown, but in the imagination induced by others' memories we see and hear her clearly as, dressed either in pink satin and flesh-coloured tights, or in the full Edwardian treatment, she carries the house in one of those jolly, full-blooded songs at the Tivoli, the Old Oxford and other homes of late Victorian vaudeville:

> London is full of elderly gentlemen who become pleasantly maudlin when they think of Dolly Henderson and the dear old days when the heart was young and they had waists (SL)

Even Lord Emsworth (who doesn't remember many things) when told the identity of Sue Brown, pays a speaking tribute:

> 'I can remember her mother. Galahad took me to the Tivoli once when she was singing there. A little bit of a thing in pink tights, with the jolliest smile you ever saw. Made you think of spring mornings. The gallery joined in the chorus, I recollect. Bless my soul, how did it go? Tum-tum tumpty-tum . . . or was it Umpty tiddly tiddly pum?' (HW)

Gally himself goes almost out of character at those moments when he remembers her as the only woman he really loved. It is the concealed playwright in Wodehouse who ensures that, coming from Galahad, the confession is the more surely authentic because made to an unsympathetic audience:

'Your attitude about young Sue infuriates me.'

'Tell me, Gally,' said his sister, 'just as a matter of interest, is she your daughter?'

The Hon. Galahad bristled. 'She is not. Her father was a man in the Irish Guards named Cotterleigh. He and Dolly were married when I was in South Africa.' He stood for a moment, his mind in the past. 'Fellow told me about it quite casually one day when I was having a drink in a Johannesburg bar . . . Out of a blue sky . . .'

So Gally in 1933 (HW). A generation later, traces of sentiment in a Wodehouse plot are rare indeed, yet it is right that in GBL (1965) Gally can muse:

> Odd, how he could still have that choked up feeling when he thought of her. Oh well, what had happened had probably been all for the best. Pretty rough it would have been for a nice girl like Dolly to be tied up with a chap like him . . . His sisters had often spoken of him as a waster, and how right they were. His disposition was genial, he made friends easily, and as far as he could recall he had never let a pal down, but you couldn't claim that as a life partner he was everybody's cup of tea. And people who knew them had described Dolly and Jack as a happy and devoted couple, so what was there to get all wistful and dreary about?

Hilsbury-Hepworths, the: a family pre-destined to inherit large fawnlike eyes, though Horace Davenport (whose mother was one) does not find them effective in mitigating the hand of justice when he stands in the Marlborough St. dock UFS)

Hoddesdon, the Rt. Hon. the Earl of: George Brent, 6th holder of the title, is distinguished, impecunious, a snob and a bore. To his salutory and frequent discomfiture he is also bro. to the equally unenthralling Vera Mace. Heir, Viscount Biskerton. Res., Edgeling Court, Kent. See also **Ask Lock** and **Loyal Royal Worcesters** (BM *et al.*)

Holbeton, the late Lord: co-founder of that celebrated food shrine Duff & Trotter Ltd., of which he formed the second (or pedal) half. Cr. 1st Baron (QS)

Holbeton, the Rt. Hon. Lord: 2nd B., a svelte and willowy young man with delicate good looks and a penchant for singing songs like *Trees* in a quivery tenor, extracting the last drop of syrup from both words and air. Such gifts tend to cloy—in Sally Fairmile's case about two days after their engagement:

'Watch that Adam's apple', advised Joss, 'and in the privacy of your chamber reflect what it would be like to spend the remainder of your life with it' (QS)

Holborn Viaduct Cabin, the: London E.C. lunchtime rendezvous for the future Lord Tilbury in his milk-and-bath-bun youth. Here he meets and woos Lucy Maynard—now referred to (if at all) as 'poor Lucy' (BC)

Holmes, Sherlock: most refs. stress his astringent dexterity. In YMS he finds himself (to his presumable surprise) coupled with Lord Peter Wimsey, q.v.

'Home Gossip': a publication which is all brown paper patterns and advice to the lovelorn, with a duke or an earl to every short story (SF)

Honourables: the shocking treatment of, see **Tan-Tantara**

Horatius, brave: (Publius Horatius Cocles, fl. c. 510 B.C.); famous international bridge expert (originated the Single Defence Theory) and inventor of the One Way Traffic System. A putative victim of the anticlimax bug (see **Ob. Dic.**)

Hungerford: family name of the Duke of Ramfurline

Hungerford, Lord Alastair: undertakes a delicate mission to Sir Roderick Glossop, who confides:

> 'His Grace, he informed me, had exhibited a renewal of the symptoms which have been causing the family so much concern.'
> 'So the Duke is off his rocker, what?'
> 'The expression is not precisely the one I should have employed myself with reference to the head of perhaps the noblest family in England, but there is no doubt that cerebral excitement does, as you suggest, exist in no small degree' (IJ)

Hunstanton, the Most Hon. the Marquess of: Sigsbee H. Waddington's terse view of this starchy and monocled sprig of nobility—a pieface—seems charitable. His opinion that they wouldn't stand for him in Arizona, no, sirree, would appear reasonable. His further supposition that in that western state hydrophobia-infected skunks would be inserted in his Most Honourable bed is (if colourful) a tenable theory (SB)

Hyde Park, W.: its many refs. range from the tranquillising influence of its ducks (FM) to the reverse effect of its orators on a noble lord (IJ). One does not pass a certain Knightsbridge hotel without remembering the solemn warning:

'Once past the Park Hotel and you're in the desert' (FM)
but Lord Bittlesham, who summed things up with

'Now the Empire isn't the place it was, I always think the Park
on Sunday is the centre of London' (IJ)

meant no reflection on the imperial theme, though speaking more
wisely than he knew

I

Ibsen, Henrik: (1828–1906); Millicent Threepwood, caught in the
toils of the laughing love god with Hugo Carmody, looks like something that might have occurred to, in one of his less frivolous
moments (SL)

Ickenham, 2nd Earl of: devotee of art in the broader sense, filled
Ickenham Hall and its grounds with statuary:

'Home isn't home', he was wont to say, running a thoughtful
hand through his whiskers, 'without plenty of nude Venuses'

Consequently the Hall and policies are reminiscent of a Turkish
bath on ladies' night (UD)

Ickenham, 3rd Earl of: gave his sons sound advice:

'Never put anything on paper, my boy, and never trust a man
with a small, black moustache' (CT)

Ickenham, 4th Earl of: e.s. of the 3rd E., died in middle life and
was s. by his bro. the 5th and present E. (CT)

Ickenham, the Rt. Hon. the Earl of: Frederick Altamont
Cornwallis Twistleton, 5th of his line, is y.s. of the 3rd E. and
succeeded on his brother's death after a varied and adventurous
career, principally in the western states of America. Shipped overseas in youth like his friend (though they nowhere appear together)
Galahad Threepwood, he worked in turn as cow-puncher, soda-
jerker, journalist and prospector. The life induced a liberal increase
in both his humanism and his innately philosophical outlook. It
probably intensified too the resolve (which he has always sedulously
fed) never to be bored, and sharpened to a fine point his talent for
stirring things up. The daily press and public have never for long
been unaware of his robust and ebullient spirit (far surpassing the
merely eccentric) which doubtless stemmed from that seething
nursery of ebullience, the London of Romans, Pink Un's and
Pelicans. In those days the Metropolis did not so much swing as take
wing. In later years this tendency towards free enterprise developed
in Uncle Fred an empyrean eye for opportunities to step high, wide

and handsome (especially on others' preserves) whilst simultaneously spreading his own version of sweetness and light on all sides. This quality is the hallmark of the character, drawing the admiration and affection of thousands of readers including, e.g., that discerning judge Hilaire Belloc (see introduction to WEW). Some have felt regret that Lord Ickenham's occasions for enterprise have been curtailed by his marriage to his much cherished Jane; others, and with reason, feel that only some such brake has delayed a 6th Earl from stepping into his shoes. Devotees may be interested to compare the means by which he gains his light-spreading ends—effrontery, provocation, 'buzzing' talk, bogus impersonation, charm and the instant imagination necessary to handle crises as they occur—with those of Gally Threepwood, to whom time and experience have imparted methods which more approximate to those of the chess-board. Had he (which heaven forfend) never appeared again, Fred Ickenham would live in fame as the central character of that classic short story (one of the funniest in English literature) *Uncle Fred Flits By* (YMS).

His author thinks of him as 'a sort of elderly Psmith' (PF). Usborne devotes a lively short chapter to him, noting his service in the Hampshire Home Guard in the last war and observing that, had the invasion happened, he would have been 'a baffling underground fighter in the English Resistance'. French thinks the mercurial peer deserves his own background and subordinate characters, and that we should now be given the full facts about that intriguing visit to the dog races (PGW). And the present editor, looking back with nostalgia to the superb uncle-nephew comedy element of the Ben Travers series of farces, has long felt it one of the compensations for living in the 20th century that Wodehouse should have been inspired to his own, very individual exercises on the same theme, and a resounding proof that good fairies do after all exist.

The present Ickenham line of earls is a revived one. Several members of the original line (see e.g. **King Richard I**) distinguished them-selves (or otherwise) in the Crusades and the French wars. Lord Ickenham's country seat (he is not allowed a town address) is Ickenham Hall, Bishop's Ickenham, Hants., a manor originally granted to the Bishops of Winchester. If you go by rail (UD) you leave the main line at Wockley Junction and take the branch line via Eggmarsh St. John, Ashendon Oakshott and Bishop's Ickenham. (YMS, UFS, UD, CT, SS)

> A tall, slim, distinguished-looking man with an alert and enterprising eye . . . Just as the years had failed to deprive him of his slender figure, so had they been impotent to quench his

indomitable spirit. Together with a juvenile waistline he still retained the fresh, unspoiled outlook of a slightly inebriated undergraduate, though to catch him at his best, as he would have been the first to admit, you had to catch him in London (UFS)

When pleasing inspirations float into Lord Ickenham's mind, prudent men make for the nearest bombproof shelter (UD)

Ickenham, the Countess of: of American birth, Jane (née Bastable) is a half-sister of that ornament of the law, Sir Raymond Bastable, Q.C. Though remaining ever offstage, Jane's character is positive enough for us to endorse the spirit of Lord Ickenham's opinion that she is probably 'the sweetest thing who ever murmured "Yes" to a clergyman's "Wilt thou, Jane…?"' She is also one of the most sorely tried. Her own original doubts about her ability to control hot springs, avalanches and earthquakes are evidenced by her lord's admission that she broke off their engagement no fewer than six times before the congregation was eventually allowed to bend a reverent gaze upon the soles of his wedding shoes. The marriage's success is her own achievement. By assuming control of the family budget, by restricting Fred's visits to the Metrop. to two per annum ceaseless vigilance and a good stock of blunt knives for skinning purposes, Jane Ickenham has effected a balance of power generally regarded as miraculous (UFS, UD, CT)

Ickenham System, the: coupled with advice 'to all young men to marry a girl whom they can tickle', is claimed by its sponsor as 100% successful—in certain cases. The Editor therefore disclaims all responsibility for such torts or malfeasances or actions for civil damages, *lis pendens* and even *pendente lite*, as may ensue upon the adoption of the System, confining himself to the terms of the claim (*parri passu* and *ad rem*) of its originator:

What you must do is stride up to the girl and grab her by the wrist. Ignoring her struggles, clasp her to your bosom and shower kisses on her upturned face. You needn't say much. Just 'My mate!' or something of that sort. I can assure you that this system will bring home the bacon. Oh, by the way, in grabbing the subject by the wrist, don't behave as though you were handling a delicate piece of china. Grip firmly and waggle her about a bit. The preliminary waggle is of the essence (UD)

It is equitable to add that, of several successful converts, Joe Cardinal (PP) gets his girl in six seconds flat (*passim*)

Iliad, the: of Homer; parallels with P. G. Wodehouse; see Usborne (WAW)

in fact, capital: 'Capital, capital, capital,' said Lord Emsworth, and would have probably gone on doing so for some little time, for he was a man who, when he started saying 'Capital', found it hard to stop (SS)

Infants' Bible Class, the: this excellent and necessary institution received some notice in WW as a reforming influence for village rozzers. In the Blandings saga it carries sadder undertones. Rarely indeed does the Shropshire of Mary Webb, or of A. E. Housman, impinge on the Shropshire of Blandings' bosky vale, yet into even this Eden some rain must fall. On those sad, successive occasions when nieces of Emsworth's noble Earl are despatched in chains to the home of their ancestors for having loved not wisely but too well, it is the Infants' Bible Class at the hamlet of Blandings Parva which they invariably convert into a field for good works. A prospective bride, torn from her betrothed on her wedding morning, is seldom lively company, and Prudence Garland is no exception:

> Her deportment would have cast a shadow on a Parisian Four Arts Ball . . . an atmosphere of doom and gloom pervaded the premises like the smell of boiled cabbage. This sombre note was particularly manifest in Lord Emsworth. A kind-hearted man, he was always vaguely pained when one of his numerous nieces came to serve her sentence; and in addition to this, one of the first of Prudence's broken utterances, as she toyed with her tea and muffins, had been the announcement that, life being now a blank for her, she proposed to devote herself to the doing of good works. He knew what that meant. It meant that his study was going to be tidied again. True, all the stricken girl had actually said was that she intended to interest herself in the Infants' Bible Class down in Blandings Parva, but . . . from superintending an Infants' Bible Class to becoming a Little Mother and tidying studies is but a step. His niece Gertrude, while doing her stretch for wanting to marry the curate, had been a very virulent study tidier, and he saw no reason to suppose that Prudence would not equal, or even surpass, her cousin's excesses (FM)

'Ingoldsby Legends, The': one of those mediaeval, silk-and-satined little boys in, is Patricia Marsh's goal for Albert the page boy (DD)

intervention in human affairs, Providence and the kindly: see **Doxology** (TP)

Ippleton, the Rt. Hon. the Earl of: George Francis Augustus Delamere Murgatroyd, 5th Earl, has refreshingly traditional views on daughters who march from Aldermaston and lie prostrate in Trafalgar Square. He also has a sufficiency of old-fashioned sense to take steps about it. In his outspoken view, Lady Mabel's conduct more condignly blots the family escutcheon than any other since his coll. ancestress Lady Evangeline forgot to say 'No' to King Charles II (PP)

Issue: you may be issue (most of us are) but unless you are Issue you haven't a hope of appearing in *Debrett* (TJ)

Ivan the Terrible: when a mediaeval Russian potentate was nicknamed the Terrible, it can be assumed that things were pretty bad (*passim*)

Ivry: Battle of (1590); its hero occurs *passim*, usually in contexts of that conspicuousness featured in Lord Macaulay's lay, where amid the thickest carnage blazed the helmet of Navarre (see **Vert Galant, le**)

J

Jabberwocky: the pug dog in whose defence an awesome weapon is unleashed in Grosvenor Square by Lady Brenda Twistleton, with momentous effects on the career of a friend of Kings (see **Lorgnettes**) (UFS)

Jacquerie, the: among such rogues and peasant slaves the Lady Brenda Bracken moves like a princess (HWA)

Jael: patron saint of absentee husbands, the wife of Heber the Kenite still gets around, collecting a good press. Some citations, stressing her superlative gifts as a hostess, couple her with, e.g., Lady Macbeth; others speak of a certain gleam in the eye of, just before she gets down to the rough work. Elsewhere Tipton Plimsoll, immured in a police cell after a Greenwich Village party,

> shook his head, and uttered a sharp howl. There are moments when shaking the head creates the illusion that one has met Jael the wife of Heber, incurred her displeasure and started her going into her celebrated routine (GBL)

James: Blandings Castle footman, gets Ideas Above his Station: 'He was a good young fellow once,' said Beach, 'and 'ad a proper respect for people, but now 'e 'as gone all to pieces. Six months ago 'e 'ad the rheumatism, and 'ad the audacity to send his picture and a testimonial saying it 'ad cured 'im of Awful Agonies to Walkinshaw's Supreme Ointment, and they printed it in half-a-dozen papers, and it 'as been the ruin of James. He has Got Above Himself and don't care for nobody' (SF)

Jane: dau. of Lord Emsworth's sister Charlotte, is not only the third prettiest girl in Shropshire but inherits all the resourceful and combative spirit of the female Threepwood *gens*. She is prepared to fight to the last ditch for her projected marriage to George Abercrombie and, when fate deals her a single trump card, she plays it resolutely:

'When I left you, Uncle Clarence, I went into the shrubbery to cry my eyes out because of your frightful cruelty and inhumanity, and I suddenly saw you creep to the library window with a hideous look of low cunning on your face and young George's air-gun in your hand. Next moment there was a shot, a cry, and Baxter weltering in his blood on the terrace. And as I stood there, a thought floated into my mind. What will Aunt Constance have to say about this when I tell her?' (LEO)

Jefferson, la Belle: of the George Edwardes chorus at the old Gaiety in 1907, is taken by punt on a river jaunt by the youthful George Uffenham. He recalls that his behaviour was so scrupulously correct as to suggest one brushing flies from a sleeping Venus. Consequently he was chagrined to hear that the lady had bruited it abroad that he was a boob, a sap, a poop, a clot, a wet ha'porth and a soppy date (MB)

Jellaby, Sir Leopold, O.B.E.: though a retired financier has not yet acquired a title. When he does, he may take as motto his favourite slogan: 'Never give a sucker an even break' (EBC)

Jellaby, Myrtle: dau. of Sir Leopold, would probably opt for an even terser motto: 'Soak him good' (EBC)

Jellicoe-Smith, K.C., Mr: his cross-examination of young Lord Stockheath in a breach-of-promise suit makes agreeable reading below stairs at Blandings Castle (SF)

Jenkins, Herbert, Ltd.: the publishing house of, is doubly blessed. Not only has it given to the world some seventy of the Wodehouse novels and short story collections (the first was **PICCADILLY JIM** in 1918) but for generations its premises themselves stood on hallowed ground in Duke St., St. James's, S.W. Galahad Threepwood has his London headquarters in the street, and a few yards from Jenkins' front portal was the spot where he was chatting with his chauffeur, preparatory to driving to Blandings for his niece Veronica's birthday, when they were joined by his godson Bill Lister (FM). Elsewhere Herbert Jenkins is listed as among that coterie of distinguished publishers who would have been sickened to see the in-and-out work among the bushes of such a publishing tick as Otis Painter (UD)

Jepp, Elaine: of the ensemble at the Alvin Theatre, New York, meets and accepts J. Phipps within twenty minutes of his arrival on American soil (PP)

Jevons, J. Horace: one of those rare characters (cf. Freddie Chalk-Marshall) of whom we suspect that most of his music is still within him. This big-hearted Chicagan millionaire acquires the services of Rupert Baxter for twelve months and then, a year or two later, takes the Wonder Boy on again for a second term of office. Even in the Windy City, surely, they don't come tougher than this? (LIP, LEO)

Jezebel: 'Well, what price her playing fast and loose with me?' cried Tipton. 'The two-timing Jezebel!'
'Don't you mean Delilah?' said Gally, none too sure himself. 'Jezebel was the one who got eaten by dogs.'
'What a beastly idea.'
'Not pleasant,' agreed Gally. 'Must have hurt like the dickens' (FM)

John the Chaplain: ranks high among those Marcher heroes of whom we were speaking under **Gladys:**

In the days before the Welshman began to expend his surplus energy in playing rugby football he was accustomed . . . to collect a few friends and make raids across the border. It was to cope with this habit that Dreever Castle, in Shropshire, came into existence. There is but one instance of a bandit's attempting to take the place by storm, and the attack was an emphatic failure. On receipt of a ladleful of molten lead, aimed to a nicety by one John, the Chaplain—evidently one of those sporting parsons—this warrior retired, done to a turn, to his mountain fastnesses, and is never heard of again (GL)

Johnson, Dr Samuel: (1709–84); there are refs. to his chair at the

Cheshire Cheese Tavern, E.C., and to his dictum on the adequacy of London. His other *mot* about the object of writing books is merrily discussed in OS (*passim*)

Jones: active assistant at the Argus Agency (SL)

Jones, Porky: goes twenty rounds with Eddie Flynn at the National Sporting Club (SF)

Jones, R.: though one of the underworld's busiest citizens, the rugged simplicity of his name helps to preserve his stainless reputation at Scotland Yard (SF)

Jonson, Ben: (1572–1637); the first poet laureate's somewhat mystified reactions as Shakespeare explains the plot of *Hamlet* are recorded in WW. Elsewhere we hear of a robust Elizabethan epithet, such as Rare Ben might have thrown at Beaumont and Fletcher over the sherris-sack at the Mermaid (BW)

Judson: garrulous and familiar valet to Freddie Threepwood (SF)

K

Kaiser Wilhelm II: sends a telegram (TS); moustache of, reminds an editor of a nightmare (PSJ); putative assassination of, (TSA)

Kate: a fleeting fancy in Lord Uffenham's past, gives him the elbow when he writes to her as 'Dear Mabel' (MB)

Keating, Mrs: of 11 Budge St., q.v., Chelsea, has only once strayed farther from home than the King's Road, around the corner. This was when Keating was laid to rest at Kensal Green:

> 'Wasted away to a shadow he did, and it wasn't two months before we were wearing our blacks' (CT)

Keeble, Lady Constance: a dau. of the 8th Earl of Emsworth and, like all the Threepwood girls (except Hermione) is tall, fair and statuesque. In youth she returned a passing fancy (its fitful shadow still lingers) for Alaric Davenport, now Duke of Dunstable. She m. (1) Joseph Keeble and (2) James Schoonmaker, q.v.; no issue. We last hear of her honeymooning with the latter at Cape Cod.
The impact of the character is, of course, out of all proportion to the scantiness of the data. Of the several units in Clarence Emsworth's monstrous regiment of sisters who, since his Countess's death, have acted as chatelaine at Blandings, Connie is by far the most familiar and probably the most likable. By those (there are many) who earn

her disapproval or incur her wrath she is regarded as a Cleopatra, a gorilla, a rattlesnake and an Apollyon. To Clarence she seems to be a wolf in permanent residence in the fold. These are biased views, engendered under stress. Her rule is milder, in actuality, than that, say, of a Tamerlane, and probably no more draconic than that of the average concentration camp kommandant. Her causes, it should be remembered, are not our causes; she represents authority, which, far from spoiling the fun, enhances it. Cast by fate for an unsympathetic role, she champions ghastly young poets and the even ghastlier Baxter; bullies the supine Earl; disapproves of pigs, pubs and pumpkins; castigates racegoers, rips and Romano's and is at permanent odds with Galahad. Haughty, censorious, feudal, unyielding, she is an affront to the 'classless society' and a wholesome corrective to the age of the common man. She is a superb hostess, but her sense of humour is somewhat embryonic and her assumption of privilege outrageous in this day and age. Yet we not only like, but approve, her. The thing is as mysterious as our devotion to that arch-villain, Falstaff, who was at least good company. Let us seek a different approach.

Connie has twice married wisely, democratically and happily. Her cajoling of Clarence is (let us admit it) mild in the circumstances. Can a 9th Earl, seigneur of a famous showplace, titular head of a historic family, overlord of a wealthy estate, patron of many livings, a landlord to whom decent peasants doff their hats while their womenfolk give respectfully at the knee—can such a figure afford to look like a heap of old clothes draped over a pigsty, to say nothing of the vacillation, the shirked responsibilities, the sagging jaw, the absent eye, the vacuousness, the pottering . . . all calculated to drive a highly organised mind to distraction? No, nature demands that where you have a Clarence you also have a Constance, lest order perish and chaos ensue. Yet, as inexorably it follows that where you have a Connie you must also have a Gally, lest a benevolent autocracy degenerate into a tyrannous dictatorship. Reviewing in turn the male minds which have come into collision with central authority at Blandings (we except the egregious Psmith as *sui generis*) we can recall only one type that is capable of meeting that dominance in equal combat and winning the day. It is the kind of mind which has battered its way around the world of men and women for forty years, living on the wits and wisdom it has garnered and applying to their use the civilised methods of the chessboard. When, as in Galahad's case, such a mind has preserved its humour and its humanism, it is doubtful whether the woman exists who can triumph over the strategy it can deploy—especially when in furtherance of some cherished cause or principle. This, too, is as it should be. (LIP, SL, HW, BCE, PHW, LEO, UFS, SS, GBL, PP)

Keeble, Joseph: men who make fortunes in the South African diamond market are not wanting in business acumen, and it speaks eloquently for both Joe and Connie Threepwood that on their marriage, and in the greensickness of love, he proposes a joint bank account. The arrangement works well until he wants to unbelt a small matter of £20,000 for his other lodestar—his stepdaughter Phyllis. Their marriage is one of genuine affection in which the Phyllis issue seems the only rift. He dies at some time (unspecified) before SS (LIP)

'Kelly's County Families': with *Landed Gentry*, *Debrett* and *Burke*, are standard reading for Cedric Mulliner (MM)

Keggs: butler to Lord Marshmoreton, resembles a particularly saintly bishop, but it is hinted with awesome relish in the servants' hall that at heart he is a Socialist (DD)

Keggs, Augustus: a butlerine family, these Keggs (there is a third pigeon-toed old sinner in CB). Augustus learned his trade at Shipley Hall, home of successive Viscounts Uffenham. He goes to the U.S. as butler to the millionaire J. J. Bunyan and, returning to a war-impoverished England, buys property in Valley Fields, S.E., and finds himself landlord to his former employer, Lord Uffenham (SFI *et al.*)

Kidderminster, the Rt. Hon. the Earl of: f. of Lady Joyce Sproule, q.v. (LEO)

King of the Amalekites: the captive; about to be interviewed by one of the less amiable elder prophets (U)

King Arthur: usu. in contexts of reproach when confronting Guinevere, but (anticipating Tipton Plimsoll some centuries later) loving her in spite of it all (FM, UD, AS, LEO *et al.*):

> No-one, in the days of King Arthur, thought the worse of a young knight who suspended all his social and business engagements in favour of a search for the Holy Grail (CC)

King of Bollygolla, the: invades England (TS)

King Charles I: plants the famous oak tree at Woollam Chersey Manor, Hants. (DS); see also **Nigel Carmody** (MN)

King Charles II: the ducal house of Dunstable owes its beginnings to an ancestress who could not say 'No' to, (UFS); for other ladies unable to apply a *nolle prosequi* to, see **Lady Barbara Belfry** and **Lady Evangeline Murgatroyd;** the Duchess of Portsmouth is also instanced:

> What a man of steely nerve, the beholder feels on looking at the imperious visage of Louise de Querouaille, this Charles Stewart must have been, that he should have been able to associate on terms of intimacy with anyone so formidable (OR)

King Claudius of Denmark: a keen playgoer, is sitting in the royal box at the first night of the new production *The Mouse Trap* when he affords an excellent example of a chap who is suddenly faced with the unpalatable (UD)

King of Denmark, the: unspecified, but apparently credulous, monarch to whom rash claimants are advised to report their beliefs. (Perhaps H.M. was Colonel-in-Chief of the Royal Horse Marines? —*Ed.*)

King Edward the Confessor: Lord Worplesdon, going down for the third time in a sea of dance champagne, sees the royal Saint plainly, and refuses to believe it (JM); Hugo Carmody conjectures that Gally Threepwood must have been pretty hot stuff, back in the days of (SL); Lord Blotsam's early forebear decorates the battlements of his castle in the reign of; (MUN)

King Edward III: says goodbye to his girl friend in aid of the Distressed Daughters of the Clergy (RHJ); graciously extends his thanks to a Mulliner (or a Molineux, or possibly a de Moulinière), for timely aid to the Black Prince on the field of Creçy (MM)

King Edward VII: a charming companion of Gally Threepwood causes something of a contretemps at a Buckingham Palace garden party given by, (see **Mabel**); his Majesty is elsewhere instanced as probably the last person to have heard a bell in working order at Lord Rowcester's stately home (RJ)

King Edward VIII: singled out by Jeeves as being allowed sartorial discretion (COJ); in the opinion of dispassionate observers Sigsbee Waddington, being a fourth-rate power in his own home, would not be able to take H.M. (as Prince of Wales) home to dinner and get away with it (SB)

King George V: graciously intervenes (in a dream) as arbiter between Lord Emsworth and head gardener McAllister (BCE); attends the homeric ball-game between New York Giants and Chicago White Sox at the Chelsea football ground (MT)

King George VI: when in need of a new top hat, was accustomed to ankle round to Bodmin's, the Bespoke Hatters, in Vigo St., W., and to say 'Good morning, Bodmin. We want a topper' (YMS); but forty-two years ago in SS His Majesty had figured, as Duke of York, as the subject under discussion by a group of late night coffee-stall customers, who finally decided by a large majority that the Duke did *not* sport a smorl dork moustorche, or indeed any other kind (SS). (The incident is placed in Pimlico, and it may be worth recording that as a matter of historic fact the non-palace-minded King, during the bombing of London, remarked modestly 'I have a house in Pimlico'—*Ed.*)

King Harold II: Jane Abbott, scanning the Walsingford High St. for Joe's remains, calls to mind Editha of the Swan Neck, searching the stricken field of Hastings for the corpse of, (SM)

King Henri IV of France and Navarre: as hero of Ivry; see **Vert Galant**

King Henry I: his inability to smile at the loss of the White Ship solely due to the fact that Larsen had not then invented his famous Exercises (SF, BW)

King Henry II: Mrs Cork's views on her wayward major-domo recall the king's attitude to his Archbishop. The words 'Will no-one rid me of this turbulent butler?' seem to hover on her lips (MB); Lord Emsworth feels much the same about the turbulent Lads Brigade (SS)

King Henry V: when calling on the chaps to close the wall up with their English dead, was not damped to hear a Twistleton remark that he didn't think he could make it (CT); see also **Agincourt:**

> 'Perform this simple task', said Gally, 'and there will be no limit to his gratitude. Purses of gold will change hands. Camels, bearing apes, ivory and peacocks, all addressed to you, will shortly be calling at the back door of Blandings Castle.'
> It was a powerful plea. Beach's two chins, which had been waggling unhappily, ceased to waggle. A light of resolution came into his eyes. He looked like a butler who has stiffened the sinews and summoned up the blood, as recommended by King Henry V. 'Very good, Mr Galahad,' he said (PP)

King Henry VII: founds Harchester College, q.v. (MM)

King Henry VIII: a lasting inspiration to all who, standing on the brink of matrimony, view the idea with misgiving (OR); didn't amount to anything until he began marrying, then you just stood back and watched his smoke (FM); must in time have become quite blasé (GL); his bedroom at Rowcester Abbey finds an appropriate tenant (RJ)

King Herod: first on the list of what the country really needs (UD); his policy of wholesale infanticide in the best public interest (DD); Freddie Widgeon's popularity equivalent to that of, at an Israelite Mothers' Pleasant Saturday Afternoon (YMS)

King Lear: the old gentleman's rollicking gaiety is frequently extolled, and there are wistful references to an England blessed with so equable a climate as that of his time (*passim*); see also **G. Ovens:**

> the only spot which the golden beams did not penetrate was the small smoking-room off the hall . . . Tipton Plimsoll, having breakfasted frugally off a cup of coffee and his thoughts, had gone there to brood. He was not in the market for sunshine. Given his choice, he would have scrapped this glorious morning, flattering the mountain tops with sovereign eye, and substituted for it something more nearly resembling the weather conditions of *King Lear*, Act III (FM)

King Macbeth of Scots: son of Doada, reigned 1040–1057. Shakespeare's play is a popular source, the king being assoc. esp. with emotions of shock (Banquo's ghost) and nervous tension. He is also identified with his lady's (see **Queen Gruoch**) natural anxiety to have the latest battle reports from the spare room (*passim*)

King Merolchazzar of Oom: wooing the lovely Princess of the Outer Isles, is coolly advised to wait his turn. A chronicler of the time, writing on a couple of paving-stones and a half-brick, records that

> it did begin to appear that our beloved Monarch . . . had been handed the bitter fruit of the citron

but that attentive fate which sees to it that kings rarely have a dull moment prepares two notable surprises—an assassination attempt and a conversion to a new religion (see **Caledonia**) (CC)

King of M'Gumbo-M'Gumbo (the last): 'And I've always sworn that if any slinking, sneaking, pop-eyed, lop-eared son of a sea-cook attempted to rob me of that girl, I would . . .'
'Er—what?' asked Osbert.
Bashford Braddock laughed a short, metallic laugh. 'Did you ever hear what I did to the King of M'Gumbo-M'Gumbo?'
'I didn't even know there was a King of M'Gumbo-M'Gumbo.'
'There isn't, now.' (MMS)

King Numa Pompilius: (in Roman legend the successor of Romulus); receives moral support nightly from the goddess Egeria (BC)

King Pausole: wisely advocates '*Ne nuis pas a ton voisin*'. So (of all people) reports Uncle Fred Ickenham, though anything less expected as reading matter for that inspired extrovert than *Les Aventures du Roi Pausole* is difficult to imagine. The satire by Pierre Louÿs (1870–1925) involves a somewhat obscure symbolism. Poet and translator, his best-known original work is *Aphrodite*. Even Larousse states that 'he celebrates the fleshly pleasures with a veritable mysticism'—*Ed.* (UFS)

King Richard I: the Earl of (good old) Ickenham cheerfully admits that some of his ancestors, when told to go off and fight the Paynim, were not above using the word 'can't', as may be verified from the Lionheart's despatches from Acre (UD)

King Robert the Bruce: at critical moments the visage of Angus McAllister (always excepting the occupied territories) takes on the look of a Scot who has not forgotten Bruce, or William Wallace, or the Battle of Bannockburn (BCE)

King of Ruritania, the former: the ex-Monarch gets around. He is to be seen e.g. ushering guests into or out of their limousines outside many West End hotels (esp. Barribault's) and summarily ejecting other guests from Soho night-clubs. He is also a guest of the Fishbeins (BCE) and arrives for the season at the Hotel Magnifique, Nice (EBC):

> Bill asked the ex-King if he was married, and the ex-King said he was. Bill then said that he himself ought to have been by now, only the bride hadn't turned up, and the ex-King said that he doubted if a bit of luck like that would happen once in a hundred years (FM)

King of Scots, the: (probably King James VI, but see **Long Sword**); sentences an ancestor of Lord Droitwich to a very unpleasant end (IWY)

King Solomon: usu. as the all-time protagonist of the married state, excelling even U.S. millionaires Jopp (CC), Chinnery (SM) or King Henry VIII (MS, OR, GL, FM, PHW); his wisdom is rebutted by Sir Herbert Bassinger, who thinks him a fool when compared with Polly Brown (IWY)

King Wenceslas: usu. as a staunch advocate of the means to combat any risk of night starvation. Many do their best (e.g. Sir Gregory Parsloe) to prove worthy disciples (PHW, VGJ *et al.*)

King William I: instanced as rather good at squaring the housemaid (UD) the Wooster (de Wocestre) family claim to have been extemely pally with (CW); his kinsman Bishop Odo's useful work with the episcopal battle-axe (MUN)

Kirkcudbrightshire, the Most Noble the Duke of: in a fit of dudgeon, walks out on his Hollywood hosts after a two months' visit when their supply of old brown sherry is exhausted (BCE)

Knubble of Knopp, the Rt. Hon. Lord: like cheerfulness, his lordship keeps breaking in, rabbit teeth and flapping ears compensating for his entire lack of chin. But for all his ubiquity we learn little about him. His baptismal name is Percy and his early ambition is to wed Amanda Biffen, dau. of the financier. Forestalled in this, he takes to Persian Monarchs on the grand scale. His main achievement is to stand godfather to a Mulliner; few members of the Upper House can boast as much. Res. Knubble Hall, near Knopp, Worcs. (NS, FO, MUN *et al.*)

Kubla Khan: see **Xanadu**

Küssnacht Castle: William Tell sentenced to durance vile in, (WT)

Kyne, the Hon. Hildebrand: suffers some damage to his aristocratic interior after a dormitory tobacco-chewing orgy (LN)

L

Lady Bishopess, the: see **Priscilla Bickerton**

Lakenheath, the late Sir Rupert: once Governor of various insanitary outposts of Empire (U)

Lakenheath, Lady (Elizabeth): spends her widowhood with her parrot Leonard, her niece Mildred and her late husband's diaries which she is editing for publication. Res., Thurloe Square, S.W. (U)

Lancaster, Duchy of: for the incredible facts about precedence of Vice-Chancellors of (probably as the result of some fiddling by the late John of Gaunt?) see **Tan-Tantara** (UD)

LEAVE IT TO PSMITH: serialised in the *Saturday Evening Post* and first published 1923, is the second Blandings novel but the fourth and last of the Psmiths. Baxter first appears in it, causing a change (see n. in WW) in Psmith's baptismal name. Writing from Great Neck, Long I., December 1922, Wodehouse noted laconically:

> I then sat down to finish **LEAVE IT TO PSMITH.** I wrote 40,00 words in three weeks (PF)

He had to rewrite the last part, however, *after* its U.S. publication, because of 'a stream of letters cursing the end of the story'. This caused 'much agony of spirit at the Herbert Jenkins office' (*ibid*)

Left Bank, the: Otis Painter, watching Bill Oakshott applying the Ickenham Method to Hermione Bostock, feels nostalgia for the old, happy days on, (UD)

Leighs, the: it is while staying with this Devon family that Lord Emsworth's niece Jane first meets her George Abercrombie, on whose behalf she is to become a gentle blackmail practitioner (LEO)

Lely, Sir Peter: (1618–1680); Restoration painter, orig. Pieter van der Faes; paints a Carolean Countess of Marshmoreton (DD); would have made a better job of painting Beatrice Chavender than does Joss Wetherby (QS)

'Leonard's Leap': 'I will call your attention', boomed Keggs, 'to this window—known in the fam'ly tradition as "Leonard's Leap". It was in the year seventeen 'undred and eighty-seven that Lord Leonard Forth, son of 'is Grace the Dook of Lochlane, 'urled 'isself outer this window to avoid compromising the beautiful Countess of Marshmoreton, with 'om 'e is related to 'ave 'ad a ninnercent romance. Surprised at an advanced hour by 'is lordship the Earl in 'er ladyship's boudoir as this room then was, 'e leaped through the open window into the boughs of the cedar tree which stands below, and was fortunate enough to escape with a few 'armless contusions' (DD)

Leopold and his Band: 'that justly famous ensemble' (v. Press) plays nightly, with rolling eyeballs, at Mario's Restaurant, W., where we are regaled by its strains in several novels. Artists like these are not easily put off their stride. The Kaiser's zeppelins left them unaffected. Slap-happy Hermann's blitz caused no interruption of their svelte cadences. It says much therefore for the impact made by the Last of the Fishes, when he visits the dining-room in search of Sue Brown in a shower of glass, that 'there were crashes which even the Band could not drown , and that Hugo Carmody, entering the battlefield a few minutes later, was interested to find waiters massaging bruised limbs, other waiters replacing fallen tables, and Leopold's Band playing in a sort of hushed undertone, like a band that has seen strange things (SL)

like Ma's? Baxter, staring through his spectacles, often gave people the impression of possessing an eye that could pierce six inches of harveyised steel and stick out on the other side (LIP) The young man in spectacles eyed them keenly—so keenly, indeed, that one might have supposed that he had found in these three fellow-travellers something to view with suspicion. This, however, was not the case. Rupert Baxter always eyed people keenly. It was pure routine (UFS)

Lindsay-Todd, Major and Mrs: dine at Blandings (HW)

Lipton, the late Sir Thomas: gets his chance; see **Lorgnettes**

Lister, William Galahad: kindly young mass of muscle with leanings towards art and the face of a gentle gorilla (in fact, what a Victorian lady novelist would have designated 'a magnificent ugly man'), Bill is the offspring of an outsize father and a music-hall strong woman who could bend pokers into lovers' knots. An ex-Amateur Heavyweight Boxing Champion, he is also a godson of Galahad Threepwood. His ardent love for the charming Prudence Garland is checked at all points until Gally's strategy brings them to the altar (FM)

Little: family name of Lord Bittlesham

Lochlane, the Most Noble the Duke of: for the romantic exploit of his collateral ancestor in 1787 see **Leonard's Leap** (DD)

Lollobrigida, Gina: the highly individual shape of, (CT)

Long Sword, Richard: (a namesake, though not a contemporary, of William Longespée, Earl of Salisbury, natural s. of King Henry I and Fair Rosamund); Scottish ancestor of the Chalk-Marshall Earls of Droitwich who, according to family tradition, pulled the nose of a King of Scots who had called him a liar, and was sentenced to be hanged, drawn and quartered for high treason. He owed his life to the courage and resource of his young dau. who smuggled into his prison cell the weapon by which he became familiarly known. With the sword he cut his way through the prison guards and made his escape. Long Sword's portrait by Franz Pourbus the Younger is a notable painting in the state drawing-room at Langley End, Worcs., home of his descendants. It depicts Richard in full armour of his period, his hand at rest on the pommel of the famous sword.

(No date or period is directly assignable but the evidence of the armour and of the Pourbus period leave us with the justifiable assumption that the King of Scots concerned is James VI (later I of England) during whose stormy reign several Sc. nobles (e.g. James Stewart, the 'Bonnie' Earl of Moray) came to untimely ends. This disclosure of the family's part-Scottish ancestry gives rise to an interesting theory. 'Marshall' rather than 'Chalk' seems to carry a Sc. connotation. If so it may be pointed out that the only Marshalls anciently in Scotland were the Marischals (Earls Marischal). Was Richard a member of this ancient and eminent line, of which the Keiths later became representative?—*Ed*.)

Lord Chancellor of England, the Rt. Hon. the: refs. to the Woolsack's occupant are fairly frequent. It is e.g. within the jurisdiction of, to jug anyone so mistaken as to marry a ward in chancery unless the Lord Chancellor has hoisted the All Right flag (JM). For a historic contribution to Wodehouse lore by the late Earl of Kilmuir (a former Lord Chancellor) see his recollections of the Nazi War Criminal Trials at Nuremberg in WW

LORD EMSWORTH AND OTHERS: first published 1937. The Blandings content is that *tour de force The Crime Wave at Blandings*, where the fusillade of airgun pellets is so fast and furious that even the two experts tend to get things mixed in WAW and PGW. Lady Constance aims at Beach (not Baxter) and misses him at short range, though she ashamedly confesses to having been the guilty party in nursery days when the target was the governess's bustle. The hapless Baxter is here (at last) driven to the realisation that he is not really wanted at Blandings, and the conclusion is added to the many more solid objects which pierce his consciousness. He is (for the record) pinked four times, by young George Threepwood, by Lord Emsworth, by Beach and by Lord Emsworth again (while bending forward over his motor-cycle handlebars on his final departure). As Usborne succinctly remarks, 'it appeals to something elemental in most of us' (LEO)

Lord Mayor of London, the Rt. Hon. the: standing on the Guildhall steps, takes a swipe at a Drone with the City Mace (YMS)

Lord's Cricket Ground: Lord Plumpton is shocked to see its sanctity violated (NS)

Lorgnettes: their efficacy as an offensive weapon is nowhere underestimated; see e.g. **Priscilla Bickerton;** but even the exploits of the Lady Bishopess are eclipsed by Lord Ickenham's boyish experience of their deadliness:

> God bless my soul, though, you can't compare the lorgnettes of to-day with the ones I used to know as a boy. I remember walking one day in Grosvenor Square with my Aunt Brenda and her pug dog Jabberwocky, and a policeman came up and said that the latter ought to be wearing a muzzle. My aunt made no verbal reply. She merely whipped her lorgnette from its holster and looked at the man, who gave one choking gasp and fell back against the railings without a mark on him, but with an awful look of horror in his staring eyes, as if he had seen some dreadful sight. A doctor was sent for and they managed to bring him round, but he was never the same again. He had to leave the force, and eventually drifted into the grocery business. And that is how Sir Thomas Lipton got his start (UFS)

Lower Isisi, the Paramount Chief of the: Lady Bassett, q.v., that intrepid hunter and explorer, is our sole authority for this incidental stray from the *Sanders* stories of Edgar Wallace. A dear, good fellow, she reports, but apt to become over-familiar under the influence of trade gin. She was once obliged to shoot him in the leg, and after a single course of this treatment he mended his ways so condignly as to be able to write a book on etiquette (MUN)

Lower Smattering-on-the-Wissel: Worcs. home originally of the Watson-Watsons and later of the Sprockett line of baronets (YMS, FO). There is a nostalgic note too in BG:

> Gertie Lawrence was back in England. Guy and Plum felt it would be advisable to see her and discuss her part in *Oh, Kay!* They drove to London through those delicious Cotswold villages, Moreton-in-the-Marsh, Stow-on-the-Wold, Lower Slaughter, Weston-sub-Edge and possibly those hamlets of which Plum had written, Chickenham-infra-Mud, Lower Smattering-on-the-Wissel and Higgleford-cum-Wortlebury-under-the-Hill

Loyal Royal Worcestershire Regiment, the: military historians are agreed that this famous old regiment of the line takes second place to none in its traditions of directness both of speech and action. The Earl of Hoddesdon, e.g., acquires proof of both when discovered loitering with intent near Major Flood-Smith's hatstand. The Major's service with the regiment may have been comparatively short; his vernacular reserves are the reverse:

Pausing only to snatch his service revolver, he had charged downstairs, and he would be damned if here wasn't another blasted feller strolling about the hall, pinching his hats.

'You!' he thundered, 'What the devil are you doing? Who are you? How did you get in?' The Major decorated the bald questions with a few of the rich expletives which a soldier inevitably picks up.

'Sneaking my hats under my very nose! Well I'll be . . .' He mentioned a few of the things he would be. Most of them were spiritual, a few merely physical. Lord Hoddesdon at last found words.

'It's quite all right,' he said.

'Quite all right? Quite all right? I catch you in my hall, sneaking my ensanguined hats, and you have the haemorrhagic impudence to stand there and tell me it's quite all right? I'll show you how all right it is, I'll . . .'

He stopped abruptly, for at this moment there came from the rear of the house the dreadful sound of splintering glass. Major Flood-Smith quivered from head to foot, and said something sharply in one of the lesser known dialects of the Hindu Khoosh. The good man loved his hat. But he also loved his windows. Barking like a seal, he disappeared down the passage (BM)

Loyal Sons of Shropshire, the: in the excellent cause of county pride most of the landowners listed as living in Shropshire attend annually to endure the ghastly speeches of old Todger and the even ghastlier ones of old Bodger. Here the portly seigneur of Much Matchingham (is he now the sitting member for the Bridgeford and Shifnal division?) does his duty by the festive board, banishing from memory those long-ago scenes at Romano's and their associations with sticks of celery and tureen covers—hoping too that no-one present is in a position to lift the lid on the story about the prawns. The annual banquet is also one of the very few events for which Lord Emsworth can be lured from his pig, his unfrilled hollyhocks and his roses; and having steeled himself to the temporary parting, he finds compensation in speaking about them to a wider and (we hope) more appreciative audience than he enjoys at home (FM *et al.*)

Loyal Sons of Worcestershire, the: as might be expected of a shire whose county town wears the titular nimbus of The Faithful City, the browsing and sluicing at the annual banquet of the Sons is of the ripest, tending to outdo even the Hampshire Hogs and the remarkable trencher talent in Shropshire, which can point with justifiable pride to such gourmands as Lord Burslem and Sir Gregory

Parsloe. However, the loyalty of Worcestershire's flesh is not always equal to that of its spirit. There is, e.g., Lord Wivelscombe, who is in a highly nervous condition on the morning after the Banquet and in no state to cope with spectres. Worcestershire's Sons do not confine their local pride to the merely fleshly talents; art and culture are also encouraged at their gatherings. Sir Reginald Sprockett, for instance, is given a standing ovation when he recites a modest saga of his own composition based on a traditional heroine in county folklore—a certain young lady of Bewdley (YMS *et al.*)

Lutz, Meyer: see the **Earl of Marshmoreton**

Lynn, Sir Claude, Bart., M.P.: the member for East Bittlesham is a man of parts who, apparently, is earmarked as a future Minister of All the Talents. Equally distinguished in debate, in Committee, at the hustings, on the links, the tennis court and the polo field, he is (like so many others) specifically unequal to coping with Roberta Wickham (MMS)

M

Mabel: Gally Threepwood, recorded as having been 'commonly knee-deep in ballet-dancers and chorus-girls' in his earlier days, escorts the engaging Mabel to a Buckingham Palace garden party given by King Edward VII and Queen Alexandra. His companion causes a minor incident on discovering she has a beetle down her back (PHW)

Mac: devil-porters it at the stage door of the Regal Theatre in Little Gooch St., Shaftesbury Avenue, W. Among his sterling qualities tact and discretion play little part. He would probably have tried to cheer up Napoleon in exile by talking about the winter sports in Moscow (SL, DD)

McAllister, Angus: head gardener at Blandings Castle, this dour, hirsute and redoubtable Glaswegian took over the portfolio from Thorne as long ago as LIP and, save for the brief interval (regretted by all) painfully dwelt on in *The Custody of the Pumpkin* (BCE), has reigned over Blandings' lawns and pleasaunces ever since. He seems to fulfil overflowingly those Scottish characteristics of which the poets Flanders and Swan remind us:

> He's bony and blotchy and covered with hair;
> He eats salted porridge, he works all the day
> And he hasn't got Bishops to show him the Way.

The poet Wodehouse has this to say:

> Concerning Glasgow, that great commercial and manufacturing city in the county of Lanarkshire in Scotland, much has been written. So lyrically does the *Encyclopaedia Britannica* deal with the place that it covers twenty-seven pages before it can tear itself away and go on to Glass, Glastonbury, Glatz and Glauber. The only aspect of it, however, which immediately concerns the present historian is the fact that its citizens are apt to be grim, dour, persevering, tenacious men; men with red whiskers who know what they want and mean to get it.

In that genre Angus holds an honoured place. We do not need to be told the details of those battles, fought remorselessly over the rose-beds and the flower garden, no quarter given or expected, in which the Threepwood pride has gone down again and again in a series of bloodless Bannockburns. There was the Pumpkin incident. There was the Hollyhock holocaust. Little wonder that the chronicler directs our attention to those signal, because so rare, fields of conflict—the Halidon Hills, the Neville's Crosses and the Floddens, when shivered was fair Scotland's spear and broken was her shield. They culminate of course in that Field of Culloden which concerns the Girl Friend and the Yew Alley. Yet because each side, happily, is careful to recognise and preserve the elements of mediaeval chivalry, the delicate balance is maintained. Neither protagonist is permitted permanently to lose face.

Factually it must be recorded that McAllister, the humble Glaswegian, is closely related to Donaldson, the U.S. millionaire. It is (had he but known it at the time) a happy day for Lord Emsworth when the great Donaldson's elder daughter came to stay as paying guest at McAllister's cottage, for it removes the ever-present fly in the Peerage's ointment—what to do with the younger son. And purists may perceive too a logical sequence of events common to Scottish sociology. For the McAllisters and the Donaldsons are both septs of the great Clan Donald, and in that small, conservatively minded country, even in the twentieth century, like will to like, and the tendency to marry within the clan is still a cardinal fact (*passim*, esp. BCE)

McGuffy, Aloysius St. X.: white-jacketed ministering angel at the smaller of Barribault's main bars, and creator of McGuffy's Special (SFE)

Mackintosh, Emily Ann: author of the romantic novel *Roses Red and Roses White* whose title calls eloquently to the deeps in that eminent rosarian, Lord Marshmoreton. He is chagrined to discover it is not a treatise on his favourite flora but a novel of stearine sentimentality about a pure English girl and an artist called Claud (DD)

McPhail & McPherson: of Edinburgh, book a substantial order with Freddie Threepwood (PP)

MacPherson: head gardener at Belpher Castle, is (not unexpectedly) a rose expert (DD)

McTeague: this ex-sergeant major of the Irish Guards is surprisingly taciturn for one of his race, but he is the decisive factor in that homeric contest, Fish v. The Rest, at Mario's Restaurant:

> Anyone who has ever been bounced from a restaurant knows that commissionaires are heavy metal. This one had a grim face made of some hard kind of wood and the muscles of a village blacksmith. A man of action rather than of words, he clove his way through the press in silence. Only when he reached the centre of the maelstrom did he speak. This was when Ronnie, leaping upon a chair the better to perform the operation, hit him on the nose. On receipt of this blow, he uttered the brief monosyllable 'Ho!' and then scooped Ronnie into an embrace of steel and bore him towards the door, through which was now moving a long, large, leisurely policeman (SL)

McTodd, Cynthia: old school friend of Phyllis Jackson, now m. to the Canadian poet, Ralston McTodd (LIP)

McTodd, Ralston: Saskatoon poet of the *avant garde* school, to whose pen (according to the *Montreal Star*) the depths of human emotion are about as plumbable as an ink-well (LIP)

Mace, the late Col. Archibald, C.V.O.: military historians record no more inarticulate wooer. His proposal of marriage is of classic economy. One summer afternoon at Hurlingham, he grabs the arm of Lady Vera Brent, turns purple and says 'Eh, what?' (BM)

Mace, Lady Vera: dau. of the 5th Earl of Hoddesdon, m. Archie Mace of the Coldstream Guards. She collects a handsome fee and expenses by chaperoning the U.S. heiress, Ann Moon, during her first London season. Res., Davies St., W. (BM)

Mad Mullah, the: leads an Islamic invading army (TS)

Magnus, Major General: former employer of butler Beach and associate of Galahad Threepwood, was (even for a soldier) of more than ordinarily homicidal bent. His dexterity with the breadknife suggests that he gave the War Office their original idea for the Commandos (SL)

Mainprice, Mainprice & Boole: law firm, Denvers St., Strand, W.C., founded in 1786 (SF)

Maltbury Hunt, the: its country is not specified but is probably in Worcs., since all Earls of Droitwich are expected to become M.F.H. (IWY)

Malvern, the Most Hon. the Marquess of: f. of Lord Pershore, q.v., res., Much Middlefold Hall, Shropshire (COJ)

Malvern, the Marchioness of: close friend of Agatha Wooster, is about six feet from o.p. to prompt side, fitting into the largest armchair as if it had been built around her (COJ)

Manchester United F.C.: by swotting up their form Freddie Threepwood achieves signal success with P. P. Wilks, the Mancunian store proprietor (PP)

Mandeville, young: main objective of the tactical exercise 'Breadknife' initiated by Major General Magnus (SL)

Mannering, Lady Clara: a dau. of the 1st Earl of Havershot and mother of Egremont M., q.v. (LG)

Mannering, Egremont: a cousin of Reggie Havershot, q.v., would take a front place in any list of Eminent Collectors. Has been told for years that it is idle to try to absorb all the alcohol in England, but pertinaciously goes on trying (LG)

Mant, Col. Horace: m. Lady Mildred Threepwood, q.v. (SF)

Mant, Lady Mildred: o. dau. of the 9th Earl of Emsworth, appears briefly in the first Blandings novel. Described ceremoniously below stairs as 'our eldest', it is deducible that she is senior to George, Viscount Bosham (SF)

Mapleton, Miss: hard-tried governess in the Threepwood nest at Blandings in nursery days, when the golden-haired little darlings included the Ladies Jane, Constance, Georgiana, Ann, Hermione, Julia, Charlotte and Dora and, to balance things up, Clarence Bosham, Galahad and Lancelot. The briefest reference to these toughs, even before they hit mid-season form, would suffice to qualify Miss M. for 1st prize in any Unpopular Jobs contest. If (as is likely) she is identifiable with the Miss M. found later at St. Monica's (VGJ) where her grey hairs are brought in sorrow to the grave by those outstanding blisters Bobbie Wickham and Prudence Carroway, our sympathy is intensified. At Blandings, as Lord Emsworth recollects, her martyrdom is brought to a head (hardly the word we want) by Connie's airgun. Fortunately, as he adds, governesses in those days were protected by bustles (LEO)

Mariana, Fr. George: (fl. 1250); held dancing (quite unilaterally) to be a mortal sin; was esp. down on the sarabande which, he thought, worked more mischief than the Plague. Ed. Leipsig University; hobbies included fishing, illuminating vellum and mangling the wurzel (SL)

Mario's: fashionable West End restaurant frequented by all that is best and fairest. As the Savoy in its time has boasted the virtuosity of the Savoy Havana and Orpheans, so Mario's is indissolubly associated with the celebrated Leopold and his Band. Normally dignified and even sedate, Mario's has had its moments, as when, e.g., its diners should have equipped themselves with smoked glasses (see **Gloria Salt**) and when Ronnie Fish arrives in a shower of glass. Diners should note that, save in the balcony, ev. dress is still oblig. (SL, SFI, BM, NS, BCE *et al.*)

Market Blandings, Shropshire: there is perhaps natural temptation to think of this consequential little town as unique in England to-day. Essentially it is so. Yet its inherent decencies have not been altogether forgotten by some of its sister townships up and down the country. When, for instance, a slight case of dope-peddling recently came to light in one of the two or three places Trollope had in mind when he created Barchester, shocked Fleet St. sub-editors accorded it top-column space and the B.B.C. quoted counsel's indignant rhetoric. There are still, in England, places innocent of 'progress', where 'planning' and 'overspill' are jargon and 'conurbations' are unknown. It cannot last; which is why (among other reasons) we must cherish our Market Blandings.

It stands a little more than two miles from the main gates of Blandings Castle. To reach it 'you turn to the right on leaving the gates', which one assumes to mean in a N.N.W. direction, towards Shrewsbury. Devotees who have been visiting it ever since SF (now a matter of fifty-two years) find that it has hardly changed in that time. The old Rector (Canon Fosberry) retired about 1933 (after HW) and the new man (the Rev. Belford) has found himself allied by marriage to the Threepwoods up at the Castle. A fourth generation of Wellbeloveds is prominent in the person of Marlene, barmaid at the Emsworth Arms, but other changes are few. The Electric Palace in the High St. still shows films on Tuesdays and Fridays, but it is respectably ivy-covered and crowned with Elizabethan stone gables. The cathedral-close atmosphere of the street indeed still retains only one objectionable element—Jno. Banks' new premises are still regarded, after forty-five years, by neighbours as an eyesore. Out on the Shrewsbury road, too, there was at one time a tendency to ribbon building. One of the new villas was taken by Admiral Fruity Biffen, but finding sleep impossible owing to the ceaseless clamour of moths, bats and nightingales, he forsook it and returned to London's peace and quiet. The next tenant of 'Sunnybrae' was of course that accommodating being, the Empress of Blandings, glad no doubt to exchange her rural retreat for a town house for the season. Things in fact are much the same as they were when Joe Keeble, having his grizzled locks shorn for the County Ball, unwisely allowed his thoughts to wander and let Jno. Banks finish off the job with a liberal anointing of heliotrope-scented hairwash; or when Eve Halliday so rightly admired the bulging second storeys of the age-old inns and the lichened Norman church with its sturdy square tower; or when Baxter, seeking the genteel first floor dining room at the Emsworth Arms, was served with a 'market ordinary' by the bald and shuffling waiter, own cousin to a tortoise. Which recalls us to an editor's first duty:

> In most English country towns, if the public-houses do not actually outnumber the inhabitants, they all do an excellent trade. It is only when they are two to one that hard times hit them and set the innkeepers blaming the Government (SF)

It had indeed been the rude forefathers' main intention to provide one public house for every inhabitant. Falling a little short in this laudable aim, they commendably insisted on quality if not quantity. Those sapient visitors who, like Mustard Pott, make it their first duty to locate the oases for future reference, need have no fears. They will find all the requirements of the district's mellow and thirsty climate catered for at the Wheatsheaf, the Waggoners Rest, the Beetle and Wedge, the Stitch in Time, the Goose and Gander, the Jolly Cricketers, the Blue Boar, the Cow and Grasshopper, the Blue Cow, the Blue Dragon, the Goat and Feathers and the Emsworth Arms (G. Ovens, Propr.) in the High Street. The last-named has collected a remarkable Press:

> Ovens' home-brewed is a liquid Pollyanna, forever pointing out

the bright side and indicating the silver lining. If King Lear had had a tankard of it handy, we should have had far less of that 'Blow, winds, and crack your cheeks!' stuff (UFS)

At the Arms, moreover, you can have your refreshment served (by Erbert the egalitarian potboy) in the garden overlooking the river, where numbers of rustic tables, tree-shaded, invite you to take tea on a summer's afternoon. Here Lavender Briggs meditated her hard lot in privacy, learning something to her advantage, and here too Galahad and Maudie Montrose exchanged happy memories of the old Criterion Bar. In most other ways (though Connie Keeble used wisely to drive to Shrewsbury for a hair-do) the little town amply supplies the needs of its own people and those of the pleasant villages which sprinkle the southern end of the Vale of Blandings. Gardeners, whether amateur or professional, are well aware of the excellencies of Smithsons, where seeds, shrubs and garden supplies of every kind are available. The firm do not need to boast about it, but it is conceded that they have materially assisted Lord Emsworth and others in their successes at the Shrewsbury Flower Show. Mr Bulstrode, the High St. chymist, is still at the old stand, and Dr Bird the best known medical practitioner in the district. P.c.s Evans and Claude Murphy are still among the sleepless guardians of the Queen's peace, the former well content with his success in performing the Wellbeloved hat trick. Visitors arriving by train will find the aged taxi-cab (Ed. Robinson, Propr.) awaiting them outside the station. The dumb chums of the neighbourhood are now looked after by Mr Smithers, who took over the veterinary practice when Mr Webber retired. The dumb chums, incidentally, now keep a weather eye open on those days when Beefy Bingham, Much Matchingham's respected Vicar, cycles over for tobacco supplies. He is invariably accompanied by the doughty Bottles, who has cleaned up every rival in the neighbourhood and is spoken of as a credit to his master's cloth as far afield as the Cow and Caterpillar on the Shrewsbury road. And finally, should you wisely resolve to flee the weary world and settle in this vale of Avalon, you will find Caine & Cooper, estate agents, more than ready to help you, and Lancelot Cooper, the senior partner, a most courteous (if slightly dressy) cicerone.

As of Blandings Castle and its rolling acres, so of the market town, the uninitiated forever inquire as to the truth of the Avalon tradition. Are (for instance) zinnias, daffodils, dahlias and roses invariably contemporaneous in lordly castle and in peasant cot? Do nightingales hymn their praises every night of the year? Does the sun forever beam, do the best birds forever sing, the most superior bees sempiternally hum about their business? The answer, I think, is almost.

If the sun is shining anywhere in England, it is shining here; and there are no half-measures; either it is high summer or (see HW, SL) a spectacular thunderstorm is in progress. As for winter weather, Market Blandings has recorded only one snowstorm. It stunned the populace, and the oldest inhabitant, Ezekiel Wellbeloved, was so shocked that he took off his trousers and gave them away to a passing stranger in the High Street, confident that the end of the world was at hand (*passim*)

Marlborough St. Police Court: a duke's heir-presumptive graces the dock at, wearing the scanty finery of a Zulu warrior, and is charged with assaulting Queen Marie Antoinette with an assegai (UFS *et al.*)

Marlowe, Sir Mallaby: of Ridgway's Inn, E.C.; the eminent lawyer discloses the first good deed he performed for his son:

> 'Your poor mother wanted to call you Hyacinth, Sam. You may not know it, but in the 'nineties when you were born children were frequently christened Hyacinth. Well, I saved you from that (GOB)

Marsh: family name of the Earl of Marshmoreton

Marsh, Lady Patricia: dau. of the 7th Earl of Marshmoreton, likeable, romantic and possessed of talents which, in her day and age, can find few outlets (DD)

Marshmoreton, 1st Earl of: stabs his Countess with a dagger to abate her tendency to curtain-lectures (DD)

Marshmoreton, 3rd Earl of: arranges for two aunts and a sister to be unobtrusively poisoned (DD)

Marshmoreton, 4th Earl of: the immediate reason for Leonard's Leap (DD)

Marshmoreton, 4th Countess of: basic cause of the same (DD)

Marshmoreton, the Rt. Hon. the Earl of: John Marsh, 7th Earl, s. his f. the 6th E. as head of a family with Hampshire estates and associations for many centuries. One cannot agree with WAW that the family's name is Bosham. The many refs to his unm. dau. Lady Patricia Marsh seem conclusive, though the close suggestion of Moreton-in-the-Marsh roots may provide a theory that the surname as in the Cotswold town, may originally have been March. However, as Usborne rightly observes:

> Emsworth is, in fact, a town in Sussex, in a district rich in

place-names that have acquired glory in song or legend. Hilaire
Belloc's Halnaker and Duncton Hill are near by . . . Obviously
Belpher Castle in Hampshire is, in the literary dimension, some-
where on the Emsworth-Corsham-Blandings road. To all intents
DD is a Blandings novel. Lord Marshmoreton is an echo of
Lord Emsworth, Lord Belpher of Lord Bosham, Lady Caroline
Byng of Lady Constance Keeble, Reggie Byng of Freddie
Threepwood, Keggs the butler of Beach the butler, and
MacPherson the gardener of McAllister the gardener (WAW)

Both peers, too, are widowers and rose-growers. Lord Marsh-
moreton has won a first prize for hybrid teas at the Temple Flower
Show. Heir, Viscount Belpher, q.v.; Club, Athenaeum; Res.,
Belpher Castle, Hants. (DD)

Marshmoreton Arms, the: offers accommodation and bait for
man and beast and is the Belpher social centre where, of an evening,
you will find the local vet smoking a pipe with the grocer, baker and
butcher. On Saturdays the inn provides a 'Shilling Ordinary', which
is rural English for a cut off the joint, boiled potato and greens,
followed by hunks of the sort of cheese which believes it pays to
advertise (DD)

Marson, Ashe: s. of the Rev. Joseph Marson, Vicar of Much
Middlefold, Shropshire, and Sarah his wife, runs the mile for Oxford
in $4\frac{1}{2}$ mins. and gets his Blue for athletics, but failing to make any
other professional mark, becomes a writer of crime fiction. Better
things are in store for him when, on meeting Joan Valentine, he
accompanies her to Blandings Castle in the roles of valet and lady's
maid—the first recorded of the many impersonations the place is to
suffer (SF)

Masefield, John: (1878–1967); the late Poet Laureate; refs. are
usually to his narrative poem *Reynard the Fox* and in contexts of the
feelings of the hunted. Tipton Plimsoll, e.g., experiences these in FM

Matchelow, the Rt. Hon. Viscount: data scanty; res., Heron's
Hill, Sussex (SL)

Maudie: Lord Uffenham's thoughts drift away to the year 1911 and
a girl in a hat like a herbaceous border whose name was, (MB)

**Maufringneuse et Valerie-Moberanne, M. le (ci-devant)
Marquis de:** to his more indulgent friends known as Old Nick,
Nicolas Jules St. Xavier Auguste occupies the position of *employé
attaché à l'expedition du troisième bureau* (meaning clerk) at the *Ministère
de Dons et Legs* (meaning Legacies), an appointment of considerable

modesty which he contrives to make even more inconspicuous by his calculated non-attendance there (FL)

Mauleverer, Colonel and Mrs: dinner guests at Blandings (HW)

Mauretania, the R.M.S.: the many for whom the Old Maurie, holder for so many years of the Blue Riband of the Atlantic, will always afford affectionate nostalgia will like to know that Jimmy Pitts, among others, discovers romance (though not her name) aboard the liner (GL) and that Lord Tilbury (SA) is a passenger

May Queen: foreshortened name of the stimulant always recommended by Lord Ickenham to timorous lovers when they shrink from trying the Ickenham System. Its full cognomen is To-Morrow'll Be Of All The Year The Maddest, Merriest Day, For I'm To Be Queen Of The May, Mother, I'm To Be Queen Of The May. Its foundation is any good dry champagne, to which are added liqueur brandy, kümmel and green chartreuse to taste (UD, SS)

meanwhile at Blandings: 'Did I ever tell you', said Gally, the story of Clarence and the Arkwright wedding? The Arkwrights lived out Bridgnorth way, and their daughter Amelia was getting married, so Clarence tied a knot in his handkerchief to remind him to send the bride's mother a telegram on the happy day.'
'And he forgot?'
'Oh, no, he sent it. "My heartfelt congratulations to you on this joyous occasion" he said. It was fine. Couldn't have been improved on. Only the trouble was that in one of his distrait moments he sent it, not to Mrs Arkwright, but to another friend of his, a Mrs Cartwright, and her husband had happened to die that morning. Diabetes. Very sad. We were all very sorry about it, but no doubt the telegram cheered her up' (PHW)

Merridew: it may well be that Blandings Castle, where time stands still, continues to maintain an under-butler in addition to Beach, but Merridew (the last known to hold that portfolio) has not been heard of for many years. His chief duty, it seems, is to deputise for Beach by supervising the dining arrangements above stairs while the noble hierarchy below stairs require Beach's presence at the head of the table in the Steward's Room (SF)

Mervo, H.S.H. the Prince of: o.s. of the late Prince, who retired to contented exile in England after the Mediterranean island declared its republican status. John, *de jure* Prince of Mervo, is a massive and cheerful young man—'one of nature's forwards', and has indeed played for Cambridge in that position for two strenuous seasons. Recalled to rule the island of his fathers at the whim of an American millionaire, he enjoys a short but idyllic reign (PB)

M'Goopi M'Gwumpi: paramount Chief of the Lesser M'Gwowpi tribe, has twenty-seven wives and a hundred spares (LEO)

Milano, Ill. et Ecc. P. il Duca di: the earliest recorded perform-ance of a ballet (1489) given to celebrate the nuptials of (MT)

Molesey, Sir Claude, Bart: becomes ruby of countenance when *Society Spice* ventilates the facts about a certain Brighton bungalow (BC)

moments with the poets: they run through the Wodehouse opus, a gleaming thread from the *Golden Treasury* as the basic motif, though the Rev. Francis Palgrave might raise a pensive eyebrow on noting contributions by e.g. the poet Coward and the poet Berlin. They prompted the tribute paid by the *Times Literary Supplement* reviewer, many years ago, 'rich in those echoes from English literature which it is always so gratifying to pick up'; though he surely missed the better point, which is that only the latent poet in Wodehouse himself could perfect the exquisite, and quite individual, use he makes of them in point counterpoint with his own gorgeous prose. Perhaps the most brilliant in this kind is the versicle use of Shakespearian poetry alternating with his own vernacular, e.g. the classic one of the sheeted dead in *Caesar* (OR). In the two latest books are:

> Wilfred Allsop's face lit up, as that of the poet Shelley whom he so closely resembled must have done when he suddenly realised that 'blithe spirit' rhymes with 'near it', not that it does, and another ode as good as off the assembly line (GBL)
> the poet Burns has pointed out this to his public. 'Gang agley' was how he put it, for he did not spell very well, but it meant the same thing (PP)
> the sun was very sultry, and the poet Coward has specifically stressed the advisability of avoiding its ultra-violet ray (GBL)

A certain Duke incidentally has also called attention to the poet Burns's idiosyncrasies, but makes a grudging concession:

> 'If Burns thought "Loch Lomond" rhymes with "before ye", he must have been a borderline case ... Not that there are many rhymes to "Loch Lomond". Got to be fair to the chap, I suppose' (UFS)

Monaco, H.S.H. the Prince of: catches a fish with telescopic eyes (PB)

Montrose, James Graham, 5th Earl and 1st Marquess of: (1612–1650); the Great Montrose; usual refs. to the foremost Scottish man of action are to his best-known poem, the 'Ode to Duty' ('Never Love Thee More') (GT, DS *et al.*)

moonlight at Blandings: he was pottering aimlessly to and fro in the parts adjacent to the rear of the Castle when there appeared in his path a slender female form. He recognised it without pleasure. Any unbiased judge would have said that his niece Angela, standing there in the soft pale light, looked like some dainty spirit of the moon. Lord Emsworth was not an unbiased judge. To him Angela merely looked like Trouble. The march of civilisation has given the modern girl a vocabulary and an ability to use it which her grandmother never had. Lord Emsworth would not have minded meeting Angela's grandmother a bit (BCE)

Moresby, Sir Joseph: a Metropolitan stipendiary magistrate, has a word or two to say about glamorous redheads (MMS)

Morrison, Sir John, Bart.: customer of the New Asiatic Bank, E.C., whose cheque occasions a crisis in two young lives (PSC)

Mountford, Rollo: the fatal allure which causes Phyllis Jackson to engage herself to him is not discernible to the reader (LIP)

Mount Anville, Lord: courtesy title of the e.s. and heir of the Duke of Havant. When the young man is sued for breach of promise, Beach is moved to comment in headlines:

> 'What with all this Socialism rampant they seem so 'appy at the idea of doing one of Us an injury that they give 'eavy damages. A few Ardent Expressions, and that's enough for them. It's all these here cheap newspapers that does it. They tempt the Lower Classes to Get Above Themselves' (SF)

Mountry, the Earl: courtesy title of Edward Beckford, e.s. and heir of the Marquess of Broxham. Pink, shy, solemn and wealthy, he owns the m.v. *Mermaid* in which Cynthia Drassilis takes a cruise (LN)

Mull, the Most Noble the Duke of: his Grace is a bright particular star in that most exclusive coterie the Twelve Jolly Stretcher Cases at Droitgate Spa (EBC)

Mulliner, the late Sir Sholto, M.V.O.: f. of Archibald M., celebrated gallinaceous impersonator. (MM) (The Mulliner saga, as a whole, is off the present canvas, those members only being included here who impinge on the Blandings scene or who possess titles—*Ed.*)

Mulliner, the Rt. Rev. Dr. Theodore, D.D.: see **Bongo Bongo**

Mulliner, the late Rt. Rev. Dr. Theophilus, D.D.: see **Bognor**

Mulliner, Lady (Wilhelmina): when a well-loved mother goes suddenly off her rocker and the tragedy involves the breaking of one's engagement to the girl one loves, one gets something Somerset Maugham could make a three-act play out of without conscious cerebration (YMS) (see **X . . . and . . . Q**)

Murgatroyd: family name of the Earl of Ippleton

Murgatroyd: butler to the innocuous Sir Jasper ffinch-ffarrow-mere, is a huge man with a cast in one eye and an evil light in the other (MM)

Murgatroyd, Edward Jimpson: despondent Harley Street medico, feels that his most pessimistic diagnosis is barely adequate in the matter of the pink spots which sprout on Tipton Plimsoll's chassis (FM)

Murgatroyd, Lady Evangeline: was not unique in finding herself unable to utter a faint *nolle prosequi* to his late Majesty King Charles II of Glorious Memory (PP)

Murgatroyd, Lady Mabel: a sedulous Aldermaston marcher, this dau. of the Earl of Ippleton. Her Titian charms win a reprieve from the coop when she appears in the dock with Bingo Little following a Trafalgar Square incident. Fortunately her noble father, q.v., is made of sterner stuff (PP)

Murphy: sleuth attached to the Argus Agency, with lair on ground floor of same (SL)

Musker, Sir Herbert, Bart., and Lady: dinner guests at Blandings (HW)

Muspratt, Beefy: the Hon. Galahad Threepwood recalls that this outsize boulevardier, with some assistance, broke a billiards table in 1898 (HW)

N

Natchez: Adela Cork's nameless poodle resembles the equally anonymous young lady from, who said, 'Where Ah itches, Ah scratches' (OR)

New York: Lord Emsworth, we were told years ago, travelled in North America in young manhood. His only other experience of the New World is his eventful holiday with his son Frederick, now a go-getter sales vice-president with Donaldson Inc. Lord Emsworth triumphantly proves that an earl's enterprise can win through to success in the sales field, too, even in the matter of selling expensive encyclopaedias:

> He was still standing in the driveway, letting 'I dare not' wait upon 'I would', as cats do in adages, when the air became full of tooting horns and grinding brakes and screaming voices.
>
> 'God bless my soul,' said Lord Emsworth, coming out of his coma.
>
> The car which had so nearly caused a vacancy in the House of Lords was bursting with blondes. There was a blonde at the wheel, another at her side, further blondes in the rear seats and on the lap of the blonde beside the blonde at the wheel a blonde Pekinese dog. They were all shouting, and the Pekinese dog was hurling abuse in Chinese.
>
> 'God bless my soul,' said Lord Emsworth. 'I beg your pardon. I really must apologise. I was plunged in thought.'
>
> 'Oh, was that what you were plunged in?' said the blonde at the wheel, mollified by his suavity. Speak civilly to blondes, and they will speak civilly to you.
>
> 'I was thinking of dog biscuits. Of dog biscuits. Of—er—in short—dog biscuits. I wonder' said Lord Emsworth, striking while the iron was hot, 'if I could interest you in a good dog biscuit?'
>
> The blonde at the wheel weighed the question. 'Not me,' she said, 'I never touch 'em.'
>
> 'Nor me,' said a blonde at the back. 'Doctor's orders.'
>
> 'And if you're thinking of making a quick sale to Eisenhower here' said the blonde beside the driver, kissing the Pekinese on the tip of its nose, a feat of daring at which Lord Emsworth marvelled, 'he only eats chicken.'
>
> Lord Emsworth corrected himself. 'When I said dog biscuits,' he said, 'I meant a richly bound encyclopaedia of Sport'.
>
> The blondes exchanged glances. 'Look,' said the one at the

wheel. 'If you don't know the difference between a dog biscuit and a richly bound encyclopaedia of Sport, seems to me you'd be doing better in some other line of business.'

'Much better,' said the blonde beside her.

'A whole lot better,' agreed the blonde at the back.

'No future in it, the way you're going,' said the blonde at the wheel, summing up. 'That's the first thing you want to get straight on, the difference between dog biscuits and richly bound encyclopaedias of Sport. It's a thing that's cropping up all the time. There *is* a difference. I couldn't explain it to you offhand, but you go off into a corner somewheres and you'll find it will suddenly come to you.'

'Like a flash,' said the blonde at the back.

'Like a stroke of lightning or sump'n,' assented the blonde at the wheel. 'You'll be amazed how you ever came to mix them up. Well, goodbye. Been nice seeing you.' (NS)

night starvation and its avoidance: some hold the view that sorrow's crown of sorrow is remembering happier things, but Sir Gregory found that it gave him a melancholy pleasure to be wafted back into the golden past by perusing the details of the sort of dishes where you start with a dozen eggs and use plenty of suet for the pastry. At the moment he was deep in the chapter about Chocolate Soufflé, and he had just got to the part where the heroine takes two tablespoonfuls of butter and three ounces of Sunshine Sauce and was wondering how it all came out in the end . . . (PHW)

He had just sat down at the dinner table when the door bell rang. He had had three excellent cocktails and was looking forward with bright anticipation to a meal of the sort that sticks to the ribs and brings beads of perspiration to the forehead. Some men, when jilted, take to drink. Sir Gregory was taking to food:

Le Diner: Smoked Salmon: Mushroom Soup: Filet of Sole: Hungarian Goulash: Mashed Potatoes: Buttered Beets: Buttered Beans: Asparagus with Mayonnaise: Ambrosia Chiffon Pie: Cheese: Fruit: Petits Fours.

Ambrosia Chiffon Pie is the stuff you make with whipped cream, white of egg, powdered sugar, seeded grapes, sponge cake, shredded cocoanut and orange gelatin, and it had been planned by the back-sliding Baronet as the final supreme gesture of independence. A man who has been ordered by his

fiancée to diet and defiantly tucks into Ambrosia Chiffon Pie
has formally cast off the shackles (PHW)

NOTHING SERIOUS: published in 1950, its ten short stories
number one Blandings episode, *Birth of a Salesman* (NS)

Not the whole Troop? He thanked Lord Ickenham for the
suggestion and Lord Ickenham said he always made a point
of doing his day's kind deed. His mother, he said, had been
frightened by a Boy Scout (SS)

'Now We Know' Dept.: 'Ever tasted a mint julep, Beach?'
'Not to my recollection, sir.'
'Oh, you'd remember all right, if you had. Insidious things.
They creep up to you like a baby sister and slide their little
hands into yours and the next thing you know the Judge is
telling you to pay the clerk of the court fifty dollars' (SL)

Jerry Vail sat down and started writing a story designed for one
of the American magazines if one of the American magazines
would meet him halfway, about a New York private detective
who was full of Scotch whisky and sex appeal and got mixed up
with a lot of characters with names like Otto the Ox and
Bertha the Body. He was just finishing it on the following
afternoon—for stories about New York private detectives,
involving as they do almost no conscious cerebration, take very
little time to write . . . (PHW)

'Yes, they're fakes, every one of them,' Mortimer Bayliss said.
'I can tell you the artists' names if you wish. This one', he
indicated the Gainsborough he had been examining, 'is
undoubtedly a Wilfred Robinson. He painted a beautiful
Gainsborough. That Constable is a Sidney Biffen. His middle
period, I should say. About this Vermeer I'm not so sure. It
might be a Paul Muller or it might be a Jan Dircks. Their style
is somewhat similar, due no doubt to the fact that they were
both pupils of van Meegeren. Ah,' said Mr Bayliss with
enthusiasm, 'there was a man, that van Meegeren. Started out
in a modest way forging de Hoochs, and then rose to Vermeers
and never looked back. Sold the last one he did for half a
million pounds. They don't make men like that nowadays.
Still, Muller and Dircks are quite good, quite good. Not bad at
all,' said Mr Bayliss tolerantly.

'Yer mean the bally things aren't worth *anything*?' asked Lord Uffenham.

'Oh, they'd fetch a few hundreds, I suppose, if you had the luck to find the right mug. Hullo, as late as that? Time for my afternoon nap. Well, glad to have been of help' (SFI)

'Don't wave the thing about like that, Clarence! It may be loaded.' 'No,' said Lord Emsworth, pulling the trigger, 'it's not loaded' (LEO)

O

Oakley, Annie: the 5th Earl of Ickenham (Old Sureshot) armed with a catapult and brazil nut at the Drones Club front window, shows himself to be England's answer to, (CT)

Oakshott, William: last of a line who have held Ashendon Oakshott, Hants., for centuries, large, sunburned and likeable, is the victim of years of oppression. (See **Sir Aylmer Bostock**). His position is not improved by his growing devotion to the marmoreal charms of his cousin Hermione, of whom even her father stands in awe. It is when Bill makes the acquaintance of his neighbour Frederick, Earl of (good old) Ickenham that his affairs enter upon a lively and enterprising phase, as Uncle Fred's protegés are prone to discover (UD)

ob. dic.: Like all patrons of coffee stalls, they were talking about the Royal Family (SA)

All babies are practically dotty. Where you and I would shrink from this cinnamon bear, the young Rockmeteller will be all over it (PP)

When two men get together who are not only crossed in love but reasonably full of McGuffy's Specials, it is inevitable that before long confidences will be exchanged. The bruised heart demands utterance (SFE)

Just as all American publishers hope that, if they are good and lead upright lives, their books will be banned in Boston, so all English publishers pray that theirs will be denounced from the pulpit by a Bishop. Full statistics are not to hand, but it is estimated that a good Bishop, denouncing from the pulpit with the right organ note in his voice, can add between fifteen and twenty thousand to the sales (CT)

Against hand-holding as a means of stimulating the creative faculties of the brain there is, of course, nothing to be said.

152

The trouble is that it is too often but a first step to other things (BC)

'Ha!' is one of those things it is never easy to find the right reply to. It resembles 'You!' in that respect (SLJ)

The arrival and departure of the supreme moment is apt to leave a feeling of emptiness. Horatius, as he followed his plough on a warm day over the cornland which his gratified country bestowed on him for his masterly handling of the traffic on the bridge, must sometimes have felt that life was a little tame (WF)

All crooners are nervous men. The twiddly bits seem to affect their moral stamina (QS)

To attract attention in the dining-room of the Senior Conservatives between the hours of one and two-thirty, you have to be a mutton-chop, not an Earl (SF)

'It couldn't be done. It would involve shaving off my moustache, to which I am greatly attached. When a man has neither chick nor child, he grows very fond of a moustache' (UD)

Average adjustors are like chartered accountants. When they love, they give their hearts forever (LEO)

A short-sighted man whose pince-nez have gone astray at the very moment when vultures are gnawing at his bosom seldom guides his steps carefully (LEO)

All publishers are sensitive, highly-strung men. Gollancz is. So is Hamish Hamilton. So are Heinemann, Chapman and Hall and Herbert Jenkins. They are also quick-witted. Hodder and Stoughton could not have acted more nimbly. Harold Pickering kissed Troon Rockett sixteen times in quick succession, and Faber and Faber say they would have done just the same (FO)

If it is true that the hour produces the man, it is also true that it remorselessly reveals the washout (HWA)

I often think the ideal life (said Lord Ickenham) would be to have plenty of tobacco and be cut by the County (UD)

Odo, Bishop of Bayeux: from whom Boko, Bishop of Stortford, claims descent, was not hitherto thought to have had legitimate Issue. When not shepherding his See with a crozier, performed prodigies with the episcopal battle-axe (MUN)

O'Hara, Donough: scion of that ancient and noble sept long established at Castle Taterfields, Co. Clare, Eire, is distinguished as the only representative of the old Irish nobility in the Wodehouse opus. He devotes his school life at Wrykin to the laudable aim of keeping the masters happy and occupied. When banished to outer space by his French master, he spends a pleasant hour with a bag of mixed chocolates and a copy of E. W. Hornung's *Raffles* (GB)

Old Battling Daphne: see **Dame Daphne Winkworth, D.B.E.**

Old Etonians, Old Rugbeians and Old Harrovians: the amatory precepts of, compared (PHW); among Old Harrovians listed are the late Sir Winston Churchill, K.G., and Frankenstein

Old George: a senior ant whose alarmed reports of a seismic disturbance are borne out by events (UD)

Old Sammy: with Young George Benedick, later Lord Uffenham, shares the dock at Bosher St. Police Court (SFI)

Oom, the King of: see **King Merolchazzar**

Otto of Saxe-Pfennig, H.S.H. Prince: leads a German invading army (TS)

Outer Isles, the Princess of the: standing on the terrace overlooking the gardens of the King of Oom on a summer's morning, perceives a godlike man who, as he pauses to pull up a sock, causes her heart to sing within her like birds (CC)

Ovens, George: landlord and licensee of that ancient and outstanding hostelry, the Emsworth Arms, High Street, Market Blandings, scene of so many stirring and dramatic events—not least the arrest of George Cyril Wellbeloved, the strange disappearance of Beach's prize watch, and the election address which causes the mouth-roofless Edwin Pott to strain a vocal chord. Even more sensational is the fact that here, the beer is still home-brewed:

> Ricky had come to the private bar in search of relief for his bruised soul, and he could have made no wiser move. Nothing can ever render the shattering of his hopes and the bringing of his dream castles to ruin about his ears really agreeable to a young man, but the beer purveyed by G. Ovens unquestionably does its best (UFS, *passim*)

Ovens, Percy: s. of the public benefactor at the Emsworth Arms, is an earthy and guileless Shropshire lad, liable to express pop-eyed approval of any chance-met ladies of classical outline (PHW)

Oxford and Asquith, 1st Earl of: MEET MR MULLINER is dedicated to,

Oxted, the Rt. Hon. the Earl of: of this philanthropic nobleman the sole recorded notice mentions his gift of a dress suit to his butler Bowles (U)

P

Packleby, Old: one of the Leicestershire Packlebys and an incandescent flame in the London of the 'nineties, is nowadays (understandably) not allowed the use of a butter-knife (SL)

Paddington Station, W.2: among devotees of that admirable if unexpected modern cult of railway history, earth has no stauncher fanatics than the friends of the old G.W.R. In hot youth one was wont to champion the Irish Mail even against the redoubtable Flying Scotsman and for years spurned the speedier New Street–Stafford–Lime-Street trip in favour of the statelier Snowhill–Chester–Rock Ferry route. And besides, isn't the Bristolian the greatest, grandest, swiftest . . . ? The point is that the Old Master seems to be with us in spirit. His many references to the Queen of London termini may by some be thought fortuitous in that Paddington happens to be the only possible take-off point for Blandings, Market Snodsbury and points west. Not so. Paddington is in a sense unique, for such references almost always bear witness to that pre-war air of calm dignity which even then had forsaken baser and less happier realms.

> At Waterloo all is hustle and bustle, and the society tends to be mixed. Here a leisurely peace prevails and you get only the best people—cultured men accustomed to mingling with basset-hounds and women in tailored suits who look like horses (UFS)

To-day's commuters may care to ponder an undeniable fact. Two world wars and a social revolution have not, even yet, quite robbed Paddington of that quality. It is still there and detectable—the shadow of a shade. There are certain times of day, on certain days of the week, when those women and those men embark at a certain platform for a certain destination—the last, tenuous pocket of privilege left in England, and long may it reign. In such passengers we see the modern successors of that assortment of travellers who once on a day caught the 2.45 (14.45 to you) for Market Blandings:

> 'Note the chap next door,' said Lord Ickenham. 'No doubt some son of the ruling classes, returning after a quiet jaunt in London to his huntin', shootin' and fishin'.'
> The individual to whom he alluded was a swarthy young man who was leaning out of the window, surveying the Paddington

scene through a pair of steel-rimmed spectacles . . . Lord
Ickenham led his nephew away down the platform, apologising
with a charming affability to the various travellers with whom
the latter collided in his preoccupation. One of these, a portly
man of imposing aspect, paused for a moment on seeing Lord
Ickenham, as if wavering on the verge of recognition.

'Who was that?' asked Pongo, dully.

'I haven't an idea,' said Lord Ickenham. 'He would probably
turn out to be someone who was at school with me, though
some years my junior. When you reach my age, you learn to
avoid these reunions. The last man I met who was at school
with me, though some years my junior, had a long white beard
and no teeth. It blurred the impression I had formed of myself
as a sprightly young fellow on the threshold of life' (UFS)

Meanwhile the swarthy young man who, as a matter of routine,
always eyed people keenly 'substituted a travelling-cap for the rather
forbidding black hat he was wearing', and prepared to follow his
noble employer's excellent and invariable example when travelling
by train.

It was at Paddington, too, that the youthful 'Biscuit' Biskerton
underwent a searing experience:

'Fusses over you, does she? They do, these old nurses. Mine
once kissed me on the platform at Paddington, ruining my
prestige at school for the whole of one term' (BM)

Nor does the Wodehouse aficionado pass the small, busy post-office
on Platform One without lively memories of an elderly, harassed
Earl who, with two minutes to go before his train left, composed a
telegram which was to cause anguish to the telegraph operator who,
on his own responsibility, crossed out 'Ariosto' and wrote 'arriving'
substituted 'teatime' for 'totem', but failed to decide whether the
sender would arrive at Blandings Castle with leprosy or landlady.
How right too is R. B. D. French when pointing out that 'hours
have been spent in college common-rooms working out the time-
tables of the old Great Western Railway between Paddington and
Market Blandings', and adding sapiently that 'the service has not
become less whimsical with nationalisation' (PGW), though the
route, nowadays, is perhaps more rational. The journey, by fast
train, used to take about three hours and forty mins. Much would
seem to have depended on whether the first stopping-place was
Oxford or (even more unexpectedly) Swindon. The Bicester–
Banbury–Leamington Spa route would be normal to-day. Another
distinguished user of the convenient 2.45 is his Grace of Dunstable

who (a Wiltshireman) normally travels from Waterloo (Salisbury first stop—eighty-seven miles in eighty-seven mins.). There are, too, those melancholy occasions (dwelt on elsewhere) when Paddington is the mise-en-scène for the departure of fair young maidens, metaphorically by-gyved, off to do their stretch at Blandings. It seems odd that this detail should have been overlooked in Frith's famous painting (*passim*)

Painter, Otis: unwisely turns publisher and finds himself at the receiving end of a substantial libel suit by Sir Aylmer Bostock, for having published, in that nabob's autobiography, the photograph of a nude female figure captioned 'Myself in the early twenties' (UD)

Painter, Sally: dau. of a talented artist who shared Fred Ickenham's chequered youth in the U.S., is one of the nicest in Wodehouse's gallery of young women. Gay or grave, adventurous, undeniably pretty, she earns enough for an occasional meal in her Chelsea studio, and is destined for a life's happiness with Pongo Twistleton (UD)

Palace Theatre: Shaftesbury Avenue, W.; appears intermittently throughout the opus. Lord Dawlish, e.g., ponders the best method of laying a golf ball dead in front of it (UM *et al.*)

Pallant, George: old crony of Gally and Clarence in the 'nineties, is disconcerted on being told by an unshaven fellow-breakfaster that not only razors, but even butter-knives, are denied to him (SL)

Pargiter: an eel expert, informs Lord Uffenham that the streams in southern England are so replete with elvers that the water has the consistency of jelly (SFI)

Parker, Julia: it is on the pipterino Julia and her pink chappie Wilberforce Robinson that Lord Ickenham, in Hilaire Belloc's words, 'showers gold, in order that they may buy their London milk round and live happily ever after—a lovely pair of lovers'. It is they, too, who provide yet one more object lesson for the hapless Pongo:

> 'I don't know how to thank you', she said, and the pink chap said he didn't either.
> 'Not at all, my dear, not at all,' said Lord Ickenham. He kissed her on both cheeks, the chin, the forehead, the right eyebrow and the tip of the nose, Pongo looking on the while in a baffled and discontented manner. Everybody seemed to be kissing this girl except him (YMS)

Parsloe-Parsloe, Sir Gregory, Bart.: with the possible exception of the Bart. of ffinch Hall, no nobleman on the canvas has been subjected to such unwarranted suspicion and indeed downright denigration than the 7th Baronet of Much Matchingham, Shropshire. He succeeded to the title on the death of a cousin, and is e.s. of the late Dean Parsloe, q.v. Appearances have ever been against poor Tubby Parsloe, so that, as Usborne points out, even the publishing house of Herbert Jenkins are convinced of his villainy:

> In the printed synopsis at the beginning of **PIGS HAVE WINGS** Herbert Jenkins say 'on previous occasions the unscrupulous baronet has made determined efforts to nobble Lord Emsworth's pig'. Not true. Sir Gregory was always innocent of the strategies which the Blandings brothers imputed to him, and Herbert Jenkins ought to have remembered it. His only sins (other than over-eating) were that, in his hot pre-title youth he had, or Galahad thought he had, nobbled Galahad's dog Towser before a rat-killing contest and, as a bloated baronet, he had taken on as his pig-man, George Cyril Wellbeloved, at higher wages. (WAW)

Galahad is pretty convinced about the Towser episode:

> 'One or two of us used to meet at the Black Footman in Gossiter Street in the old days, and match our dogs against rats in the room behind the bar. Well, I put my Towser, an admirable beast, up against young Parsloe's Banjo on one occasion for a hundred pounds a side. And when the night came and he was shown the rats, I'm dashed if he didn't just give a long yawn and roll over and go to sleep. I whistled him . . . called him . . . no good, fast asleep. And my firm belief has always been that young Parsloe took him aside just before the contest and gave him about six pounds of steak and onions. Couldn't prove anything of course, but I sniffed the dog's breath and it was like opening the kitchen door of a Soho chophouse on a summer night' (SL)

Tubby's life in fact, to his misfortune, has always been an open book to Gally, but he has lived it and enjoyed it as fully as that gay boulevardier himself, despite slings and arrows that would have daunted a lesser man. He has allegedly 'lived one jump ahead of the gendarmerie'; is believed to slice bread with a corkscrew; is a hornswoggling highbinder, the world's worst twister, as slippery as a greased eel, a confirmed what-whatter, a 'sheep-faced, shambling exile from hell who would dope his own grandmother's bran mash and acorns', and looks like a captive balloon poised for its flight. He has walked round Romano's with a soup tureen on his head and a stick of celery on his shoulder, announcing that he is a Buckingham Palace sentry; has purloined Lord Burper's false teeth, and been thrown out of the Café d'Europe for trying to raise the price of a bottle of champagne by raffling his trousers, and is 'as wide as Leicester Square'. In other words, a lively and rather likeable chap —in his creator's words 'a practically blameless bart.—one of those who start their lives well, skid for a while and then slide back on to the straight and narrow path and stay there'. He did *not* (despite all appearances) break faith with his Maudie at the church door, and that he is a sportsman is made clear when he loses the first prize for pumpkins to Lord Emsworth after winning it three years running:

> There was the right stuff in Sir Gregory. In the Parsloe tradition there was nothing small or mean.
> 'Congratulate you, Emsworth', he said huskily.
> 'Eh? Oh, thanks. Thanks, my dear fellow, thanks, thanks. Er—can't both win, eh?'
> Sir Gregory puzzled it out and saw that he was right.
> 'No,' he said, 'no. See what you mean. Can't both win. No getting round that' (BCE)

Uncle to both Monty Bodkin and to Monica Simmons, he marries, at long last, Beach's niece, Maudie Stubbs. Res., Matchingham Hall, Much Matchingham, Shropshire (Tel. Matchingham 83) (SL, HW, BCE, PHW)

Parsloe-Parsloe, the Very Rev. Dean: f. of the Bart.-to-be, takes stern measures with young Tubby, of whom Gally relates:

> 'He hadn't a penny except what he could get by telling the tale, and he always did himself like a prince. When I knew him first, he was living down on the river at Shepperton. His old father, the Dean, had made arrangements with the keeper of the pub there to give him breakfast and bed and nothing else. "If he wants dinner he must earn it," the old boy said. And do you know how he used to earn it? He trained that mongrel of his, Banjo, to go and do tricks in front of parties that came to the place in steam-launches. And then he would stroll up and hope his dog was not annoying them and stand talking till they went in to dinner and then go in with them and pick up the wine list, and before they knew what was happening he would be bursting with their champagne and cigars' (SL)

Pashley-Drake, Col. Sir Francis: completes the executive staff at the rural abattoir known as Bludleigh Court, Goresby-on-the-

Ouse. He claims to have exterminated more gnus than any hunter in history. The surviving relatives (if any) of these unfortunate beasts, like those of the moose, elk, oryx, waterbuck, springbok, eland, hartebeeste, giraffe, zebu and other wildfowl whose glassy eyes peer reproachfully from every wall in Bludleigh Court, have now received a permanent reprieve by reason of the Colonel's lumbago. Incidentally, the intrepid soldier lives to learn that much of the fascination of shooting depends on whether one is at the giving or receiving end of the gun (MMS, PP)

Passfield, the late Lord: seldom danced in Soho night-spots (YMS)

Patzel, Fred: hog-calling champion of the Western States, whose expertise averts a tragedy at Blandings (see **bringing home**) (BCE)

Pearce, Jonathan Twistleton: godson of Lord Ickenham, engaged to Belinda Farringdon. His home, Hammer Lodge, Dovetail Hammer, Berks., is leased to Sir Raymond Bastable (CT)

Peasmarsh: family name of the Earl of Bodsham

Peasmarsh, Lady Mavis: dau. of Lord Bodsham, returns Freddie Widgeon to store in favour of a lady in a pink negligée picked out with blue lovebirds (NS)

Peasmarsh, the Hon. Wilfred: schoolboy s. of Lord Bodsham and a discerning critic of headgear (NS)

Peavey, Aileen: one of Connie Keeble's literary finds, introduced at Blandings as a brilliant poetess of the younger school, is better known in other circles as Smooth Lizzie (LIP)

Peckham, the Most. Hon. the Marquess of: distinguished member of the Twelve Jolly Stretcher Cases (EBC)

Peebles, the Rt. Hon. Viscount: head of a well-known firm of whisky distillers (DD)

Pegler, Hermione Winthrop: *ci-devant* (in a double sense) Marquise de Maufringneuse, *ci-aussi-devant* Mrs L. J. Quackenbush; a lady, in fact, who counts that day lost on which she doesn't divorce somebody (FL)

Pendlebury-Davenport: family name of the Duke of Dunstable

Pendlebury-Davenport, Horace: neph. and heir-pres. to the 6th Duke of Dunstable, q.v. Res. Bloxham Mansions, Park Lane, W. Club: Drones. An engaging young man, slender as a meridian of longitude whom Euclid, on seeing him approach, might have used as an example of his definition of a straight line having length but no breadth. Darts champion of the Drones. Is one of the few characters linking the Blandings with the Wooster saga. His appearances in the former, though brief, are colourful—his appearance in the dock at Marlborough St. in the guise of a Zulu warrior, and subsequently in the Drones Club, more than ordinarily so. In UFS he is the victim of his uncle's pokerwork, and in UD a victim of Uncle Fred's recipé for May Queen. Engaged to Valerie Twistleton (see also WW) (*passim*)

Pendlebury-Davenport, the late Lady Horatia: it is while examining critically the noble proportions of the Empress of Blandings that the Duke of Dunstable recalls the melancholy facts about his aunt:

> 'Much too fat. Look at her. Bulging.'
> Lord Emsworth started violently. 'She has already been given two medals for being fat.'
> 'Don't be silly, Clarence. What would a pig do with medals? There's only one word for that pig—gross. She reminds me of my Aunt Horatia, who died of apoplexy during Christmas dinner. Keeled over halfway through her second helping of plum pudding and never spoke again. This animal might be her double. You stuff her and stuff her and stuff her, and I don't suppose she gets a lick of exercise from one week's end to another. What she wants is a cracking good gallop every morning, and no starchy foods. That would get her into shape.'
> (UFS)

Pendlebury-Davenport, the late Lord Rupert: y.s. of the 5th Duke of Dunstable. In the opinion of his bro. the 6th Duke, resembled his father, his aunt, his nephews, Archie and Ricky, Lord Emsworth and Myra Schoonmaker, in that they were each and severally potty (SS)

perils of heredity, the: the master of Blandings was one of those fluffy-minded old gentlemen who are happiest when experimenting with strange drugs. It was not until he had retired to bed that he discovered the paper-wrapped bottle on the table by his side. Then he remembered that the pest Popjoy had mumbled something at dinner about buying him something or other for his injured ankle. He tore off the paper and examined the contents of the bottle with a lively satisfaction. The liquid was a dingy grey and sloshed pleasantly when you shook it.

The name on the label—Blake's Balsam—was new to him, and that in itself was a recommendation.

His ankle had long since ceased to pain him, and to some men this might have seemed an argument against smearing it with balsam; but not to Lord Emsworth. He decanted a liberal dose into the palm of his hand. He sniffed it. It had a strong, robust, bracing sort of smell. He spent the next five minutes thoughtfully rubbing it in. Then he put the light out and went to sleep.

It is a truism to say that in the world as it is at present constituted few things have more far-reaching consequences than the accident of birth. Lord Emsworth had probably suspected this. He was now to receive direct proof. If he had been born a horse instead of the heir to an earldom, that lotion would have been just right for him. It was for horses, though the Rev. Rupert Bingham had omitted to note the fact, that Blake had planned his balsam; and anyone enjoying even a superficial acquaintance with horses and earls knows that an important difference between them is that the latter have the more sensitive skins. Waking at a quarter to two from dreams of being burned at the stake by Red Indians, Lord Emsworth found himself suffering acute pain in the right leg.

He was a little surprised. However, being a good amateur doctor he bore up bravely and took immediate steps to cope with the trouble. Having shaken the bottle till it foamed at the mouth, he rubbed in some more lotion. It occurred to him that the previous application might have been too sketchy, so this time he did it thoroughly. He rubbed and kneaded for some twenty minutes. Then he tried to go to sleep.

Nature has made some men quicker thinkers than others. Lord Emsworth's was one of those leisurely brains. It was not till nearly four o'clock that the truth came home to him. When it did, he was just on the point of applying a fifth coating. He stopped abruptly, replaced the cork and, jumping out of bed, hobbled to the cold water tap and put as much of himself under it as he could manage (BCE)

Pershore: family name of Lord Worlingham

Pershore, the Earl of: courtesy title of the e.s. and heir of the Marquess of Malvern, Wilmot (Motty) is thin, chinless and deceptively meek-looking, having suffered all his life from parental domination and a sheltered existence in a Shropshire village. Given a conditional freedom in New York, he steps high, wide and handsome to such a degree that a term in a police cell probably saves his life (MJ)

Pershore, the Hon. Aubrey: a s. of Lord Worlingham, is infatuated with a person at the Gaiety Theatre (DD)

Peters, Aline: with Ashe Marson, George Emerson and her own millionaire father, belongs to the initial and part-experimental Blandings intended as a playful satire on life above and below stairs in an English country house, as acceptable to the reading public of the day. The Freddie Threepwood of the period was not worthy of Aline, whose heart and hand go to the sturdy, intelligent George (SF)

Peters, J. Preston: has the dyspepsia which is the concomitant of commercial wealth and is an avid collector of antiquities, like his host Lord Emsworth. A 4th Dynasty Egyptian scarab forms the basis of an extended hunt-the-slipper session (SF)

Peterson's Pup Food: though not such an abomination as Todd's Tail Waggers Tidbits, mention of its name nevertheless occasions the air of a man bitten in the leg to Freddie Threepwood, English ambassador for Donaldson's Dog Joy (FM)

Petherick-Soames, Major General Sir Masterman: horsewhips Capt. Walkinshaw on the steps of the Drones Club for trifling with the affections of his niece Hester; horsewhips Rupert Blenkinsop-Bustard on the steps of the Junior Bird Fanciers for slighting the feelings of his niece Gertrude; asks searching questions of Osbert Mulliner (see WW) as to whether his club is equipped with steps (MMS)

Petite, Pauline: world famous film star, the screen idol of Freddie Threepwood and heroine of a succession of shattering epics including *Passion's Slaves, Silken Fetters, Purple Passion, Bonds of Gold, Seduction* and other masterpieces of which Lord Emsworth has never heard (BCE)

Pevensey, the Most Noble the Duke of: an empirical nobleman who, when speaking at a public dinner, is reminded by a mere earl (a *soi-disant* one at that) that he is not the only onion in the mince (IWY)

Pharaoh, King of Egypt: his notorious unwillingness to let people go is his long suit, but in MM he all but loses one of his prophets to the dumb chum William. Believing that all things bright and beautiful were made for him to eat, William makes a sustained effort to devour a plaster statuette of the Young Joseph Prophesying Before Pharaoh, but desists on receiving A Present From Clacton in the short ribs.

Phipps, Judson: some think this bimbo as crazy as his sister Julia; others think him even more so. A bachelor with a long trail of breach-of-promise suits, becomes engaged to a complete stranger within twenty minutes of landing in New York and is already having grave doubts ten minutes after. (See **Drones Club**) (PP)

'Pig At Bee, The': hitherto undiscovered masterpiece by Sir Edwin Landseer, out of Gally Threepwood (FM)

'Pigs And How To Make Them Pay': a treatise by one of the minor prophets who preceded the masterly Whiffle in Lord Emsworth's notable collection (SL)

PIGS HAVE WINGS: published 1952. One of the most joyous of the Blandings-Matchingham saga. It is when one has the dubious privilege of taking apart a Wodehouse story for broadcasting purposes that one comes fully to appreciate the patience and skill of the plot construction. Approaching the climax, the knots seem inextricable. One loose string is pulled and the whole thing comes out straight, with happy endings all round (PHW)

Pilbeam, Percy Frobisher: this former editor of the Tilbury weekly scandal sheet, *Society Spice*, has collected, over the years, a varied but always graphic and colourful press. Perhaps the most charitable description is that he is a reptilian squirt with narrow eyes and his hair done in distressing ridges. Candour compels one to add that his pimples are normally offset by a red tie, his moustache is small and revolting; he is a slimy, slinking, marcelle-waved by-product; he is odious and thrusting; he is at once and severally a poison sac, a bacillus, a snake in the grass, a pestilence, a pustule, a blister, a wen and a yam. He is also (in Ronnie Fish's view) a Lothario who has lowered all speed records in underhand villainy by breaking up a man's home before he has got one. Yet his success cannot be denied. Despite nature's handicaps and his own shortcomings, he gets by. As proprietor of the highly dubious Argus Private Enquiry Agency in Beeston St., S.W., he gets quite handsomely by. Time and again, retribution closes in. Ruin stares him in the ferret-like face. Always he escapes, to point the moral of the green bay tree, a reminder to all whom he encounters that into each life some rain must fall (*passim*)

Pinfold, Lady: relict of the late Sir Ramsworthy and mother of that virulent do-gooder Dora, is (for the statutory day or two) mother-in-law-elect to Freddie Widgeon (LEO)

Ping Pong Pang, H.I.H. Prince: Chinese general (TS)

Pinkney, Arlene: selected for the British Curtis Cup team (PP)

Pinkney, Arnold: a tightwad tycoon and in Bunting's opinion a super-fatted poop, for whom Fate waits with a well-stuffed eelskin (PP)

Pink Un's and Pelicans: to-day's readers (I was myself one of the under-informed) may be glad of a little guidance in regard to Galahad Threepwood's effervescent memories of the brave days of old. The old buster scatters his stories round with such *éclat* that it is usually impossible to detect which of the characters are historic and which fictional. The Pelican Club was of course an actuality, as are a half-dozen of the gay boulevardiers with whom he peoples not only the Club itself but those other lively *fin-de-siècle* hot-spots, the National Sporting Club, Romano's, the old Empire, the Oxford and Tivoli music-halls and the old Gaiety. The Pelican Club was founded by 'the Shifter' (William Farm Goldberg) in Denman St., Piccadilly Circus, and when bought out by Ernest 'Swears' Wells he became the first secretary of the National Sporting Club and the Pelican moved to new premises in Gerrard St., Soho. At our first introduction to Gally (SL) Wodehouse cites him as 'a brother-in-arms of Hughie Drummond and Fatty Coleman, of the Shifter, the Pitcher, Peter Blobbs and the rest of an interesting but not strait-laced circle'; and in so doing he pinpoints with precision the clubland level on which the extrovert younger son of an earl, in those days, would be most likely to find his métier. 'Peter Blobbs' was the pseudonym of Reginald Shirley Brooks. Hughie Drummond once figured in an incident which parallels Gally's story about Plug Basham at Romano's, but Hughie's offensive weapon was not a side of beef but a glazed boar's head. 'The Pitcher' was Arthur M. Binstead. When I was gathering information for this entry, Macdonald Hastings, well-known author, broadcaster, and last editor of the ever-lamented *Strand* magazine, told me: 'As a very small boy I remember meeting Arthur Binstead ("The Pitcher") in our house. He was a friend of my father. He was indirectly famous for the polish on his shoes. I think he painted varnish on them.'

In an inaugural address at the Pelican, Sir John Astley said: 'I believe in a man takin' his own part an' bein' able to put 'em up if he wants to. What's the use of carryin' a damn great stick about, or one of those blasted six-shooters? So long as he's got his two bunches of dukes hangin' down by his sides an' can put 'em up he don't want anything else and God damn all other inventions.'

The membership numbered many coroneted heads and the general impression one gets is of an uninhibited version of the Pirates of Penzance (They are all Noblemen who have Gone Wrong) and of a studied attempt to revive the Corinthian tradition of the previous century. It was Hughie Drummond, incidentally, who was once thought to have gone a little far when he drove a four-wheeler cab filled with fellow members into the Club common-room, to give a twenty minute rendering of the Club anthem. Interested readers should consult the splendidly racy books of J. B. Booth (especially *Old Pink Un' Days*) and Tom Girtin's lively *The Abominable Clubman*. As for Romano's in the Strand (almost opposite the old Tivoli) the famous red plush, known to King Edward VII as Prince of Wales, vanished little more than a decade ago. But it remains true that from outside the now rebuilt Romano House, Gally Threepwood could to-day win his dinner wager that one can see the time by the Law Courts' clock. Most men of the world who knew their host and his nickname were rigid in pronouncing it *RO*mano's. That legal luminary, Sir John Simon, once so referred to the restaurant in the High Court of Justice, and his adversary, Sir Ernest Wild, was quick to comment:

> 'The learned Solicitor-General shows every indication of a well-spent youth by calling it ROmano's.'

And it is with quiet satisfaction that I record that I myself have been told, by the head waiter of Scotts in Coventry Street:

> 'If his Majesty King Edward the Seventh was to drop in here once again, this evening, I reckon we could still show him to his usual table.'

London Pride—what can compare with it! (*passim*)

Pirbright, Percy James: second in the noble dynasty of mentors and janitors to Empress of Blandings, though the first to appear (the faithless George Cyril having already deserted her) is a mono-syllabic Shropshire lad, even thinner, taller and scraggier than her owner (HW, PHW)

'Pitcher, The': Arthur Binstead; see **Pink Un's**

Platt, Rhoda: waitress at the Buffers Club, S.W., stirs matrimonial ambitions in the elderly Earl of Yaxley, q.v. (VGJ)

Plimsoll, Tipton: this engaging young U.S. millionaire is the s. of the late Chester (Chet) Plimsoll, close friend of Gally Threepwood and owner of a chain of multiple stores straddling the States. Twenty years have passed since he entered the Blandings scene in FM, to reappear in GBL (1965) as effervescent a character as any in the opus. To sketch his dossier, he is the son of parents who, having married each other, at once started marrying other people with a perseverance worthy of a better cause; had one of those childhoods where the bewildered offspring finds himself passed from hand to hand like a medicine ball; mother of, divorced father of, because he got her to the station at 10.7 to catch a train which had left at 7.10; has seen far too much of that EX-WIFE'S HEART-BALM—SOCIETY LOVE TANGLE stuff; is as soused as a herring; has the voice of one who at no distant date has been wandering long and far across the hot sands; pink spots sprout on the chest of; has advanced alcoholic poisoning; picks a lemon in the Harley St. garden of medicine; throws soft-boiled eggs at the electric fan at the Angry Cheese Club; love comes to, but green-eyed monster runs up leg of, biting him to the bone; wishes Lord Emsworth would trip over moonbeam and break his neck; sees Veronica Wedge's lovely features with burning spectacles; has to answer snakes who speak to him but sees no reason to do so sunnily; resigns his hip flask with something of resignation of Russian peasant throwing infant son to pursuing wolf-pack; feels that phantom faces, wired for sound, are going too far; is firm with a phantom . . . Of romance, he has seen much. Like Kipling's hero, he had learned about wimmen from Doris Jimpson, Angela Thurloe, Vanessa Wainwright, Barbara Bessemer, Clarice Burbank and Marcia Ferris; especially Marcia Ferris, the Russian Ballet one, and Clarice Burbank, who made him read Kafka; which is why (as he explains) he likes Vee Wedge, dumbest brick in Shropshire and the adjoining counties, so much:

> 'She probably thinks Kafka's a brand of instant coffee,' said Sandy, 'with 97% of the kaffein extracted.'
> 'Exactly. She's just a sweet, simple English girl,' said Tipton, 'with about as much brain as would make a jay bird fly crooked, and that's the way I want her.' (FM, GBL)

PLUM PIE: aptly named in a double sense, was published in 1966 when the author (incredibly) was 85. A *Times* leader, the same year, spoke of 'the incredible Mr Wodehouse'. It contains the short story *Sticky Wicket at Blandings* and the Freddie Threepwood long-short-story *Life With Freddie*. Both are instinct with such springlike zest that one interprets literally the phrase in Wodehouse's letter of some years ago; 'I still feel like a young fellow of twenty-five or so trying to get on, and not so good . . .'

Plumpton, the Rt. Hon. Lord: Everard Biddle looks like a mass murderer, except that his face lacks the genial expression one often sees in mass murderers. On the committee of the M.C.C., he knows the batting average of every first-class cricketer back to the days when they played in top-hats and whiskers, and has a cricket-loathing but dependent nephew on whom to inflict them (see **Conky Biddle**) (NS)

Poffin, Lord Percy: arrives at Nice (EBC)

Pond-Pond, the Rev. Alistair: vets the souls of the peasantry in the pleasant Worcs. village of Rudge-in-the-Vale. Ever a happy phrase-maker, the Vicar winds up the annual sports with an impressive appeal:

> We must not consider ourselves as belonging to this section of Rudge-in-the-Vale or to that section of Rudge-in-the-Vale. Let us recollect that we are all fellow-members of one united community. Rudge must be looked on as a whole. And what a whole it is. (MN)

Poole, the Rt. Rev. the Bishop of: stays at Blandings (HW)

Popgood & Grooly: publishers and public benefactors, it is they who give to the world Whiffle's monumental work *On The Care Of The Pig* at a modest 35/- (GBL *et al.*)

Poppenheim, the Graf von: A.D.C. to Prince Otto, q.v. (TS)

Portwood, Sir Chester: one of the last actor-managers, takes the Leicester Square theatre for a season and sets it, if not the Thames, on fire (JR)

Pott, Claud (Mustard): f. of the delectable Polly, is (and looks) a retired Silver Ring bookie who has done himself well on the starchy foods for years; expert also in improvising means of relieving other people's wallets of their burden. One shares Usborne's doubts as to whether even Fred Ickenham (his sole champion) could have sustained Mustard's limitations over a period of years. Retribution has a field day however when he sits down to teach the Duke of Dunstable how to play Persian Monarchs (UFS *et al.*)

Pott, Edwin: third in the devoted dynasty of valets to the Empress, Edwin holds the portfolio after Percy Pirbright's departure for the Canadian prairie. Factually he has a poorish press. Phrases such as 'niffy to a degree', 'well stricken in years', 'an odiferous gargoyle', 'either a smelly centenarian or an octogenarian prematurely aged by trouble', cling to him like the fragrance of the Empress's residence. Lady Constance calls him 'a gnome of a man who smells worse than the pig'. Nature herself has been unkind to him, but though he has no roof to his mouth, it does not prevent his addressing a general election meeting in the Tory interest in the Emsworth Arms bar. Edwin however has one friend in Gally Threepwood, who is moved to observe (and sermons have been preached on less worthy texts) 'After all, we can't all have roofs to our mouths' (probably one of the most humanistic *obiter dicta* in all Wodehouse). More potent still is the goddess Fortune who sees to it that Edwin wins a substantial football pool and retires to private life (PHW)

Pott, Polly: 'If Polly had had a respectable father', said Lord Ickenham, 'everything would be simple, but his greatest admirer couldn't call him a social asset to a girl.' It says the more for Polly that she wins the heart and hand of Ricky Gilpin:

> Lord Ickenham patted her hand, put his arm about her waist and kissed her tenderly. Pongo wished he had thought of that himself. He reflected moodily that this was always the way . . . If ever there had been any kissing or hand-patting or waist-encircling to be done, it had always been his nimbler uncle who had nipped in ahead of him and attended to it (UFS)

Pott, Sir Wandesbury: endows the Abbey Museum at Bottesford Mortimer (YMS)

Potter, Sir Preston: proud owner of that surpassing moustache Love In Idleness. Res., Wapleigh Towers, Norfolk:

> Except for a few outlying ears and the tip of a nose, the fellow was entirely moustache. Until he had set eyes on it he had never really appreciated the full significance of Longfellow's 'This is the forest primeval' (LEO)

Potts, Freddie: The only safe way to get through life (said Gally) is to pickle your system thoroughly in alcohol. Look at Freddie Potts and his brother Eustace the time they ate the hedgehog. They were living on the Riviera at the time and they had a French chef, one of whose jobs was to go to market and buy supplies. On the way to Grasse that day, as he trotted off with the money in his pocket, he saw a dead hedgehog lying by the side of the road. Now this chef was a thrifty sort of chap and he saw immediately that if he refrained from buying the chicken he'd been sent to buy and stuck to the money, he'd be that much up, and he knew that with the aid of a few sauces he could pass that hedgehog off as chicken all right, so he picked it up and went home with it, and served it up next day *en casserole*. Both brothers ate heartily, and here's the point of the story. Eustace, who was a teetotaller, nearly died, but Freddie, who had lived mostly on whisky since early boyhood, showed no ill effects whatsoever. I think there is a lesson in this for all of us, so press that bell, Clarence (GBL *et al.*)

Pourbus, Franz: (the Younger; 1569–1622; Flemish portrait painter. Among his best known works are four portraits of King Henri IV of France and Navarre). The only landscape attributed to him is an early painting of Blandings Castle, Shropshire, seat of the Threepwoods (later Earls of Emsworth). The picture (27 ins. by 16 ins.) hangs in the gallery at Blandings. More typical is his portrait of Richard 'Long Sword' Marshall (or Marischal), an ancestor of Lord Droitwich, to whom a romantic legend attaches. Depicting the subject in full armour of the period, this is in the Droitwich collection in the state drawing-room at Langley End, Worcs. (See **Long Sword**) (IWY *et al.*)

Powick, the Rt. Hon. the Earl of: it is in the Earl's library that the butler Phipps makes a stimulating acquaintance with Lyly's *Euphues* (OR)

Prenderby, Sir Mortimer, Bart.: maintains at his Oxfordshire seat, Matcham Scratchings, a clowder of cats, a kindle of kittens, a Donnybrook of dogs and an anthropoid ape (assiduously scratching away with the rest). In point of ferocity the baronet probably ranks second to Wilhelm, the cat-eating Alsatian, but his natural talents are stimulated by unexpectedly receiving a cat in the back of the neck (YMS)

Prenderby, Lady: consort of the foregoing, a tall, rangy type with tight lips and cold, blancmange eyes (YMS)

Price, Major: one of three minds with but a single thought whose verdict none can set at nought (PHW)

Price's Hygienic Toilet Saloon: in its Knightsbridge setting and traditions ranks in our minds with Tattersalls, Knightsbridge Green, Number One London and other landmarks. Known to generations of Londoners as Price's, *tout court*, and pointed out to provincial and overseas visitors with reverence in the small *cul-de-sac*, Mott St., off the Brompton Road. For most of the nobility and gentry living south of the Park, their first visit to Price's for the ceremonial shearing of their Fauntleroy locks stands out in memory like their first day at school, first hat-fitting at Bodmin's or first dinner-date at Mario's. Yet the founder had his doubts, when obeying fortune's command to go west, young man, whether this was not a little too far west, though his intuition in establishing a business well outside the sphere of the two famous firms in Bond St. and Curzon St. was justified. Soon, famous and historic figures—Sir Rowland Hill, W. M. Thackeray (who figures in the firm's books as still owing a few pence for whisker-trimming) among them—were customers. His fame was assured when the Iron Duke himself became a patron, continuing to come despite the momentary lapse which caused Price to nick his chin, occasioning thereby a flow of invective unequalled by his Grace since the field of Waterloo. Until recent street widening operations a mounting-stone of the Duke's (similar to those still seen elsewhere) stood in Mott St. The firm's modern history is high-lighted by its owner's remarkable and all-but-successful claim to the Earldom of Droitwich (IWY)

Pride of Matchingham: Sir Gregory Parsloe's portly nominee for the Fat Pigs Class at the Shropshire Show, though a match for Lord Tilbury's Buckingham Big Boy, is patently no match for the blimp-like Empress of Blandings, and is relegated to second string when the ambitious Bart. imports from foreign parts (Essex or Lincs. suspected) the more curvaceous Queen of Matchingham (HW, PHW)

Prosser, Alexander (Oofy): whose riches are outweighed only by his pimples, is cautiously conditioned into buying the stately Great Swifts property (see **Bagshot**) for his wife out of the millions his f. made from Prosser's Pep Pills (GBL *et al.*)

Psmith, Ronald Eustace Rupert: e.s. of R. E. Smith of Ilsworth Hall (later of Corfby Hall), Much Middlefold, Shropshire. Psmith's bright particular star illumines the Blandings scene only in LIP, though his exploits in MP, PSC and PSJ are perennially enjoyable. It is perhaps curious to reflect that the whole Blandings saga could have been completed with Psmith as the *Eminence Grise*—no Gally to compose lovers' differences, no Ickenham catalyst to drop time-bombs or to illumine the castle walls with moonbeams from the larger lunacy. Psmith's methods are smooth and decorous, yet they extract from deserving cases (whether evildoers or stuffed shirts) a maximum flow of innocent merriment. We would not, of course, have had it otherwise. The world needs its Gally and its Uncle Fred. Yet this febrile age of ours needs its Psmith too, for he is a sublime instrument of common sense (LIP *et al.*)

Pulteney-Banks, Mrs: only a cocoon of shawls is visible to the outer world of this aged mother of Lady Widdrington:

> 'They know! They know! Cats are cleverer than we think!' (MUN)

Pumpkin Phase, the: in his introduction to BCE the author observes that *The Custody of the Pumpkin* shows Lord Emsworth passing through a brief vegetable condition which succeeds the antiquarian era and precedes the more lasting pig seizure. As already observed, his late Majesty, King George V, was graciously pleased to intervene as arbiter between his English and his Scottish subjects:

> On the tenth night after McAllister's departure Lord Emsworth dreamed a strange dream. He had gone with King George to show his Gracious Majesty the pumpkin, promising him the treat of a lifetime; and, when they arrived, there in a corner of the frame was a shrivelled thing the size of a pea. He woke, sweating, with his sovereign's disappointed screams ringing in his ears.

and as a result of the royal disapproval persuades McAllister to return (BCE)

Punter, Lady: m. of the spirited Diana, retires to bed at her Berkeley Square home with a digestive tablet and a sex novel (YMS)

Pyke: family name of Viscount Tilbury

Pyke, Sir George Alexander, Bart.: see **Tilbury**

Pyke, the Hon. Roderick: e.s. and heir of Viscount Tilbury, is a tall, thin intellectual. Though not over-fond of his aunt Frances, feels that almost anyone who makes a third at an interview with his father is welcome (BC *et al.*)

Q

Quackenbush, L. J.: see **Pegler**

Quaglino's, W.: lunching at, Lady Hermione Wedge marks down Tipton Plimsoll for the complaisant Veronica (FM)

Queen Boadicea: (Boudicca of the Iceni); prototype of regal militancy, esp. applicable to women hunters and explorers. Crocodiles, lions, boa constrictors and other wildfowl, with time on their hands, usually repair of an evening to the tents of such ladies. At the Empire Exhibition at Wembley however, Britain's warrior queen unexpectedly wears a Tudor ruff (COJ *et al.*)

Queen Cleopatra: (B.C. 60–30); occurs *passim;* on the present canvas her most prismatic appearance is at Mario's Restaurant where she gives Jerry Vail a pep talk even excelling her advice to a laggardly soldier before the battle of Actium:

> When girls like Gloria Salt, planning dinner with an old friend, say they are going to dress, they use the word in its deepest and fullest sense, meaning that they propose to extend themselves and that such of the populace as are sharing the *salle a manger* with them will be well advised to wear smoked glasses. Jerry, waiting in the lobby, was momentarily stunned by what came floating through the revolving door twenty minutes or so after the time appointed for the tryst . . . Gloria Salt was tall and slim and the last word in languorous elegance. Though capable of pasting a golf ball two hundred yards and creating, when serving at tennis, the impression that it was raining thunderbolts, her dark beauty made her look like a serpent of Old Nile. A nervous host, encountering her on the way to dine, might have been excused for wondering whether to offer her a dry Martini or an asp (PHW)

Queen Elizabeth I: presents a silver salt to Amyas Carmody of Rudge in respect of services rendered (MN)

Queen Elizabeth: (H.M. Queen Elizabeth, the Queen Mother); implicitly depicted as handling with royal tact an incident at a Buckingham Palace dinner party (see WW)

Queen Gruoch: (Gruoch *nighean* Bode, Queen of Scots, called 'Lady Macbeth'; fl. 1050); as a prototype of royal hospitality, executive ability, and decisive action in dealing with a crisis; is also assoc. with her husband the Mormaer of Moray in her curiosity to get the latest battle reports from the spare room (*passim*)

Queen Guinevere: usu. in contexts of Arthurian reproach (cf. Caesar vis-à-vis Brutus) (*passim*)

Queen Isabella of Castile and Aragon: takes a hand in discovering America (*passim*)

Queen Jezebel: see **Jezebel**

Queen Marie Antoinette: a Zulu warrior inadvertently uses the softer portions of, as target for his assegai at the Albert Hall (UFS)

Queen Mary I: Lord Rowcester shares the traditional chagrin of, the words in his case being 'Three thousand and five pounds, two and six' (RJ)

Queen of Matchingham: Sir Gregory Parsloe's stupendous entry for the Shropshire Show is acquired in foreign parts (Essex or Lincs. according to rumour) to supersede Pride of Matchingham and topple Empress of Blandings from her coveted throne as the fattest pig in Shropshire (except Lord Burslem). A horrified Clarence relates the facts:

> 'From an inside pocket he produced a photograph . . . It was of an enormous pig. He thrust it under my nose with an evil leer and said "Emsworth, old cockywax, meet the winner of this year's Fat Pig medal!" His very words . . .'
> 'You don't mean it's fatter than the Empress?' said Gally, marvelling that such a thing could be possible.
> Lord Emsworth looked shocked. 'I would not say that. No. No, I certainly would not say that. But the contest will now become a desperately close one. It may be a matter of ounces' (PHW)

Queen of Sheba, the: perceiving Clarence, Earl of Emsworth, in sponge-bag trousers and morning coat, realises that the half was not told her (LEO); Prudence Garland is, (FM)

Queen Victoria: butler Phipps's mother resembles (OR); those little attentions which were all the go in the reign of (YMS)

Queensberry, the Marquess of: and the Rules so carefully mapped by (HK)

Queen's Hall: London W., and the late Sir Henry Wood (FM, SL); Yascha Prysky gives recital at, (HWA)

Querouaille, Louise de: Duchess of Portsmouth; see **King Charles II**

R

Rainsby, Viscount: courtesy title of the Earl of Datchet's e.s. and heir. His courtesy title at the Drones is Dogface. When at Oxford, was an earnest candidate for the Seekers Club (IJ)

Ramfurline, the Most Noble the Duke of: for the disturbing facts, see **Hungerford** (IJ)

Rampling, Hartley, M.D.: one of the full house of medicos to whom Tipton Plimsoll takes his pink patches (FM)

Ranelagh, Lord Frederick: a noble victim of Soapy Sid at Monte Carlo (IJ)

Rattigan, Terence: like the late Ian Hay is instanced by Wodehouse, vertically speaking, as all his admirers could desire, though barely discernible when seen sideways (SFE)

Raviogli, the Princess della: is (perhaps) rescued from a ravening covey of sharks by Capt.(?) Jack Fosdyke (NS)

Reddish, Hartley, M.P.: retiring member for the Bridgeford parliamentary division of Shropshire (LIP)

Regal Theatre, the: Shaftesbury Avenue, W.; it wears the likeness of first-hand reportage and is redolent of real stage life. Of its many appearances the most memorable is that in which, on a sweltering day in high summer, when chorus girls pray their show may see them through the dead season, Sue Brown goes to the manager's office to resign her job (SL)

rem acu: 'My dear child, mine has been a long life,' said Galahad, 'in the course of which I have frequently been bothered by experts. And always without effect. Bothering passes me by as the idle wind, which I respect not.'
'That's Shakespeare, isn't it?'
'I shouldn't wonder. Most of the good gags are.' (FM)

Renshaw, Clarence: an expert on the trochaic spondee (sic). Research suggests that he is the sole authority on this elephantine metrical foot (SFE)

reverting to the agenda: The morning sun shone down on Blandings Castle, and the various inmates, their breakfasts digested, were occupying themselves in their various ways. One may as well run through the roster to keep the record straight. Beach the butler was in his pantry reading an Agatha Christie; Voules the chauffeur was chewing gum in the car outside the front door. The Duke of Dunstable, who had come uninvited for a long visit and showed no signs of ever leaving, sat spelling through *The Times* on the terrace outside the amber drawing-room, while George, Lord Emsworth's grandson, roamed the grounds with the camera which he had been given on his twelfth birthday. He had been photographing—not that the fact is of more than mild general interest—a family of rabbits down by the west wood. Lady Constance was in her boudoir writing a letter to James Schoonmaker. Lord Emsworth's secretary was out looking for Lord Emsworth, and Lord Emsworth himself was on his way to the headquarters of Empress of Blandings . . . (SS)

'Reynard the Fox': John Masefield's epic should be consulted by those desiring clarification of Tipton Plimsoll's conviction that he is a hunted thing (FM)

Riggs' Superfine Emulsion: Sir Francis Pashley-Drake employs, for his lumbago; but the complaint yields more rapidly to treatment by a well-handled air rifle (MMS)

Robbins, Cousin Alfred: would probably die of shame if his niece Julia married a common eel-jellier (YMS)

Robert: has the influential post of Chief Assistant Torturer to the Lord High Executioner on the official establishment of his Excellency the Imperial Governor-General of Switzerland (WT)

Robinson, Ed.: his invaluable (if superannuated) taxi, drowsing in the sun outside Market Blandings railway station, is a cogent link between the Metropolis and Blandings Castle. It is likewise in occasional use as a rubbish repository for unwanted guests on the return route (HW *et al.*) and as a Black Maria for be-gyved nieces (*passim*)

Robinson, Wilberforce: this fairly pink young man (by occupation an eel-jellier) is doubly blest, being predestined not only for marital bliss with the pipterino Julia Parker but also for imperishable fame. Of the classic short story *Uncle Fred Flits By* (YMS) Hilaire Belloc observed:

> Then there are the immortal, vivid glimpses of suburban life, for example the glorious adventures of the uncle who breaks loose once a year and showers gold upon the young man who jellies eels, and his devoted would-be spouse, as vivid as a strong transparency on one small screen; a lovely pair of lovers, yet not a dozen adjectives between them (Introduction to WEW)

Rockmeteller, Bream: has recently added a Jun. to the strength:

> 'Well, actually,' said Freddie, 'Mrs Bream did most of the heavy work, but Bream gets his name on the bills' (PP)

Rockmeteller System, the: diametric opposite of the Ickenham System, is designed to wear down the victim's resistance. It has been known to produce results in six years, but see IWY for an even more protracted case (PP)

Roedean, the Pride of: that muscular hockey-knocker, Monica Simmons (PHW *et al.*)

Roegate, the Rt. Hon. Lord: like Lord Matchelow in the case of her cousin, is deservedly left at the post in the marriage stakes for Lord Emsworth's excellent niece, Jane (LEO)

Roland: hero of Roncesvalles, emulated by Syd Price (IWY)

Rollo, the Rt. Hon. Lord: pupil at Sanstead House (LN)

Rosherville Gardens: There is a story about Sir Stanley Gervase-Gervase (said Florence Craye) which is ghastly—I can't tell you! (COJ)

Romano's: Strand, W.C.; see **Pink Un's**

Ross, the Thane of: remarked of Macbeth 'His highness is not well', and would have said the same had his glance fallen on Pongo Twistleton (UD)

Rossiter, Jno.: popular purveyor of provisions, groceries and home-made jams, High St., Blandings Parva (BCE)

Rossiter, Mrs: wife of the grocer, is 'a nice, quiet, docile woman who on meeting you or any other member of the gentry, gave at the knees respectfully as you passed'. But when infected by the general spirit of *fiesta* at the annual School Treat in Blandings Castle Park:

> flushed in the face and with her bonnet on one side, seemed to have gone completely native. She was . . . drinking lemonade out of a bottle and employing her mouth, when not so occupied, to make a devastating noise with what he believed was termed a squeaker. The injustice of the thing wrung Lord Emsworth. How would Mrs Rossiter like it if one afternoon he suddenly invaded her neat little garden in the High Street and rushed about over her lawn, blowing a squeaker? (BCE)

'Round Britain Quiz': B.B.C. programme; see **Xanadu**

Rowcester, 2nd Earl of: (pron. 'Roaster'); the commendable suavity of, when mounting the scaffold in Cromwellian days, he bowed and waved a gloved hand to admirers in the front row of the stalls (RJ)

Rowcester, 3rd Earl of: known to discerning ladies-in-waiting at Charles II's court as Tabasco Rowcester (RJ)

Rowcester, 8th Earl of: host to King Edward VII at Rowcester Abbey, was never known to put on his own boots and, when in need of domestic help, threw his head back and howled like a timber wolf (RJ)

Rowcester, the Rt. Hon. the Earl of: William Egerton Bamfylde Ossingham Belfry, 9th of his line, is fully documented in WW. He suffers the results of the economic pressures best summed up by his sister's dictum that 'all the Rowcester men have been lilies of the field', but is fortunate in securing Jeeves as butler, at which point (not surprisingly) his fortunes begin to mend. Res. Rowcester Abbey, Southmoltonshire (RJ)

Royal Albert Hall, W.: the Bohemian Ball at, has a colourful sequel at Marlborough St. (UFS); falls on the Crystal Palace (COJ); All-In Wrestling Championship at, (FO); *mise* for the twenty-rounds contest between welterweights Rodd and Warburton (MN)

Rudel, the Seigneur Geoffrey: (or Galfridus), Prince of Blaye-en-Saintonge. Only Madeline Bassett, that superlative drip, dau. of the chief blister at Bosher St. Police Court, could liken any young man to, and she does it with a sigh that comes straight up from the cami-knickers (CW)

Rudge-in-the-Vale: Worcs., is a prototype of all the pleasant villages which star the Severn Vale. A quiet (some would say unconscious) place, it stands in the area where the grey Cotswold stone begins to give place to the mellow red brick of Worcestershire. It is somnolently content with its pop., 3,548 (*v. Automobile Guide*), its eleven pubs, Norman church, eloquent Vicar (see **Pond-Pond**) and most of all with the eighteen m. that separate it from Birmingham, feeling doubtless that its own sole effort—the emporium of Chas. Bywater, its popular and courteous chemist—sufficiently serves the cause of modern commercialism (MN)

Rumbelow, the Rt. Hon. Lord: though a mere Baron, entitled to only two white fur guards on his Parliamentary robes, suffers from that distinguished disease, Telangiectasis, and is therefore admitted to the Twelve Jolly Stretcher Cases on whose behalf (as junior member) he is deputed to make overtures to Sir Aylmer Bastable (EBC)

Rumtifoo, the Rt. Rev. the Bishop of: presents the prizes at Eckleton College (is this in the interim between attending the 'Synod called Pan-Anglican' and his re-embarkation for his faithless See?) and works off a totally inaudible speech lasting seventy minutes. (Of the good man's signature there can be no possible, probable shadow of doubt. It is, as all Gilbertian addicts are aware, + PETRUS RUMTIFOO) (HK)

Runyan, Damon: and the welldoer (UD)

S

St. Andrews: the Royal and Ancient figures largely off the present canvas. See however **Gloria Salt** (FM, PHW, *passim*)

St. Anthony: himself would have reeled at such a charge (SL); there is at times to be noted on the face of Pongo Twistleton an austere, wary look, such as might have appeared on that of, just before the Temptations began (UD)

St. Beowulf-in-the-West: parish church of, London W.; the Vicar writes to his Bishop saying he wants to know about incense, and is told he mustn't (MM)

St. Botolph's, Knightsbridge, S.W.: the saintly Bishop of Bongo Bongo once Vicar of, (MUN)

St. George's, Hanover Sq., W.: Lady Florence Craye selects, for her coming nuptials to Bertram W. Wooster (JFS)

St. James's St., S.W.: main stamping ground for generations of the Wodehouse nobility. Of Clubs, only the orthodox ones find footing in this perimeter. The extrovert clubs are scattered about Greater London while the subterranean ones are chiefly confined to Soho. Here portly gentlemen are to be seen on fine days, wheezing a little as they make the grade from one water-hole to the next. Prominent among them (and even more prominent when seen sideways) are Lords Blicester, Burper, Burslem, Plumpton, Bittlesham and (when U.S. sherry supplies run out) the Duke of Kirkcudbrightshire. Here too that festive old egg, Sir George Wooster, toddling from the Devonshire Club to Boodles, is shocked to see the ghost of his nephew Eustace (*passim*)

St. John, Florence: at the Old Gaiety (DD)

St. John's Wood, N.W.: in hot youth, George Uffenham is trailed by a private eye from, as far as Berkeley Square (MB)

St. Jude the Resilient: the church of, in Eaton Square, S.W., is chosen for fame as the public platform from which the venerable Bishop of Stortford, preaching with the right organ note in his voice, sternly denounces the novel *Cocktail Time* as impure, indecent, ribald, scabrous, unclean, immodest, lascivious, immoral and obscene, thereby causing its sales to soar by tens of thousands (CT)

St. Mihiel: where Archie Moffam gets his first bite in eight hours (IA)

St. Louis Post-Democrat, the: comments favourably on Mabel Potter's bird imitations (BCE)

St. Peter's, Eaton Square, S.W.: scene of the nuptials of Oliver Sipperley and Gwendolen Moon (VGJ); of the Hon. Roderick Pyke and Felicia Sheridan (BC); and of Wilmot Byng and Gwendolen Poskitt, when (we learn) the Bishop has never been in better voice (LEO)

St. Rocque: (or Roc, Rock or Roche; fl. 1327); making a pilgrimage from Montpellier to Rome, devoted himself to victims of the Plague; becoming infected, bore pain with patience and joy; returned to France where he practised piety and penance, dying at Montpellier. Esteemed as patron of sufferers from the Plague (*Golden Legend*):

> who that calleth to Seynt Rocke mekely he shal not be hurte with ony hurte of Pestylence

His feast day is August 16 (HWA)

St. Saviour's, Pimlico, S.W.: the ham-fisted message on Tubby Parsloe's note to Maudie Stubbs causes her to r.v. for their wedding on June 7, he having turned up, arrayed like Solomon, on the 4th. Some twenty sad, penitential years go by before the mistake is discovered (PHW)

St. Sebastian: Lord Chuffnell looks like, on receipt of about the fifteenth arrow (TJ)

St. Thomas's, New York City: 'Quite suddenly,' said Molly, 'he asked me to marry him, outside the cage of the Siberian yak.' 'No, sir,' exclaimed Sigsbee H. 'You'll be married in St. Thomas's like any other nice girl' (SB)

St. Vitus: Lady Abbott in her theatrical days had little in common with (SM)

salad—with dressing: Did I ever tell you about Clarence and the salad? It was in the days when he was younger and used to let me take him about London a bit. Well, of course, even then it wasn't easy to get him absolutely shining and glittering in lively society and being the belle of the ball, but he did have one unique gift. He could mix a superb salad. As his public relations man, I played this up on all occasions. When men came to me and said, 'Tell me, Gally, am I correct in supposing that this brother of yours is about as outstanding a dumb brick

and fathead as ever broke biscuit?' I would reply 'To a certain
extent, my dear Smith or Jones or whatever the name might be,
the facts are as you state. Clarence has his limitations as a social
ball of fire—except when it comes to mixing salads. You just
get him to mix you a salad one of these days.' So his fame grew.
People would point him out in the street and say 'That's
Emsworth, the chap who mixes salads.' And came a day when
I took him to the Pelican Club, feeling like the impresario of a
performing flea on opening night, and they handed him the
lettuce and the tomatoes and the oil and the vinegar and the
chives and all the rest of it, and he started in. He was a sensational success. He had cut his finger that morning and was
wearing a finger-stall, and I had feared that this might cramp
his style, but no, it didn't seem to hamper him a bit. He chopped
and mixed and mixed and chopped, with here a drop of oil and
there a drop of vinegar, and in due season the salad was
prepared in a lordly bowl and those present flung themselves
upon it like starving wolves. They loved it. They devoured it to
the last morsel. There wasn't as much as a shred of lettuce or a
solitary chive left in the bowl. And then, when everyone was
fawning on Clarence and slapping his back, it was noticed that
he was looking disturbed and unhappy. 'What's the matter, old
man?' I asked. 'Is something wrong?' 'Oh, no,' he said,
'everything is capital, capital . . . only I seem to have lost my
finger-stall' (PHW)

Salt, Gloria: the discerning male reader will have a special
category for this bewitching Serpent of Old Nile. So doubtless will
the wary female reader. Temperamental, extrovert and highly
decorative, she is more like a volcano than a girl with a handicap of
six at St. Andrews. On the beach at Cannes, or dashing about a
tennis-court, she invites the use of field-glasses. But making her
Cleopatrine entrance by night at Mario's, and looking like a snake
with hips, she is best seen through smoked glasses. Her engagement
to the multi-chinned Baronet of Matchingham is the chance result
of her impulsive temperament and a sore trial to them both, and her
subsequent reunion with Orlo Vosper is full of promise, though of
what, it would be difficult to predict (FM, PHW)

**Sarawak & New Guinea Rubber Estates Exploitation Co.,
the:** neighbours of R. Jones in the Strand, and none the happier
for it (SF)

Saviours of Britain, the: popularly (or otherwise) known as the

Black Shorts; see WW for details of this Fascist organisation founded and led by Roderick Spode, later Lord Sidcup

Savoy Theatre, the: Strand, W.C.; Lord Marshmoreton recalls the original production of Gilbert and Sullivan's *Yeomen of the Guard* at, and probably remembers the theatre's erection from the proceeds of Mr d'Oyly Carte's theatrical investments (DD)

Saxby, Howard: titular head of a literary agency, bird-watcher and chief gargoyle of the Demosthenes Club, Dover St., W., is amiably gaga and suggests something stationed in a cornfield to discourage crows (CT)

Scalpo: an alleged hair-restorer favoured by Lord Uffenham, though without discernible results (MB)

Schlossing-Lossing, H.S.H. the Prince von: looking bronzed and fit, is (possibly) amused by the practical jokes played on his princely person (LEO)

Schoonmaker, James R.: this hardy American millionaire is an old mutual friend of Galahad Threepwood and Fred Ickenham, both of whom cherish memories of their days with him in downtown New York. Gally, who on occasion also calls him 'old Johnnie', remembers him as a notable mixer of mint juleps (SL) and it must be a red-letter day when his sister Connie (GBL) becomes Lady Constance Schoonmaker. Uncle Fred recalls:

> When I was earning my living in New York, Jimmy was my great buddy. I don't get over to God's country much now— your aunt thinks it better otherwise. But even then, he was able to shoot a cigar across his face without touching it with his fingers, which we all know is the first step to establishing oneself as a tycoon. I expect by this time he's offended if he isn't investigated every other week by a Senate commission (SS)

An All-American footballer in youth, Jimmy still looks capable of busking a line, though to-day he would probably do it, not with a bull-like rush, but with an authoritative glance which would take all the heart out of the opposition. Res. Park Avenue, New York, and The Dunes, Westhampton, Long Island (SL, GBL, SS)

Schoonmaker, Myra: dau. of James R., is prevented from visiting Blandings in SL, but is ably (if unwittingly) impersonated by Sue Brown. She materialises in SS to elope (against all the odds) with the Rev. 'Bill' Bailey:

> 'Do I know her!' said Lord Ickenham. 'Many's the time I've

given her her bath. Of course I'm coming to her wedding. She would never forgive me if I were not there to hold her hand when the firing-squad assembles' (SS)

Seacliff, the Rt. Hon. Lord: as a nephew of Gen. Mannister, Squiffy Seacliff has a natural talent for the wassail bowl and a genius for lapping it up (IA)

Seltzerpore, H.H. the Rajah of: benefactor (but strictly in the historical sense) of Beckford College (PU)

Senior Conservative Club, the: Northumberland Avenue, W.C. (where it doubtless keeps a watchful eye on the National Liberal Club). We make its acquaintance in PSC when Psmith, nominated for membership at a tender age, is found nestling elegantly amongst its dukes, earls and elder statesmen. Here too we first meet that country member, Clarence, Earl of Emsworth, lecturing the head waiter (see **Adams**) on the need to masticate one's food, and absent-mindedly pocketing the cutlery (PSC, SF, FM, BCE *et al.*)

SERVICE WITH A SMILE: published in 1962. The walls of Blandings Castle are stout enough—just—to contain the convulsions of nature which follow Lord Ickenham's kindly promise to rid its owner of an unwanted secretary, a domineering sister, a despotic duke and an encamped Church Lads Brigade (SS)

Severn, the River: like a protective girdle Sabrina circles the far bounds of the Blandings countryside, a silver ribbon twining through the meadows of the verdant, drowsy Vale of Blandings, and receiving the lively confidences of her tributary streams, the brook Wipple, the River Wopple and the Skirme (FM, SM, MN)

Shelley, Percy Bysshe: (1792–1822); did not rhyme very well (see **moments,** (*passim*)

Shipton-Bellinger: family name of the Earl of Brangbolton

Shipton-Bellinger, the Hon. Joseph: bro. of Lord Brangbolton, with the usual remission for good conduct, should be in circulation again about July (MUN)

Shipton-Bellinger, Lady Millicent: y. da. of Lord Brangbolton, her radiant blonde beauty is often featured in the shiny weeklies. Her wedding to Adrian Mulliner, though beatified by the presence of the Dean of Bittlesham, has a startling sequel (MUN)

short snorts: so their author describes the stories in **BLANDINGS CASTLE AND ELSEWHERE:**

The stories . . . represent what I may term the short snorts in between the solid orgies. From time to time I would feel the Blandings Castle craving coming over me, but I had the manhood to content myself with a small dose (BCE)

Shropshire: see **Infants' Bible Class; Loyal Sons of**

Shropshire County Ball, the: glittering gathering of the gallant and fairest of the county, at which Vee Wedge hopes to make a coruscating entrance, looking like a chandelier bedecked with the Crown Jewels (FM)

Shropshire dialect, the: there is some evidence that etymologists are now inclining to the view that the work and research which was devoted to the evolving of Esperanto and other international linguistic efforts was wasted, since the Salopian *lingua franca* as a world tongue would be both simple and economical. What e.g. could be easier than a language in which the monosyllable 'Gur!' means 'You come along of me while I shut you up somewhere and go and tell his lordship what has been happening'. Even Latin cannot express twenty-one words at the price of one. If one has a cleft palate, as one exponent has, the whole thing becomes even easier and more explicit. 'Car yar har' for instance means 'Cotched you, have I?', and for concise and euphonious assonance, 'Wah yah dah?' as implying the speaker's desire for more precise information as to the present activities and future intentions of the person addressed, has probably never been equalled. (FM) (It seems a little odd that the poet Housman made so little use of the native tongue of Wenlock Edge and Clun, since with its aid he could have produced narrative verse with one-tenth the effort—*Ed.*)

Shropshire, Herefordshire and South Wales Pig Breeders' Association, the: the keenness and hardiness of these suilline addicts enable them to sit through an address by the noble owner of Empress of Blandings, buoyed up no doubt by the pleasurable anticipation of a pint or two of beer over which to discuss the latest folk-research into the adventures of that local heroine, the young lady from Bewdley (FM)

Shortlands, the Rt. Hon. the Earl of: Claude Percival John Delamere Cobbold, 5th Earl, stands at his study window, moodily rattling in his pocket the two shillings and eightpence which are all that remain of his month's pocket money. A couple of rays of sunshine, of adventurous disposition, start to muscle into the room, but back out again hastily at sight of this stout, smooth-faced man who

(with some reason) looks like a discontented butler. Res., Beevor
Castle, Kent. (SFE) (The practised Wodehouse reader has long
since ceased to feel surprise that not only the events, but even the
names, common to real life tend to justify even the seemingly
fantastic elements in Wodehouse. Barely a month goes by but what
some paragraph in the daily press echoes, or even surpasses, his
liveliest imaginings of years ago. Yet who in 1932 (HWA) or 1948
(SFE) could have foreseen that even the Peerage would conform to
the pattern, and that e.g. Bracken and Cobbold would one day
figure in capital letters in *Debrett*. Doubtless there will be many
more—*Ed.*)

Sidcup, the Rt. Hon. Lord: Roderick Spode, leader of Britain's
Black Shorts and backroom *modiste*, succ. to the barony on dec. of
an uncle. Looks as though nature had intended to make a gorilla
but changed her mind halfway through the job (see WW for dossier)

Simmons: retires as land agent for the Blandings estates. No
relationship is indicated with the extrovert Monica S. (LIP)

Simmons, Monica: hearty and muscular hockey-knocker, takes
over the Empress's portfolio on George Cyril's defection. One of the
six daus. of a rural dean (every one of whom played hockey for
Roedean) she is at first deeply suspect when it is revealed she is a
niece of Tubby Parsloe. Lord Emsworth too resents her flippant
attitude to what should be a dedicated mission:

> 'Hullo, Lord Emsworth,' she said. 'Hot, what? Have you come
> to see the piggy-wiggy? Well, I'll be buzzing off and getting my
> tea and shrimps. I've a thirst I wouldn't sell for fifty quid.'
> She strode off, her large feet spurning the antic hay, and Lord
> Emsworth . . . gazed after her with a smouldering eye (PHW)

But Monica is of sterling metal, and her romance with the Shelley-
esque Wilfred Allsop is, beneath a flippant surface, tenderly drawn
(GBL)

Simmons, Susan: from a London private detective agency, is
installed at Blandings as parlour-maid by the Efficient Baxter (LIP)

Simpson's in the Strand: 'nowhere are the meals squarer' (CT)
there is only one Simpson's . . . Here, if he wishes, the Briton
may, for the small sum of half-a-dollar, stupefy himself with
food . . . Country clergymen visiting London for the annual
Clerical Congress come here to get the one square meal which
will last them till next year's Clerical Congress. A restful temple
of food, no strident orchestra forces the diner to bolt beef in

ragtime . . . There he sits while white-robed priests, wheeling their smoking trucks, move to and fro, ever ready with fresh supplies (SF)

Sitwells, the: Lord Ickenham suspects that Bill Oakshott is at least one, if not more, of, (UD)

Slingsby: drives the Blandings Castle's majestic Hispano-Suiza car until Voules takes over the wheel (SF)

Slurk, Major General Sir Everard: arrives at Nice (EBC)

Slythe and Sale, the Rt. Hon. Lord: on Capt. Fosdyke's alleged adroitness (NS, also LEO, MMS)

Slythe and Sale, Lady: Adelaide Cynthia is a distant cousin of Chloe Downblotton—not that the point is of interest save to Adrian Mulliner (MMS)

Smith, Dopey: Lord Emsworth is not, (BCE)

Smith, R. E.: f. of the egregious Psmith, settles in Shropshire with the intention of raising the standard of the county's cricket. A man of sudden enthusiasms, with a generosity which probably conduces to the embarrassment of his estate on his demise. We hear a great deal of him in the Mike and Psmith books. Lord Emsworth, remembering him as a neighbour and friend at Much Middlefold and at Corfby Hall, is thereby predisposed to offer Psmith appointment as his secretary:

> 'Bless my soul! I won the first prize for roses at the Shrewsbury Flower Show the year he won the prize for tulips' (LIP *et al.*)

Smithers, Mr, M.R.C.V.S.: Market Blandings' excellent veterinary surgeon, acquires the practice on Mr Webber's retirement. The general euphoria which pervades the Blandings region nullifies of course any disposition to serious disorders among its blissful fauna. Beach's pet bullfinch has not been known to suffer from croup or the gapes; the deer, cattle, horses and sheep who roam the Threepwood acres are refreshingly immune from glanders, footrot, the staggers, the lampass, the fives, the fashions, spavins, the yellows and the bots. A harassed look may occasionally cross Mr Smithers' face when Lady Alcester's travelling menagerie is visiting the Castle for a protracted stay, but his normal visits are confined to the maintenance of Empress of Blandings in County Show condition. It is, for instance, to telephone him that Lord Emsworth puts on a rare burst of speed (GBL) when the sardonic George Cyril mentions the words swine fever, but his best efforts are unavailing after the Empress's portly rival at Much Matchingham has feasted not wisely but too well on Slimmo (GBL, BCE)

Smithsons Ltd.: if Market Blandings is your nearest shopping centre you do not need to be told that everything for the garden is to be had from this old-established firm. Modesty would prevent their making any claims, but most people are well aware that the reputations of well-known exhibitors, like Lord Emsworth and Sir Gregory Parsloe, owe much to the excellence of the seeds, trees and fertilisers supplied by them (FM)

Snettisham, the Rt. Hon. Lord and Lady: serpentine guests of Tom and Dahlia Travers at Brinkley Court, Worcs., follow up their attempt to nobble a favourite by trying to steal an incomparable chef (VGJ)

'Society Spice': the circulation of this weekly scandal sheet owned by Lord Tilbury's Mammoth Publishing Corporation leaps phenomenally under the unscrupulous guidance of Percy Pilbeam. Many injured parties, including Galahad Threepwood, take active steps to discover the editor's identity, only to learn that it is foreign to the firm's policy to disclose such details to visitors armed with horsewhips (SL, BC *et al.*)

Something, Frederica: haunts Gally Threepwood's memory as a redhead who acted resourcefully to renew her betrothal (SL)

Something, Yvonne: one-time girl friend of Hugo Carmody, is walking with him in Piccadilly Circus when she is suddenly overcome by a painful attack of neuralgia, so causing an old lady to stop and tell Hugo that it is brutes like him who cause all the misery in the world (SL)

SOMETHING FRESH: first of the Blandings novels, was published in September 1915 (Methuen) though it had earlier appeared in the U.S. as **SOMETHING NEW.** New and fresh it assuredly was, as had been evident to that discerning critic G. H. Lorimer, editor of the *Saturday Evening Post*:

> I was plugging along like this (wrote Wodehouse later) when suddenly everything changed and the millennium set in. The *S.E.P.* took my serial **SOMETHING FRESH,** an amazing bit of luck which stunned me, as it had never really occurred to me that a long story by an unknown writer would have a chance there (PF)

But Lorimer was astute enough to take three more serials from Wodehouse in quick succession (with more to follow) raising the fee each time:

> So now I can afford an occasional meat meal, not only for self but for wife and resident kitten and bulldog, all of whom can do with a cut off the joint (*ibid*—see also WAW and PGW)

Southbourne: family name of the Duke of Hampshire

Southbourne, Lady Monica: dau. of the Duke of Hampshire and a client of the society photographer, Clarence Mulliner (MM)

South Kensington, S.W.: where (Lord Ickenham opines) sin stalks naked through the dark alleys and only might is right (SS)

Sparta: in the trad. connotation of keeping up appearances and hiding private emotions:

> there was a widely press-agented boy in Sparta who went so far as to allow a fox to gnaw his tender young stomach without permitting the discomfort to interfere with his facial expression. Historians have handed it down that, even in the latter stages of the meal, the polite lad continued to be the life and soul of the party (DD)

Spatchett: valet to Gally Threepwood, gives notice every time he backs a losing horse (HW)

Spenlow, George: U.S. citizen in the lumber business, is given to throwing (in his wife's absence) those neo-Babylonian parties which are so frequent when blondes and men in the lumber business get together. Is not surprisingly known as the Timber Wolf. He materially (if unexpectedly) assists in making Lord Emsworth's reputation as a go-getter sales representative (NS)

Spettisbury: family name of the Earl of Wivelscombe

Spettisbury, Lady Geraldine: takes a resourceful line with a Roman father. When Lord Wivelscombe separates her (initially by 11 ft. 2 ins.) from Adolphus Stiffham, she finds means of persuading him that ouija boards cannot lie, and that a corporeal son-in-law is preferable to a phantom secretary (YMS)

Spink: butler at Beevor Castle, Kent. Nature is an indifferent caster, and when called upon to provide an earl and a butler, produces a butler who looks like an earl and an earl who looks like a butler. Spink is tall, aristocratic and elegant; Lord Shortlands square, stout and plebeian (SFE)

Spode: family name of Lord Sidcup

Spofforth: family name of the Duke of Gorbals and Strathbungo

Spofforth, Lord Ronald: y.s. of his Grace the Duke of Gorbals and Strathbungo, considered a more suitable match for Lady Catherine Duseby than the bridegroom of her choice (DD)

Sprockett, Ebenezer: Blandings Parva worthy, causes Lord Emsworth to reflect, not for the first time, what ghastly names some of his tenants possess (BCE)

Sprockett-Sprockett, Sir Murgatroyd, Bart.: is on occasion no mean performer in the metrical foot known as the anapaestic trimeter (see **Loyal Sons of Worcestershire**). Res., Smattering Hall, Lower Smattering-on-the-Wissel, Worcs. (YMS)

Sproule: family name of the Earl of Kidderminster

Sproule, Lady Joyce: dau. of the Earl of Kidderminster, engaged to one of the Devonshire Dalrymples (LEO)

Stableford, the Rt. Hon. the Earl of: lives with his Countess in a highly contented state of mutual loquacity. Res., Worbles, Dorset (HWA)

Stableford, the Countess of: an always appreciative audience for the sporting anecdotes flowing from her lord's ample store, and herself no mean fount of parish gossip gleaned from the Dorset grapevine (HWA)

Stockheath, Lord: not (for some years) easy to identify with accuracy in the Threepwood family tree (*cf.* Wilfred Allsop); his is a courtesy title—his noble father's remarks on Percy Stockheath's breach-of-promise suit are discussed with relish below stairs. Beach moreover categorically states that he is 'a nephew of ours', and it later appears logical that he is heir to the Marquess of Alcester, who had m. Lady Georgiana Threepwood (SF)

Stokeshaye: later **Stokeshaye-Whipple:** family name of the Duke of Devizes (see **Augustus Whiffle**)

Stokeshaye, Lord Ronald: y.s. of the Duke of Devizes, takes additional surname of Whipple like the rest of his Grace's family (LN)

Stokeshaye-Whipple, Lord Percival: y.s. of the Duke of Devizes, is selected by Eugenia Crocker as an admirable companion for Piccadilly Jim. The two young men unfortunately have already had a brief but brisk encounter (PJ)

Stooge, Sir Godfrey: President of the Amalgamated Society of Bulb Squeezers, eulogises and toasts a Mulliner (MM)

Stortford, the late Lord Bishop of: the Rt. Rev. Dr. Brimble, D.D., preaching with the right organ note in his voice, sternly denounces the novel *Cocktail Time* (see **St. Jude**). He is the f. of the divine Hermione B., q.v. (CT, FO)

Stortford, the Lord Bishop of: the Rt. Rev. Percival Bickerton, D.D.; educ. Harchester College and New College, Cambridge, was V. of St. Barnabas the Resilient, W., before being enthroned as Bp. of the See of Stortford on the death of Dr. Brimble. No summary can do justice to this enlightened and enterprising prelate, who stands to the cloth of which he is such an outstanding ornament in much the same relation as do such catalysts as Fred Ickenham and Bobbie Wickham to the world at large. He m. Priscilla, known widely to the minor clergy as the Lady Bishopess q.v. Signs + BOKO: STORT: (MM, MUN *et al.*)

Stretchley-Budd, Sir Percival, Bart.: of Kingham Manor, Pershore, Worcs., has one fair dau. (RHJ)

Struggles, Buffy: of the many boys of the old brigade who figure in the memory of Gally Threepwood, Buffy, with Plug Basham, Puffy Benger and Fruity Biffen, holds a special place, and is the only one to be spoken of as 'poor, dear old chap'. It was in 1893 that some misguided welldoer

> lured poor old Buffy into one of those temperance lectures illustrated with coloured slides, and he called on me next day ashen, poor old chap, ashen. 'Gally,' he said, 'what would you say the procedure was when a fellow wants to buy tea? How would a fellow set about it?' 'Tea?' I said, 'What do you want tea for?' 'To drink,' said Buffy. 'Pull yourself together, dear boy,' I said, 'you're talking wildly. You can't drink tea. Have a brandy and soda.' 'No more alcohol for me,' said Buffy. 'Look what it does to the common earthworm.' 'But you're not a common earthworm,' I said. 'I dashed soon shall be if I go on drinking alcohol,' said Buffy. Well, I begged him with tears in my eyes not to do anything rash, but I couldn't move him. He

ordered in ten pounds of the muck and was dead inside the year . . . Dead as a door-nail. Got run over by a hansom-cab, poor, dear old chap, as he was crossing Piccadilly (SL *et al.*)

Stubbs, Cedric: private eye, m. Maudie Beach, and now dwells with the morning stars (PHW)

Stubbs, Maudie: Beach by birth, Montrose by adoption, Stubbs by marriage, Digby by profession, 'might be termed the Bohemian member of the family', says Sebastian Beach of his niece. She carries on her late husband's private inquiry agency and finally becomes Lady Parsloe-Parsloe by remarriage. For the girls who graced the bar of the old Criterion, even though their golden bird's nest hair fades through twenty years to a vivid orange, get their man in the end (PHW)

Sturridge, the Rt. Hon. the Earl of: see **Wingham**

SUMMER LIGHTNING: published 1929, had appeared earlier in the U.S. under the equally apt title of **FISH PREFERRED.** (The British Museum has a copy under this title with the Herbert Jenkins imprint—probably a copyright measure.) Here with the first appearance of that dedicated, suave old chevalier, Galahad Threepwood, we enter the mellowed, vintage Blandings period. The vein is to continue to the present day, alternating with the crazy-quilt pattern of plot in which Fred Ickenham and Alaric Dunstable are the catalysts. Latterly they have come alternately with the moonstruck corybantics of SS, succeeded by the gay and hilarious maturity of GBL

Sugg's Soothine: of Sugg the Unguent King it may be said that he was there forty ways from the jack. Use Soothine and laugh at gnat-bites (FM)

sunt lachrymae: her brow was furrowed, and the large brown eyes, which rested on George Cyril Wellbeloved, had in them something of the sadness one sees in the eyes of a dachshund which, coming to the dinner table to get its ten per cent, is refused a cut off the joint (SS)

Swartzheir, H.S.H. the Prince von: his morning departure to enjoy the air (his major domo recollects) was an event filled with stir and pomp (PB)

Swithin: family name of the Earl of Havershot

T

I myself am a hell of a fellow—a first-class earl who keeps his carriage (UD)

TAN-TANTARA! TZING-BOOM!

Blotsam Castle, a noble pile, is situated at least half a dozen miles from anywhere, and the only time anybody ever succeeded in disgracing the family name, while in residence, was back in the reign of Edward the Confessor, when the then Earl of Blotsam, having lured a number of neighbouring landowners into the banqueting hall on the specious pretence of standing them mulled sack, had proceeded to murder one and all with a battle-axe, subsequently cutting their heads off and—in rather loud taste, sticking them on spikes along the outer battlements (MUN)

'What makes them haughty?' asked Lord Ickenham warmly. 'Are they Earls?'
'No, they aren't Earls.'
'Then why the devil are they haughty? Only Earls have a right to be haughty. Earls are hot stuff. When you get an Earl, you've got something.' (YMS)

He was not the son of the fourth Baron; he was simply something his mother had picked up in the course of a former marriage and, consequently, did not come under the head of what the Peerage calls Issue. And in matters of succession, if you aren't Issue you haven't a hope (TJ)

'I was with Sir Ralph Dillingworth, a Yorkshire baronet,' said Baxter.
'Yours has been a very steady rise in the social scale,' said Lord Ickenham admiringly. 'Starting at the bottom with a humble baronet—slumming, you might almost call it—you go on to an earl and then to a duke. It does you credit. I think I've heard of Dillingworth. Odd sort of fellow, isn't he?'
'Very,' said Baxter.
'There was some story about him shooting mice in the drawing-room with an elephant gun.'
'Yes.'
'Painful for the family. For the mice, too, of course.' (UFS)

The canny peer of the realm, when duty compels him to lend his presence to the ceremony of the opening of Parliament, hires his robes and coronet from that indispensable clothing firm the Brothers Moss of Covent Garden (SS)

'Say, what time do you reckon an English peer would be waking up in the morning?'

He had come to the woman who knew. 'Eleven, Mr Cobbold.'

'*Eleven?*'

'That's the time young Lord Peebles wakes up in the novel I'm reading. 'He props his eyes open with his fingers and presses the bell, and Meadowes, his man, brings him a bromo seltzer and an anchovy on hot toast' (SFE)

'The whole set-up sounds extraordinarily like Devil's Island.' A strange light had come into Lord Ickenham's eyes. Pongo would have recognised it. It was the light which had so often come into them when his uncle was suggesting that they embark on one of their pleasant and instructive afternoons. 'What you need, it seems to me,' he said, 'is some rugged ally at your side, someone who will quell the secretary, look Connie in the eye and make her wilt, take the Duke off your hands and generally spread sweetness and light.'

'Ah,' said Lord Emsworth with a sigh, as he allowed his mind to dwell on this utopian picture (SS)

'Even in the post-war days,' said Bill Rowcester, 'with the social revolution turning handsprings on every side and civilisation in the melting-pot, it's still quite an advantage to be in big print in *Debrett's Peerage*.'

'Unquestionably so, m'lord. It gives a gentleman a certain standing' (RJ)

'You've got to impress these pig-breeding blighters,' said Gally. 'Give them the morning coat, the spongebag trousers, the stiff collar and the old top hat, and you have them saying to themselves "Golly, these Earls are hot stuff!" Whereas, seeing you dressed as you are now, they would give you the bird and probably start a revolution. You must cow them, Clarence, overawe them, make them say "The half was not told me," like the Queen of Sheba when she met King Solomon' (PHW)

We may say what we will against the aristocracy of England, but we cannot deny that in certain crises blood will tell. An English peer of the right sort can be bored nearer to the point where mortification sets in, without showing it, than any other person in the world. From early youth he has been accustomed to staying at English country houses where, though horses bored him intensely, he has had to accompany his host round the stables every morning and pretend to enjoy it. This Spartan discipline stands him in good stead in after years (SF)

'Is an Earl the same as a Duke?'
'Not quite. A Duke is a bit higher up.'
'Is it the same as a Viscount?'
'No. Viscounts are a bit lower down. We Earls rather sneer at Viscounts. One is pretty haughty with them, poor devils.' (LG)

He was the old buster who, a few years later, came down to breakfast one morning, lifted the first cover he saw, said 'Eggs! Eggs! Eggs! Damn all eggs!' and instantly legged it to France, never to return to the bosom of his family. This, mind you, being a bit of luck for the b. of the f., for old Worplesdon had the worst temper in the county (COJ)

Curious how prejudiced some people are against humble suitors. When I was courting your Aunt Jane, her parents took the bleakest view of the situation, and weren't their faces red when one day I became that noblest of created beings, an Earl. Her father, scorning me because I was a soda-jerker at the time, frequently, I believe, alluded to me as 'that bum', but it was very different when I presented myself at his Park Avenue residence with a coronet on the back of my head and a volume of *Debrett* under my arm. He gave me his blessing and a cigar (SS)

The discovery of a man in Sir George Pyke's position engaged in writing is surely enough to attract the most blasé. For who can say what literary task it is that occupies him? It may be anything from a snappy column article on 'Should Engaged Couples Kiss?' for *Pyke's Weekly* to an editorial for the *Daily Record*, a page of helpful thoughts for *The Sabbath Hour* or even a bedtime story for *Tiny Tots*. But, as a matter of fact, it is none of these things. What Sir George is busily jotting down on that large pad is a list of names. He has already written Ilfracombe, Forshore, Waynscote, Barraclough, Wensleydale, Creeby, Woodshott, Marlinghue. And now he adds to the collection the word *Michelhever*. This one seems to please him particularly, for he places against it a couple of crosses . . .
'What did you want to see me about?' asked Mrs Hammond.
Sir George drew a deep breath. He had tremendous news.
'What do you think, Francie, old girl?' he cried. 'They've offered me a peerage!' (BC)

'Were you at that thing this morning?' Lord Emsworth asked.
'I was indeed,' said Lord Ickenham, 'and looking magnificent. I don't suppose there is a peer in England who presents a posher appearance when wearing the reach-me-downs and the comic hat

than I do. Just when the procession got under way, I heard Rouge Croix whisper to Bluemantle "Don't look now, but who's that chap over there?", and Bluemantle whispered back "I haven't the foggiest, but evidently some terrific swell".' (SS)

These times in which we live are not good times for Earls. Theirs was a great racket while it lasted, but the boom days are over. A scattered few may still have a pittance, but the majority, after they have paid their income tax and their land tax and all their other taxes, and invested in one or two of the get-rich-quick schemes thrown together for their benefit by bright-eyed gentlemen in the City, are generally pretty close to the bread line. Lord Shortlands, with two-and-eightpence in his pocket, was more happily situated than most. But even he cannot be considered affluent (SFE)

The Earl of Biddlecombe's town residence was in Berkeley Square. Lancelot rang the bell and a massive butler appeared.
'No hawkers, street criers or circulars,' said the butler.
'I wish to see Lord Biddlecombe.'
A voice made itself heard. 'Fotheringay! Bung him in.'
Lancelot found himself confronting a dignified old man with a patrician nose and small side-whiskers.
'Can I interest you', said Lord Biddlecombe, 'in an ingenious little combination mousetrap and pencil-sharpener?'
Lancelot was a little taken aback. Then, remembering what Angela had said about the state of the family finances, he recovered his poise. He thought no worse of this Grecian-beaked old man for ekeing out a slender income by acting as agent for the curious little object he was holding out. Many of the aristocracy, he was aware, had been forced into similar commercial enterprises by recent legislation of a harsh and Socialistic trend.
'I should like it above all things,' he said courteously. 'I was thinking only this morning that it was just what I needed.'
'Highly educational. Not a toy. Fotheringay, book one Mouso-Penso' (MM)

'Daphne Winkworth was made a Dame in the last Birthday Honours,' explained Gally, 'a thing that's never likely to happen to you or me, Clarence. I often wonder who had the idea of calling these women Dames. Probably an American. There's nothing like a dame, he told them, and they agreed with him, and so the order came into being' (GBL)

'I was just coming out then,' said Jill, 'and I expect I looked more of an excrescence than ever.'

Monica sighed. 'Coming out. The dear old getting-ready-for-market stage. How it takes one back. Off with the glasses and the teeth-braces!'

'On with things that push you in or push you out, whichever you needed.'

'What I remember best are those agonised family conferences about my hockey-player's hands. I used to walk about the house for hours, holding them in the air.' (RJ)

And so in due course, in the blue and apricot twilight of a perfect May evening, she arrived in England with a hopeful heart and ten trunks and went to reside with Lady Vera Mace at her cosy little flat in Davies Street, Mayfair. And presently she was busily engaged in the enjoyment of all the numerous amenities which a London season has to offer.

She lunched at the Berkeley, tea-ed at Claridges, dined at the Embassy, supped at the Kit-Kat.

She went to the Cambridge May Week, the Buckingham Palace Garden Party, the Aldershot Tattoo, the Derby, and Hawthorn Hill.

She danced at the Mayfair, the Bat, Sovrani's, the Café de Paris and Bray's on the river.

She spent weekends at country houses in Bucks., Berks., Hants., Lincs., Wilts., and Devon.

She represented an Agate at a Jewel Ball, a Calceolaria at a Flower Ball, Mary Queen of Scots at a Ball of Famous Women.

She saw the Tower of London, Westminster Abbey, Madame Tussaud's, Buck's Club, the Cenotaph, Limehouse, Simpson's in the Strand, a series of races between consumptive-looking greyhounds, another series of races between goggled men on motor-cycles, and the pelicans in St. James's Park.

She met soldiers who talked of horses, sailors who talked of cocktails, poets who talked of publishers, painters who talked of surrealism, absolute form and the difficulty of deciding whether to be architectural or rhythmical.

She met men who told her the only possible place in London to lunch, to dine, to dance, to buy an umbrella; women who told her the only possible place in London to go for a frock, a hat, a pair of shoes, a manicure and a permanent wave; young men with systems for winning money by backing second favourites; middle-aged men with systems that needed constant toning up with gin-and-vermouth; old men who quavered compliments in her ear and wished their granddaughters were more like her.

And at an early point in her visit she met Godfrey, Lord Biskerton,

and one Sunday morning was driven down by him in a borrowed
two-seater to inspect the ancestral country seat of his family . . .
They took sandwiches and made a day of it (BM)

'People see me now the dickens of a fellow with five Christian names
and a coronet hanging on a peg in the hats and coats cupboard
under the stairs, and they forget that I started at the bottom of the
ladder. For years I was a younger son. A mere Honourable. A worm
of an Hon. In *Debrett*, yes, but only in small print.'
'You're making me cry.'
'I can't help that. Do you know how they treat Hons., Sally? Like
dogs. They have to go into dinner behind the Vice-Chancellor of
the County Palatine of Lancaster. The only bit of sunshine in their
lives is the privilege of being allowed to stand at the bar of the House
of Lords during debates. And I couldn't even do that, my time
being earmarked for the cows I was punching in Arizona . . . But was
I happy? No. Because always at the back of my mind was the thought
that I had to go into dinner behind the Vice-Chancellor of the
Palatine County of Lancaster. In the end, by pluck and perseverance, I raised myself from the depths and became what I am to-day.
I'd like to see any Vice-Chancellor of the Palatine County of
Lancaster try to squash in ahead of me now' (UD)

'Bruises or no bruises,' said Sir Herbert portentously, 'you have got
to learn to ride. Are you aware that as the Earl of Droitwich you
will naturally become M.F.H. of the Maltbury?'
'If I 'ad my way,' said Syd sullenly, 'I'd stop the Maltbury 'Unt
and shoot the foxes.'
A heavy silence followed the remark. Sir Herbert turned with a
dreadful calm.
'It's no use, Lydia,' he said, 'we shall have to give him up.' (IWY)

The Duke of Dunstable was looking for someone to talk to, and
Connie, though in his opinion potty, like all women, would be
better than nothing. He reached his destination, went in without
knocking, found Lady Constance busy at her desk, and shouted
'Hoy!'
The monosyllable, uttered in her immediate rear in a tone of voice
usually confined to the hog-rearing industry of western America,
made her leap like a rising trout. But she was a hostess. Concealing
her annoyance, not that that was necessary, for her visitor since
early boyhood had never noticed when he was annoying anyone,
she laid down her pen and achieved a reasonably bright smile.
'Good morning, Alaric.'

'What do you mean, good morning, as if you had not seen me before to-day?' said the Duke, his low opinion of the woman's intelligence confirmed. 'We met at breakfast, didn't we? Potty thing to say. No sense to it. What you doing?'

'Writing a letter.'

'Who to?' said the Duke, never one to allow the conventions to interfere with his thirst for knowledge (SS)

'Clear out? That is no way for a member of a proud family to talk. Did Twistletons clear out at Agincourt and Crecy? When the Old Guard made their last desperate charge up the blood-soaked slopes of Waterloo, do you suppose that Wellington, glancing over his shoulder, saw a Twistleton sneaking off with ill-assumed carelessness in the direction of Brussels? We Twistletons do not clear out, my boy. We stick around, generally long after we have outstayed our welcome' (UFS)

Mild though the 9th Earl was by nature, a lover of rural peace and the quiet life, he had, like all Britain's aristocracy, the right stuff in him. It so chanced that during the years when he had held his commission in the Shropshire Yeomanry, the motherland had not called to him to save her. But, had that call been made, Clarence, 9th Earl of Emsworth, would have answered it with as prompt a 'Bless my soul! Of course! Certainly!' as any of his Crusader ancestors. And in his sixtieth year the ancient fire still lingered.

'I have you covered, my dear fellow,' he said mildly.

Rupert Baxter had not yet begun to stick straws in his hair, but he seemed on the verge of that final piece of self-expression.

'Don't point that damned thing at me!'

'I shall point it at you,' replied Lord Emsworth with spirit. He was not a man to be dictated to in his own house. 'And at the slightest sign of violence . . .' (SL)

'Uncle Fred! Fancy meeting you again after all these years. Though I suppose I ought to call you Mr Twistleton.'

'You would be making a serious social gaffe if you did. I've come a long way since we last saw each other . . . I am the Lord Ickenham about whom there has been so much talk. And not one of your humble Barons or Viscounts, mind you, but a belted Earl, with papers to prove it.'

'Like Lord Emsworth?'

'Yes, only brighter.' (SS)

'You have probably noticed yourself,' said Lord Ickenham, 'that the

British Gawd-help-us seems to flourish particularly luxuriantly in the rural districts. My wife tries to drag me to routs and revels from time to time, but I toss my curls at her and refuse to stir (UD)

'He's got a thing about the British aristocracy. He admires them terrifically.'
'I don't blame him. We're the salt of the earth.' (SS)

The conversation in the bar-parlour always tends to get a bit deepish towards closing time (MMS)

TAVERNS IN THE TOWN

With the above pregnant observation as text we may recommend (with occasional reservations) the following, which cover the whole corpus:

Angler's Rest (Hq. of the world's most recherché raconteur) (MM, MUN, MMS)
Beetle and Wedge, Dovetail Hammer, Berks. (CT)
Beetle and Wedge, Market Blandings
Black Footman, Gossiter St. (PHW)
Black Mike's Bar (for White Hunters) Pago-Pago (RJ)
Blue Anchor, Tulse Hill, S.W. (SS)*
Blue Boar, Belpher, Hants. (DD)
Blue Boar, Market Blandings
Blue Boar, Much Matchingham
Blue Boar, Walsingford Parva, Berks. (SM)
Blue Boar, Windlehurst, Hants. (GOB)
Blue Boar, Wrykin, Shropshire (for boxers) (WF)
Blue Cow, Market Blandings
Blue Dragon, Market Blandings
Blue Lion, Tudsleigh, Worcs. (YMS)

*the high incidence of 'Blue', both here and on the general English scene, if not of armorial derivation, indicates the political persuasion of the local bigwig. One northern nobleman a century ago ordered every pub on his estates to turn blue, with the result that the entire contents of Noah's Ark appeared to have been painted with woad —*Ed.*

Bodega, W. (YMS)
Bollinger's Bar, New Bond St., W. (JM)
Bull, Redbridge, Berks. (U)
Bull and Bush, Market Snodsbury, Worcs. (JO)
Bull's Head, Ashendon Oakshott, Hants. (UD)
Bunch of Grapes (MM)
Bunch of Grapes, E.C. (HW)
Bunch of Grapes, Rudge-in-the-Vale, Worcs. (MN)
Bunch of Grapes, S.W. (U)
Bunch of Grapes, W. (HW)
Cap and Feathers, Llunindnno (U)
Carmody Arms, Rudge-in-the-Vale (MN)
Caterpillar and Jug, Mott St., S.W. (IWY)
Cheshire Cheese, E.C. (actual and historic) (*passim*)
Chuffnell Arms, Chuffnell Regis, Som. (TJ)
Coal Hole, Strand, W.C. (actual and historic) (U)
Cow and Caterpillar, Much Matchingham, Shropshire (BCE)
Cow and Cornflower, Biddlehampton (PU)
Cow and Horses, Twing, Glos. (IJ)
Cow and Wheelbarrow, East Wobsley, Worcs. (MM)
Crown, Kennington, S.E. (U)
Dog and Duck, Pondlebury Parva, Worcs. (MM)
Droitwich Arms, Langley, Worcs. (IWY)
Emsworth Arms, High St., Market Blandings (for best home-brewed) (*passim*)
Feathers, Sanstead, Hants. (LN)
ffinch Arms, ffinch, Yorks. (MM)
Goat and Bottle, Fulham Rd., S.W.
Goat and Feathers, Market Blandings
Goat and Grapes, East Bermondsey, E. (VGJ)
Goose and Cowslip, King's Deverill, Hants. (MS)
Goose and Gander, Market Blandings (SS *et al.*)
Goose and Gander, Walsingford Parva, Berks. (SM)
Goose and Gherkin, Bottleton, E. (YMS)
Goose and Grasshopper, Maiden Eggesford, Som. (YMS)
Goose and Grasshopper, Market Blandings (SS)
Goose and Grasshopper, Rising Mattock, Hants. (EBC)
Grasshopper and Ant, Worfield, Shropshire ('I want lunch for 550') (MW)
Green Goose, Bottleton, E. (LEO)
Green Lion, Valley Fields, S.E. (SFI)
Green Pig, Hockley-cum-Meston, Hants. (rendezvous for giants) (VGJ)

Jolly Cricketers, Market Blandings
Jolly Harvesters, Esher (BM)
Jolly Miller, Shepperton-on-Thames (for performing dogs) (SL)
Jug and Bottle, East Bermondsey, E. (for performing Bertie) (VGJ)
Little Bindlebury Arms (PU)
Marshmoreton Arms, Belpher, Hants. (DD)
Mermaid Tavern (the late) Bread St., Friday St., City (PF, BM *et al.*)
Mike's Place, San Francisco, Cal. (for Dynamite Dewdrop, Dreamland Special and Undertaker's Joy) (MM)
Mulberry Tree, Oxford (FM)
Net and Mackerel, Combe Regis, Dorset (LAC)
Patio, Meadowhampton, Long Island, N.Y. (SFI)
Pig and Whistle, Rupert St., Soho (FM)
Plough and Chickens, Rudge-in-the-Vale (MN)
Prince of Wales, Ratcliff Highway (U)
Red Lion, Tulse Hill, S.W. (PSC)
Rose and Crown, Loose Chippings, Sussex (QS)
Stag and Antlers, Shipley, Kent (MB)
Stitch in Time, Market Blandings
Three Pigeons, Little Weeting, Hants. (DD)
Two Goslings, Haymarket, W. (SL)
Waggoners Rest, Market Blandings
Waggoners Rest, Rudge-in-the-Vale (MN)
Wheatsheaf, Market Blandings
White Boar, Lower Borlock (MP)
White Hart, Barnes, S.W. (U)
White Stag, Barnes, S.W. (FO)
Wickham Arms, Skeldings, Herts. (MMS)

Thackeray, William Makepeace: still owes twopence to Price's of Knightsbridge for trimming his whiskers (IWY); nocturnal excitement of, on thinking of title of *Vanity Fair* (SL)

'that thing this morning': see Lord Emsworth's casual reference to no less an occasion than the State Opening of Parliament, under **Tan-Tantara,** for a masterly and percipient example of the traditional English cult of meiosis. Few other writers of eminence have (obliquely or otherwise) stressed or instanced the national addiction to the great playing-down game. But so (we may imagine) may Lord Cardigan, e.g., having led the great charge into and out of the Valley of Death, have later inquired from some subordinate in the Cavalry Mess: I say, old boy, were you at that thing this morning?'

Thistleton: family name of Lord Bridgeworth

Thorne: details are sparse of this predecessor of McAllister as head gardener to Lord Emsworth at Blandings. Indubitably he was a doubtful starter in the matter of azaleas. Not (we recollect) that his successor was so hot on hollyhocks, or for that matter yew walks (SF)

Threepwood: family name of the Earl of Emsworth

Threepwoods, the: (*see family tree between pages 200 and 201*) the derivation of the name allows of little latitude. The first element is almost certainly one of the many metathesized forms of *throp* or *thorp*, akin to Thripp, Tripp, Thrupp, Throup and Tropp (a Ralph de Trop is recorded in 1263) and derives either from one of the many places named Thorpe or from residence in an outlying hamlet or dairy-farm, in or near a wood. A second possible derivation is from *threap* and would mean (of or near) the 'debatable wood'.

On the eve of publication I find Threapwood (sic) as a place name. Those acquainted with P.G.'s extraordinary sense of accuracy will not be surprised to learn that it is plum spang in the middle of the Welsh Marches (National Grid map J96). In its case the *Dictionary of English Place Names* plumps for 'the debatable wood' as derivation from the Middle Eng. verb *threpen* to contend.

The family's West Sussex associations are evidenced by its two principal titles of Emsworth and Bosham. The present heir resides still on the family's extensive estates there. But the Shropshire association is of long standing and Blandings Castle has for centuries been the Threepwoods' principal residence. How well documented the later history of the family has been is seen in the family tree, which illustrates the proliferation of no fewer than five successive generations; and although the earlier and mediaeval history is touched upon only here and there in the annals, there is no reason to doubt the present peer's reflection that

> for generations back his ancestors had been doing notable deeds; they had sent out from Blandings Castle statesmen and warriors, governors and leaders of the people (BCE)

The date of the creation of the present Emsworth earldom is nowhere stated, but it is possible to make a conjecture. Clarence Threepwood is (as we are so often reminded) the ninth of his line. Making a list from the current *Whitaker* of the sixteen other living noblemen who are Lord Emsworth's fellow ninth-earls (beginning with the Earls of Annesley and Buckinghamshire and ending with the Earls of St. Germans and Shannon) one may find that the dates of creation vary between the years 1684 (Granard) and 1815 (St. Germans) but that the great majority attained their comital status around the year 1750. The precise average is the year 1747. (The Viscounty of Bosham may precede that date, and there is little doubt that a Bosham Barony goes back further still). But the extraordinary longevity so evident among recent generations of Threepwoods, to which Lord Emsworth himself has called attention, is a strong argument for placing the creation of the senior title a good deal further back, and perhaps as far as 1670–1680. Here admittedly we are in the realm of conjecture, but the date raises the interesting speculation whether Clarence, like the Duke of Dunstable and the Earls of Ippleton and Rowcester, had an ancestress who could not say no to King Charles II. If so, and if she resembled the latter-day Threepwood ladies, it would seem that Louise de Querouaille is not alone in calling forth the onlooker's admiration for the Merry Monarch's 'steely nerve'

Threepwoods' family crest, the: see **Blandings Parva** for a tenable theory. It is significant that the same sign is carried by a tavern at Market Blandings. It may be seen *inter alia* at Chipping Norton, Oxon.

Threepwood, Lady Ann: see **Warblington**

Threepwood, Lady Charlotte: a dau. of the 8th Earl of Emsworth, m. and has issued one dau., Jane, q.v.

Threepwood, the late Claude: s. of the Hon. Harold Threepwood and a first cousin of the present Lord Emsworth, d. prematurely at the age of eighty-four, breaking his neck when jumping (pres. on horseback) a five-barred gate (BCE)

Threepwood, Lady Constance: see **Keeble**

Threepwood, Lady Dora: see **Garland**

Threepwood, the Hon. Frederick: second s. of the 9th Earl of Emsworth, like all the original Blandings characters who descend from SF and LIP, started life as a lightly drawn caricature. As French rightly diagnoses, (PGW):

> mildly satirical of the upper classes . . . (He) is 'a heavy, loutish-looking youth'. He is idle and vacuous and devours sensational thrillers . . . There are silly letters to chorus girls and a suggestion of breach-of-promise suits and blackmail

But while his elder brother, George Bosham, has remained dumb and negligible, Freddie has personified, in his own way, the growth and development of the Blandings idea. From being one of the Peerage's 'unwanted' class—the younger son—he has developed quite plausibly, under the stimulus of an attractive American wife and a (fairly) patient tycoon of a father-in-law, into a breezy, go-getting salesman and vice-president of Donaldson Inc. who (we are sure) is much more than a mere nodder, or even a yes-man, at the conference table. Acquiring self-confidence and *savoir faire*, he even inspires his noble father, in *Birth of a Salesman*, to emulate his own commercial acumen. Freddie and his Niagara, with the redoubtable Lana Tuttle, late of Bottleton, E., as cook, now live in conjugal bliss at Great Neck, N.Y., and his membership of the Bachelors and the Drones Clubs, if it survives, is doubtless of country status (SF, LIP, LEO, BCE, PP *et al.*)

Threepwood, the Hon. Galahad: second of the three s. of the 8th Earl of Emsworth. Educ. Eton; is unm.; town res., Duke St., St. James's, S.W. His youth followed a course all too familiar to students of the Threepwood *gens*. A West End club venture failed expensively, and his father also settled his racing debts of some £1,000. Galahad was usually 'knee-deep in actresses and ballet dancers', but remained comparatively heart-whole until he met the one serious love of his life, the petite Dolly Henderson, q.v., serio-star of the old Oxford and Tivoli music-halls and a reigning toast of the day. Victorian family pride then stepped in with heavy tread and in a stormy scene at which his mother wept and his father hammered the table, Gally was banished to South Africa where he later learned (with still remembered shock) that Dolly had married Jack Cotterleigh of the Irish Guards. When he eventually returns, Dolly and her husband are dead, and Gally's accidental meeting with their delectable daughter Sue is the basis of the first novel (SL) in which he appears. Through his masterly handling, she and his nephew Ronnie win their way to the altar. As different physically as he is mentally from his brother Clarence, Galahad is

> a short, trim, dapper little man of the type one associates automatically with checked suits, tight trousers, white bowler hats, pink carnations and race-glasses bumping against the left hip . . . a jaunty little gentleman, quite astonishingly fit and rosy . . . How a man who ought to have had the liver of the century could look and behave as he did was a constant mystery . . . Instead of a blot on a proud family he might have been a teetotal acrobat (SL)

That was Gally in 1929. Nearly forty years later he is just as euphoric and still the same master-tactician, the same humanist, the civilised man of the world, in fact (in the dramatic sense) the norm around which the Blandings orb revolves. Occasionally (starting with UFS) he is understudied by his old friend Fred Ickenham, causing the Blandings world to rock slightly on its axis, but at the end (GBL and PP) Gally is there again to extricate Clarence neatly from his neighbour's coal cellar. He is at once the agent-provocateur and the *éminence grise* in Clarence's life; the one man on whom (though often deceived) Clarence has implicitly relied all his life. And if Gally's tactics are shady, even sometimes shameless, his major strategy is both selfless and excellent. To score off a Draconian sister, or to finance a worthy pair of lovers, he will bamboozle the innocent Clarence with a Stag at Bay posing as a Pig at Bée, or impute to Clarence an autumnal love affair for a young and ineligible lady that has no substance in fact; but only to avert a much worse catastrophe and to bestow general happiness where it is most deserved. With Gally, the end always justifies the means, and the means are rarely so black as those of the opposition.

He is that *rara avis* in Wodehouse, a 'straight character'. His youthful escapades with his fellow sabreurs of the Pelican, Romano's and the National Sporting Club are as valid as might be expected from the pen of a young author-journalist of lively imagination and wit whose profession in the City and the West End, at the beginning of the new century, gave him every opportunity of first-hand reportage. But, as a character, Gally is very much more than a Corinthian or an elderly raconteur. His suave ingenuity, confidence and all but fault-less judgment of men (long prejudice causes him to misjudge Tubby Parsloe) his innate sense of charity—all these qualities and more, though never overtly displayed, are held in balance, in every plot in which he matches his worldly wits against the establishment. His charm is his own. Sentiment has been taboo for a generation and more from the Wodehouse formulary, but significantly the ban is lifted, as late as GBL, in Gally's case, where he is allowed to meditate pensively on his old love for Dolly Henderson, and to conclude, characteristically enough, that she was well out of it. One remembers too that most humanistic comment on the odiferous Edwin Pott: 'After all, we can't all have roofs to our mouths'. Many sermons must have been preached on less worthy texts (*passim*)

Threepwood, George: y.s. of George and Cicely Bosham and owner of the airgun which causes the crime wave at Blandings:

> a short-sighted man whose pince-nez have gone astray at the very moment when vultures are gnawing at his bosom seldom guides his steps carefully. Anyone watching Lord Emsworth

totter blindly across the terrace would have foreseen that he would shortly collide with something . . . This proved to be a small boy with ginger hair and freckles who emerged abruptly from the shrubbery carrying an airgun.

'Coo!' said the small boy. 'Sorry, grandpa.'

But George's intuitions are as sound as the Earl's. At sight of his new tutor, Rupert Baxter, his judgment is immediate:

'Looks a bit of a blister,' said George critically.

The expression was new to Lord Emsworth, but he recognised it at once as the ideal description (LEO)

Threepwood, Lady Georgiana: see **Alcester**

Threepwood, the Hon. Harold: y.s. of the 7th Earl of Emsworth, f. of Claude Threepwood and an uncle of the 9th Earl (BCE)

Threepwood, Lady Hermione: see **Wedge**

Threepwood, James: e.s. of George, Viscount Bosham, and second heir to the Emsworth earldom

Threepwood, Lady Jane: a dau. of the 8th Earl of Emsworth, m. and has issue one dau., Angela, q.v.

Threepwood, Lady Julia: see **Fish**

Threepwood, the late Hon. Lancelot: y.s. of the 8th Earl of Emsworth and bro. of Clarence and Galahad. He m. and has issue one dau., Millicent, q.v.

Threepwood, Lady Mildred: see **Mant**

Threepwood, Millicent: o. dau. of the late Hon. Lancelot Threepwood. Tall and fair like most Threepwoods, she inherits also the inflexible purpose of their womenfolk. She has

soft blue eyes and a face like the Soul's Awakening. Not even an expert could have told that she had just received a whispered message from a bribed butler and was proposing at six sharp to go and meet a quite ineligible young man among the rose bushes.

But only a posse of Threepwood aunts could consider Hugo Carmody ineligible. He is nephew and heir to the wealthy Lester C. of Rudge Hall, though currently working his passage as Clarence's secretary (SL)

Threepwood, the Hon. Richard: period uncertain but perh. fl. 1860. Known to the family as Daredevil Dick and mentioned (if at all) in undertones as 'the one who married an actress' (HW)

Threepwood, the Hon. Robert: y.s. of the 7th Earl of Emsworth. The present peer recalls that his uncle d. when nearly ninety (BCE)

Tidmouth, the Rt. Hon. the Earl of: an immaculate but subtly battered peer in his early thirties but already four marriages to the bad. Res. Albany, W. (DS)

Tilbury, the Rt. Hon. Viscount: George Alexander Pyke, Bart., cr. 1st V., is to the discerning few (including Gally Threepwood) still known as Stinker Pyke. From inauspicious beginnings, builds up the powerful Mammoth Publishing Co. of Tilbury House, E.C., whose publications include a Fleet St. daily (the *Daily Record*) and a varied assortment of weekly magazines ranging from *Tiny Tots* and *Pyke's Weekly* to the *Sabbath Hour* and the scandal sheet *Society Spice*. Despite his frequent incursions over the years he has not noticeably grown upon the reader's notice, but he has long forgotten the milk-and-bath-bun days when he lunched frugally at the Holborn Viaduct Cabin, and wooed and won the simple heart of Lucy Maynard. *m.* (1) Lucy Maynard (d); (2) Gwendoline Gibbs. Res. The Oaks, Wimbledon Common, S.W. (*passim*)

Todd, Sir Jasper: when a chap is called Jasper a certain amount of oompus-boompus may be expected. In the original short story figuring this financier in *The Strand*, he had bought himself, on retirement, a country mansion which he re-named, significantly, Dunrobin. The name proved premature, though Sir Jasper meets his match in his niece and ward, Amanda Biffen (FO)

Topham, the Rt. Hon. Viscount: On the other hand (said Bill) don't overlook the fact that if you marry Topham, you'll have half-a-dozen imbecile children, saying 'Absolutely, what?' all the time in an Oxford accent (OR)

Topping, Lady Adela: e.d. of the Earl of Shortlands, though m. to the U.S. millionaire, Desborough Topping, declines to lend her father pin money to the extent of even £200 (SFE)

to return for a moment . . . : having been carefully informed that his brother would be calling for him shortly before one and it being now twelve fifty-four, Lord Emsworth was naturally astounded to see Gally. He was sitting in the lounge when Gally reached Barribault's Hotel, his long, lean figure draped like a wet sock on a chair, and he appeared to be thinking of absolutely nothing. His mild face wore the dazed look it always wore when he was in London, a city that disturbed and bewildered him . . . He rose like a snake hurriedly uncoiling itself and his pince-nez flew from his nose . . , 'God bless my soul! Galahad!' (GBL)

Trevelyan, the Rt. Hon. Viscount: though not identified as a Drone, it is unlikely that his expertise could have been acquired in any other hotbed of talent. He picks off, unerringly, with six consecutive bread rolls, six waiters at Mario's Restaurant (BCE)

Trotter: family name of Lord Holbeton

Tuttle, Lana: emigrating from Bottleton, E., now cooks for the Freddie Threepwoods at Great Neck, N.Y., and when dealing with burglars never misses a shot (PP)

Twemlow, Mrs: Blandings Castle's euphoric, dignified and kindly housekeeper twins as harmoniously with Beach as to suggest a pair of vases. She has the same appearance of imminent apoplexy, the same air of belonging to some haughty branch of the vegetable kingdom, as she greets Ashe Marson, the supposed valet to Freddie Threepwood:

> 'Mr Marson, welcome to Blandings Castle!'

Though we have not seen her since SF there is evidence that she still lends grace to the ritual below stairs

Twistleton, Gladys: we are not told that this intriguing girl is a connection of the Ickenham family, but the central 't' in her name (against standard practice) seems to suppose it:

> 'Lots of girls are afraid of thunder,' said Gally. 'I knew one once who, whenever there was a thunderstorm, used to fling her arms round the neck of the nearest man, hugging and kissing him till it was all over. Purely nervous reaction of course, but you should have seen the young fellows flocking round as soon as the sky began to get a little overcast. Gladys, her name was. Gladys Twistleton. Beautiful girl with large, melting eyes. Married a fellow in the Blues called Harringay. I'm told that the way he used to clear the drawing-room during the early years of their married life at the first suspicion of a rumble was a sight to be seen and remembered' (HW)

Twistleton-Twistleton: family name of the Earl of Ickenham

Twistleton, Beau: celebrated Regency dandy who, like his descendant Pongo, has occasion to feel that spiders are walking up and down his spine when he hears faint, rustling sounds from a cupboard (UD)

Twistleton-Twistleton, Lady Brenda: a dau. of the 3rd Earl of Ickenham and an aunt of the present peer, is known to fame as owner of the pug dog, Jabberwocky, on whose behalf, in Grosvenor Square, she unconsciously laid the foundations of the fortune of the millionaire businessman, philanthropist, international yachtsman and friend of kings, the late Sir Thomas Lipton (see **Lorgnettes**) (UFS)

Twistleton, Sir Gervase: (fl. c. 1180); this blot on an otherwise (fairly) unstained escutcheon got the family a bad name in the Crusades when, being invited by the Lionheart to come and do his stuff at the Siege of Joppa, he curled up in bed and murmured 'Some other time'. (UD)

Twistleton-Twistleton, the Hon. Marmaduke: on Lord Ickenham's authority his late uncle had whiskers of a nature and plenitude which no pure-minded person would credit. He also owned the enormously valuable Mitching Hill estate covering much of what has since become south-east London. It is to those same rolling acres (now swarming with red-brick villas) that Lord Ickenham returns with Pongo in the classic *Uncle Fred Flits By*, to impersonate in turn a vet come to cut the parrot's claws, a suburban householder and an estate agent. No-one doubts his assertion that he could also, if necessary, have impersonated the parrot (YMS)

Twistleton-Twistleton, Reginald (Pongo): nephew and heir pres. of the 5th Earl of Ickenham, res. (somewhat hand-to-mouth) in Albany, W. Romantic and dreamy, his i.q. at the Drones is held to be in the lower reaches, though his susceptibilities to female charms are almost as tender as those of Freddie Widgeon. It is he who (as Usborne observes) suffers most acutely from his uncle's enlargements. He is suborned, on his first appearance, to impersonate a deaf and dumb anaesthetist to a veterinary surgeon ('Tap your teeth with a pencil, my boy, and try to smell of iodoform') though the ghastly thought of an earlier occasion at the dog races still hammers like fate at his memory. Pongo has conservatively rigid ideas about people who, like Lord Ickenham, believe that to stay at someone else's house or castle under one's own name is not playing the game; his respectability is revolted by such innocent deceits, by the tenderer forms of blackmail, by ebullience in any shape and, above all, by triumphantly getting away with it. He is also, and perpetually, aggrieved by Uncle Fred's smooth successes with nubile maidens who would be so much better employed in casting a melting eye in his own direction than in returning so gratefully the avuncular kisses of his accomplished senior. Nevertheless it is due to Lord Ickenham's masterly handling of matters that Pongo, on coming into a long-awaited inheritance, is finally united to the superlative Sally Painter (YMS, UFS, UD)

Twistleton-Twistleton, Valerie: sister to Pongo, and niece to Lord Ickenham, is a girl not easy to evaluate. Her appearances are used either to apply the needful (if somewhat forceful) hose of common-sense to situations set ablaze by her expansive uncle, or to moments when the uncertain Davenport temperament has wrought havoc in her relations with her suitor Horace, heir to the Dunstable coronet and fortune. No single tender scene is allowed her, and one is conscious, when she tells Uncle Fred 'with a nasty tinkle in her voice' that his stories can never be too long, that that tinkle is seldom absent (UFS, JFS, NS, CT)

U

Uffenham, the Rt. Hon. Viscount: George Benedick, 6th of his line, pear-shaped and ponderous, leases his home, Shipley Hall, Kent, to the American, Roscoe Bunyan, and rents a villa in Valley Fields, S.W., from his former butler Keggs. Though pensive at times, addicted to encyclopaedias of natural history, and to thinking up ways of living on batter to get even fatter, he has not shaken off his lifetime habit of filling in a lull in any conversation with a girl by proposing marriage. He stands somewhat alone in the Peerage, too, as a Viscount who says 'yerss' and 'tell yer what'. He takes the firm Ickenham line in matchmaking tactics. Served in the Guards Brigade in the first world war and is a mine of information on assorted fauna (SFI, MB)

unbreakable alibi: 'Will you stop maundering on about your
insufferable pig? I tell you that Angela—your niece Angela—
has broken off her engagement to Lord Heacham and expresses
her intention of marrying that hopeless ne'er-do-well, James
Belford.'
'She can't. He's in America.'
'He is not in America. He is in London.'
'No,' said Lord Emsworth, shaking his head sagely. 'I remember

meeting his father two years ago out on the road by Meeker's twenty-acre field, and he distinctly told me the boy was sailing for America next day. He must be there by this time.' (BCE)

UNCLE FRED IN THE SPRINGTIME: published 1939, concerns the goings on at Blandings when Lord Ickenham invades the place in the guise of Sir Roderick Glossop, with the reluctant and bodeful Pongo, and the highly decorative Polly Pott as his secretary

Underhill, Sir Derek, Bart., M.P.: a not very pretty example of privilege in action in the days when a baronetcy was a safe pass to a seat in Parliament. Even Winchester and New College have their shady products, and this is one. When he discards the sterling Jill Mariner many regret that Fate always seems to let its Dereks down lightly, but Fate, in effect, does not forget (JR)

Underhill, Lady: mother of the tick Derek, has much in common with the Black Widow spider (JR)

Uppingham School: Bimbo (Bwana) Biggar and Beau Sycamore were both in the army class there (RJ)

V

Vail, Gerald Anstruther: of Flat 23, Prince of Wales Mansions, Battersea Park Rd., S.W., makes a modest livelihood from writing detective fiction. In love with Penny Donaldson, he wins Galahad Threepwood's support when it transpires he is a nephew of Plug Basham. Appointed secretary to Lord Emsworth, he talks pigs ardently and eruditely and subsequently obtains a loan enabling him to join a friend in a health resort project (PHW)

Vale of Blandings, the: at its head, on rising ground, stands the late mediaeval pile of Blandings Castle. In the blue distance the only prominent features are the silver line of the Severn and the lonely eminence of the Wrekin:

The Vale of Blandings, dim and misty, dreamed beyond (SL)

Valentine, Joan: aspiring journalist, is one of the earliest band of impostors to seek harbourage at Blandings. She competes with Ashe Marson in a complicated hunt-the-scarab session after Lord Emsworth has absent-mindedly abstracted the antique from an American guest (SF)

Vaughan, Kate: see **Earl of Marshmoreton**

Velasquez, Diego Rodriguez da Silva y: (1599–1660); reluctant though her many admirers would be to admit it, there is perhaps one field in which the Noblést of her Species has her limitations. In the matter of portraiture, she is not a satisfactory sitter. That eminent artist of the younger school, William Galahad Lister (known to Lord Emsworth as Landseer, painter of the 'Stag at Bay') though spurred by a lover's devotion, fails signally to obtain a likeness:

> in the Empress's mild face, as it leered from the canvas, there was a distinct suggestion of inebriation. Her whole aspect was that of a pig which has been seeing the New Year in.
> 'You've no notion, Freddie, how disheartening it is for an artist to come up against a sitter like that. She just lay on her side with her eyes shut and bits of potato dribbling out of the corner of her mouth. Velasquez would have been baffled' (FM)

Venables, Major General Sir Everard, V.C.: a headstrong and formidable warrior, though hardly warranting his son-in-law's fear that they may have to sit on his head and cut the traces (TSA)

Venables, Lady: practising member of the Mayfair grapevine and a crony, consequently, of Vera Mace (BM)

Venner, Sir Alfred, M.P.: it is some slight compensation for later generations that a seat in Parliament no longer entitles a landowner to behave as despotically as this one does. If the modern squire had the time and opportunity to persecute schoolboys, he would be very ill-advised to do so. Res., Badgwick Hall, Glos., 49a Lancaster Gate, W. (TP)

Vert Galant, le: entrances by his Most Christian Majesty of France and Navarre are rare. He has been seen however issuing from the Dover Street entrance of the Demosthenes Club, tall and florid, wearing his top hat as, in battle, he wore his helmet (CT) and he has likewise been noted on the terrace of Blandings Castle in the small hours, hurling flowerpots through Lord Emsworth's bedroom, his lemon pyjamas flaring as incandescently in the moonlight as on the field of Ivry waved the White Plume of Navarre (LIP)

Vine St. Police Court: London W.; Gally Threepwood once a regular customer (*passim*); Lord Uffenham, in hot youth, presented in court at (MB); Lord Belpher issued with the regulation ball and chain (DD)

Viollet-le-Duc, Eugène Emmanuel: (1814–1879); 'has written of its architecture', says SF in describing Blandings Castle. He was the French architect and authority on mediaeval architecture and castellation whose works (finely illustrated) and two dictionaries are still standard books of reference (SF *et al.*)

Vodkakoff, H.I.H. the Grand Duke: leads a Russian invading army (TS)

Vokes, Stiffy: dedicated member of the Old Brigade, once strongly adjured by Gally Threepwood, after a bad City and Suburban, to drop the false beard and face the music (HW *et al.*)

Vosper, the Rt. Hon. Lord: his dark, Byronic beauty makes him the Peerage's handsomest ornament, suggesting even something which has escaped from the Metro-Goldwyn lot; but competent judges regard him as more than a bit of a poop. Marriage to Gloria Salt, one feels, will improve him, if anything can (PHW)

W

Wade-Beverly, Lady Edith: dinner guest at Belpher (DD)

Waffles, Eddie: reigning Bad Boy of Much Middlefold, on whose repertoire Ashe Marson draws for after-dinner entertainment (SF)

Walderwick, the Hon. Hugo: the toffee-nosed Drone would be surprised to hear himself referred to as a humble instrument, but his only claim to attention is when he unwittingly supplies the umbrella which effects an introduction between Psmith and his future bride (LIP)

Walls: family name of the Earl of Ackleton

Walls, Lady Evelyn: dau. of Lord Ackleton, contemplates a mésalliance with her brother's tutor (DD)

Warblington, Lady Ann: e. dau. of the 8th Earl of Emsworth, acts as chatelaine for her bro. Clarence in the first Blandings novel. Of refreshingly retiring habits among the shock squadron of sisters, she divides her time between letter-writing and nursing a sick headache (SF)

Watkins, Orlo: throaty crooner with sideburns and feet of clay (BCE)

Wattiers: the famous and fashionable gaming club of Regency days, which saw the beginning of the end of so many noble families' original fortunes, stood at the corner of Bolton St., Piccadilly, 1807–1819. It is traditionally held that the Prince Regent asked his cook Wattier, to take a house and organise a club. The favourite game was Macao (a gambling game resembling vingt-et-un). Mr Raikes in his *Journal* remarks of the Club that 'its pace was too quick to last'. The Cocoa Tree Club, often associated with Wattiers as a rapid solvent of young men's fortunes, was at 64 St. James's St., S.W., succeeding a chocolate house of that name which stood on the site in Queen Anne's reign (HW *et al.*)

Waveney, her Grace the Dowager Duchess of: former employer of butler Wrench who, whilst prepared to tolerate her Grace's regrettable habit of entertaining Members of the Lower House, drew the line at her keeping open house for monkeys (UM)

Wedge, Colonel Egbert: late Shropshire Light Infantry, m. Lady Hermione Threepwood, dau. of the 8th Earl of Emsworth; one dau. Veronica, q.v. Where others quail before Hermione's compelling eye, the Colonel merely admires it (FM, GBL)

Wedge, Lady Hermione: only member of Clarence's monstrous regiment of sisters who is not statuesquely handsome. Short and dumpy, she looks like a cook and, when stirred (not infrequently) to anger, like a cook about to give notice. It is a red-letter day in the Earl's life when, furious at his treatment of Dame Daphne Winkworth, she sweeps out of Blandings Castle forever (FM, GBL)

Wedge, Veronica: o.c. of Col. and Lady Hermione W., the dumbest blonde in Shropshire and the adjacent counties burst on our view when she was preparing to irradiate the County Ball (FM) glittering like a chandelier in borrowed diamonds. Highly decorative, she is 'the most beautiful of all the girls mentioned in small type among the collateral branches in *Debrett*'. Enormous blue eyes, a sylphlike figure and all the fixings, are attended by the brain of a peahen which has been mentally retarded by being dropped on its head when just out of the egg. Society photographers fight for her custom. But though her intellectual resources are strictly limited, she conforms precisely to Tipton Plimsoll's ideal of wifehood:

> thinks seldom and with the greatest difficulty; has voice like clotted cream; expression of, like that of cow staring over hedge at mangold wurzel; is capable, given time, with no hustling, of a rudimentary process of ratiocination; is given for her pains a

world of sighs; leers over her shoulder with rose in mouth . . . in dealing with the first romantic stroll together of Tipton and Vee Wedge, the chronicler finds himself faced with the necessity for pause and reflection. It would be possible for him to record their conversation verbatim, but it is to be doubted whether this would interest, elevate and instruct . . . Tipton started off well enough by saying that the garden looked pretty in the moonlight, and Veronica said 'Yes, doesn't it'. He followed this up by remarking that gardens always look kind of prettier when there is a moon—sort of—than when, as it were, there isn't a moon, and Veronica said 'Yes, don't they'. So far the exchanges would not have disgraced a *salon* such as that of Madame Récamier. But at this point Tipton suddenly ran dry of inspiration, and a prolonged silence followed. Some little time later Veronica said that she had been bitten on the nose that afternoon by a gnat. Tipton said that he had never liked gnats. Veronica said that she, too, did not like gnats, but that they were better than bats. Yes, assented Tipton, oh, sure, yes, a good deal better than bats. Of cats Veronica said that she was fond, and Tipton agreed that cats as a class were swell. On the subject of rats they were also at one, both holding strong views regarding their lack of charm. The ice thus broken, the talk flowed pretty easily until Veronica said that perhaps they had better be going in now . . . and Tipton said 'Well, okay, if we must.' His heart was racing and bounding. If ever there had been any doubt in his mind that this girl and he were twin souls, it no longer existed. It seemed to him absolutely amazing that two people should think so alike on everything—on gnats, bats, cats, rats, in fact absolutely everything (FM, GBL)

Weeks, Dogface: champion liar of the Pelican Club (SL, HW)

Wellbeloved, Ezekiel: senior member of the well-known Market Blandings family (see WW for its southern counties branches). George Cyril's grandfather was a philanthropic old gentleman whose details, if scanty, are not unilluminating. Ezekiel, we learn, divested himself of his trousers one snowy afternoon in the High Street and gave them away to a passing stranger, observing that he would not be needing them any longer since the end of the world was due at five-thirty sharp. (Not to labour the point, any sapient native of Market Blandings might be excused, on seeing snow fall in that sunblest paradise, for believing the end was at hand—*Ed.*)

Wellbeloved, George Cyril: Shropshire points with pride to its

Wellbeloveds, whose enterprise does so much to keep the local constabulary on its toes. George Cyril comes first in the line of dedicated pigmen whose aim is to minister to the needs of a certain noble animal at Blandings Castle, and is also, regrettably, the first to betray his trust, selling his soul for filthy lucre to the squire of Matchingham. He is

> no feast for the eye, having a sinister squint, a broken nose acquired during a political discussion (he is an outspoken Communist) at the Goose and Gander, and a good deal of mud all over him. He also smelt rather strongly. George Cyril might rather closely resemble someone for whom the police were spreading a dragnet in the expectation of making an arrest shortly, but nobody could deny his great gifts. He knew his pigs (PHW, SS *et al.*)

Wellbeloved, Marlene: of the fourth generation of the eminent family, is the ornament behind the bar at the Emsworth Arms and a niece of the perfidious George Cyril. On the disappearance of Sebastian Beach's most treasured possession she emits an 'EEE-EEE!' equalled only by that of Vee Wedge under somewhat similar circumstances (GBL)

Wellbeloved, Orlando: Sir Gregory Parsloe does not want to hear about George Cyril's father, and many citizens of Market Blandings agree with him (PHW)

Wellington, the first Duke of: perhaps it was when taking the overland route from Apsley House (Number One, London) rather than the underground tunnel, to his favourite retreat, the Grenadier Tavern, that the Iron Duke formed the habit of dropping in at Price's celebrated toilet saloon in Mott Street, later to be conducted by the *soi-disant* Earl of Droitwich. The staff still discuss the gentlemanly emphatics with which his Grace embroidered his comments when great-grandfather Price inadvertently nicked a pimple on the ducal chin (IWY) eliciting a flow of invective unequalled since the field of Waterloo; it is a matter for conjecture what his reactions would have been had Napoleon burst into tears on the battlefield (SS); see also **Tan-Tantara.**

Wensleydale, the Dowager Viscountess: with more discernment than discretion, Jane Wensleydale scores a palpable hit with her *Sixty Years Near the Knuckle in Mayfair* (HW)

Westbourne, the Rt. Hon. the Earl of: see **Drassilis**

Wetherby, the Rt. Hon. the Earl of: a genial young peer whose finances are so precarious that he can scarcely be said to possess an income at all. Possibly Algie Wetherby is the only earl who is poorer than his old friend Bill Dawlish (UM)

Wetherby, the Countess of: née Pauline (Polly) Davis of Carbondale, Ill., replenishes the Wetherby coffers (emptied at Wattiers and the Cocoa Tree in Regency days) by the sensational success of her cabaret act at Reigelheimers, New York. Dancing with nothing on her feet and very little anywhere else, her triumph is such that before long it takes three vans to carry her salary to the bank (UM)

Whiffle, Augustus: (now **Whipple**); internationally celebrated suilline expert, principally known to the general public for his standard work *On The Care Of The Pig* (Popgood & Grooly, 35/-). The section on feeding standards, based largely on the Wolff-Lehmann Scale, q.v., is considered generally to be a masterpiece. There was general surprise, not unmixed with some astonishment, in 1965 when, after some thirty-two years of near-anonymity, it was disclosed by the Hon. Galahad Threepwood that the expert's christian name was Augustus, his club the Athenaeum (where he is known to the boys as Gus) and his real name Whipple. The explanation of the last is of course tied up with the similar change of name in the ducal family of Devizes. As has been seen, relatives, even sons, of the present Duke were some years ago calling themselves Stokeshaye or Whipple at will. Augustus, head of a cadet branch of the family, declared as long ago as 1930 that he would take the name of Whiffle 'until the dashed Duke makes up his mind'. The College of Heralds was nonplussed; Garter King of Arms pursed his lips; finally, as will be remembered, the Court of Chivalry was convened and the name Stokeshaye-Whipple was accepted by the family as a whole, with the logical result that Augustus reverted to his original patronymic. It remains doubtful, however, whether his famous work will ever be known as anything but Whiffle *On The Care of the Pig*.

For details of his remarkable uncle, who grew a second set of teeth in his eightieth year and used to crack Brazil nuts with them, see Galahad Threepwood in GBL. The old gentleman perished of a surfeit of Brazil nuts at the age of eighty-two (*passim*)

Wickham, the late Sir Cuthbert, Bart.: if only one detail emerges, it is one which would suffice most men. He was f. of Roberta (JO *et al.*)

Wickham, Lady: relict of the foregoing, is necessarily a woman of blood and iron and, alone on the world's canvas, has been known to exercise a modicum of control over that redheaded catalyst Bobbie. Res., Skeldings Hall, Herts. (BCE *et al.*)

Wickhammersley, the Rt. Hon. the Earl of: f. of the superlative Cynthia. Res., Twing Hall, Twing, Glos. (IJ)

Widdrington, Lady: widow of Sir George W., entertains, with fell purpose, that saintly and unworldly prelate the Bishop of Bongo Bongo. Her revolting cat Percy is the lifeline by which the good man escapes a fate worse than death. Res., Widdrington Manor, Bottleby-in-the-Vale, Hants. (MUN)

Widgeon: family name of the Earl of Blicester

Widgeon, Farmer: of the Home Farm on the Belpher Castle estate, makes a generous offer to Albert the page-boy (DD)

Wigan, the Most Noble Duke of: like so many dukes of his era, his Grace passes, slowly, through Hollywood (BCE)

Wilberforce, Rupert: a connection of the Threepwoods who (*teste* Gally) being advised to touch his toes fifty times a day before breakfast, is found writhing in agony, his heart having run into his liver (PHW)

Wilks, P. P.: of Wilks Bros., Manchester, strews cigars all over Freddie Threepwood in admiration of his sales methods (PP)

Willard, George: neighbour and crony of Lord Emsworth and a fellow rose enthusiast (LIP)

Willie: village blacksmith of Little Weeting, Hants., lends assistance in the social education of Viscount Belpher (DD)

Wimsey, Lord Peter Death Bredon: y.s. of the late Duke of Denver and brother of the present holder of the title; speculation on his conjectural views on a kid's frock, no kid inside it, floating on the river. Res., Duke's Denver; 110a Piccadilly, W. (YMS, JM)

Wingham: family name of the Earl of Sturridge

Wingham, the Hon. and Rev. Hubert: y.s. of the Earl of Sturridge, has a cure of souls in the delightful Gloucestershire parish of Twing, where he wins the hand of Mary Burgess in a canter (Bingo Little unplaced) (IJ)

Wingham, Sir Mortimer, Bart.: entertains a Mulliner at Barkley Towers, Sussex (MUN)

Wingham, Lady: wife of Sir M., affects strange religions, notably Ba-ha-ism (MUN)

Winkworth, Dame Daphne, D.B.E.: many might suppose her past dossier (see WW) a sufficient exercise, for one lifetime, in the understudying of Simon Legree or Captain Bligh. She still conducts (at time of going to press) the school whose unfortunate moppets must think longingly of a holiday on sunny Devil's Island. That she should be brought to Blandings for the purpose of marrying Clarence Emsworth seems one over the odds:

> 'And Daphne', said Gally, 'is all for it. She feels that little Huxley needs a father.'
> Lord Emsworth . . . was looking like the Good Old Man in old-fashioned melodrama when the villain has foreclosed the mortgage. Over in a corner of the grillroom a luncher was dealing with madrilene soup. It quivered beneath his spoon, but not so whole-heartedly as Lord Emsworth

The coming doom is beyond the powers even of a Gally to avert, but not, triumphantly, beyond the resources of an aggrieved Empress (GBL)

Winkworth, Huxley: revolting offspring of the late P. B. and of Dame Daphne, and the sole example of deserved retribution by the tenant of a certain bijou residence (GBL)

Witherspoon, Sir Reginald, Bart.: m. Lady Katherine Wooster, sister of Lord Yaxley, q.v., and open host to her nephew Bertie. Res., Bleaching Court, Upper Bleaching, Hants. (VGJ)

Witherspoon, Lady: Bertie Wooster's 'Aunt Katherine', sister to Agatha Worplesdon and Dahlia Travers (VGJ)

Wivelscombe, the Rt. Hon. the Earl of: Ferdinand James Delamere Spettisbury, 6th of his line, is, on his mother's side, a Ballindalloch of Portknockie—a race traditionally gifted with 'the Sicht'. Having separated his dau. Geraldine (by 11 ft. 2 ins.—a Midland Counties record for the standing place-kick) from his secretary Stiffy Stiffham, the Earl begins to see phantoms, especially after attending the annual banquet of the Loyal Sons. Told by the astute girl that the spectral secretary under the breakfast-table is a Cautionary Projection of a Distant Personality, he is persuaded to exchange the ghost for a son-in-law. Res., Wivelscombe Court, Upton Snodsbury, Worcs. (YMS)

Wivelscombe, the late Dowager Countess of: frequently saw visions of her friends in winding-sheets. Her son recalls that it got her disliked in the County (YMS)

Wivenhoe, the Rt. Hon. the Earl of: after the Bachelors' Ball, one of his pigs, purloined by Puffy Benger and Gally Threepwood, materialises in Plug Basham's bedroom in the small hours, glowing luminously. Res., Hammer's Easton, Essex (SL, GBL *et al.*)

Wocestre, the Sieur de: (or **Wooster**); fights with vim in the French campaigns of Henry V (see WW)

Wolfe, Nero: Arnold Pinkney doesn't in the least mind looking like, (PP)

Wolff-Lehmann, Herr: international pig-breeding expert, crowns a career devoted to improving the suilline species by laying down his famous Feeding Standards. Summarised, these state that a pig, to achieve and maintain its full perfection, must consume a daily food intake of 57,800 calories (proteins 4 lbs. 8 ozs., carbohydrates 25 lbs.). If Wolff-Lehmann has a more dedicated disciple than Lord Emsworth, it can only be the Empress herself (*passim*)

Wooster: family name of the Earl of Yaxley

Wooster, Sir George Bart.: see **Earl of Yaxley**

Wooster, Algernon: guest at Blandings Castle, is of interest to students of the opus as a blood link between the Threepwoods and the Woosters. He is a cousin both of Lord Stockheath (nephew of Lord Emsworth) and of Bertie Wooster (SF)

Wopple, Sir Oscar: 'How about that financier fellow who lives out Ditchingham way?'
'He shot himself last Friday, m'lord.'
'Oh, then we won't bother about him.' (RJ)

Worlingham, the Rt. Hon. Lord: lacks the wise counsel of butler Keggs in the matter of his son, Aubrey Pershore (DD)

Worplesdon, the Rt. Hon. the Earl of: Percival Craye, cr. 1st Earl, wealthy Southampton shipowner whose interests include the well-known Pink Funnel Line, m. the widowed Agatha Spenser Gregson (see WW) (COJ, JFS, JM)

Worplesdon, the Countess of: for full dossier of Bertie Wooster's Aunt Agatha see (with caution) WW (*passim*)

Wragges: London private inquiry agency, supplies Blandings Castle with a new parlourmaid (LIP)

Wrekin, the: (1,335 ft.); famous Shropshire landmark, and the only hill visible from Blandings Castle. Doubtless it was a Threepwood of the day who held the Queen's commission to order the lighting, in 1588, of that beacon celebrated by Lord Macaulay:

> Till twelve fair counties saw the blaze on Malvern's lonely height,
> Till streamed in crimson on the wind the Wrekin's crest of light

X

X . . . and . . . Q: The 'X' was an almost inaudible murmur, produced through pouting lips. What made everything seem so sad and hopeless was the 'X'. As she emitted this, Lady (Wilhelmina) Mulliner drew her mouth back in a ghastly grin till the muscles of her neck stood out like ropes. And she went on and on and on. She refrained from Q-ing the 'Q' only to X the 'X', and when she wasn't X-ing to beat the band she was Q-ing away like a two-year-old. Well, of course, Archibald understood now why Aurelia's manner towards him had changed of late. Obviously she must have come upon the poor old parent unexpectedly in the middle of one of these spells of hers and perceived, as he did, that she was as loony as a coot. Enough to make any girl think a bit (YMS)

Xanadu: in point of actual distance only a mile or two separate Barribault's palatial hotel in Clarges St., W., from the site of St. Martin's Church on Ludgate Hill. The literary connection is a little more involved, and might tax the ingenuity of the protagonists in the B.B.C.'s 'Round Britain Quiz' programme. Wodehouse points out (PP) that the hotel's directors, in planning the sumptuous lobby to satisfy the tastes of duchesses, maharajahs and Texan oil millionaires, had in mind the sort of thing Kubla Khan envisaged when passing the plans for his stately pleasure dome at Xanadu. Most of us would never have heard of the place save for Coleridge's poem, and he came across it in 'Purchas His Pilgrimes', published in 1625, which describes the 'royall House on pillars gilded and vernished, built in a faire wood by the great Chan Cublay'. Its author, the worthy Sam Purchase, was Rector of St. Martin's Ludgate, and if Barribault's directors have not placed a blue plaque there to say so, there is no justice in this world (*Ed.*)

Yaxley, the Rt. Hon. the Earl of: the available biographical details of George Wooster are listed in WW, the main point of interest being his late but romantic marriage to Maud Wilberforce, long lost friend of his youth. But a certain amount of intriguing surmise may here be permissible with regard to his identity and to the descent of the earldom. For such facts as are available seem to point to certain very interesting conclusions.

Compared with the Threepwoods, the Woosters as a family are not too well documented. On Bertie's authority, Lord Yaxley is his 'Uncle George'. But so, too, was, some years earlier, Sir George Wooster, Bart. It is virtually certain therefore that, having the same Christian name and the same father, they are one and the same person, i.e. Sir George inherited the earldom, in which the baronetcy is now merged. It would seem both relevant and cogent to point out that the Wodehouse family (in which P.G.W.'s branch is a cadet one) is also headed by an Earl (of Kimberley) and that that earldom likewise embodies a baronetcy—one of the oldest in the country.

From whom, then, did the Sir George Wooster of IJ inherit the title of Yaxley? Of his generation of Woosters (the one senior to that of Bertie and his cousins) we have records of eight members who are brothers and sisters. Disregarding the girls Agatha, Dahlia and Katherine, these are the late Henry (father of Claude and Eustace), Clive (who gives temporary refuge to the twins at his Worcs. home), Sir George, who becomes Lord Yaxley, Bertie's late (unnamed) father, and Bertie's 'Uncle Willoughby' who years ago (in COJ and unmentioned since) was living in comfort at Easeby Hall, Shropshire, where he was engaged in writing a history of the family. The two facts—that he never reappears and that he is never referred to as 'Mr Wooster'—add some semblance of reason to the supposition that *he* was the last Earl, that he died some time between 1925 and 1930 and that his brother George (first referred to as Lord Yaxley in 1930) succeeded him in the earldom. We now come to the really intriguing point. Who is George Yaxley's heir? He has married late in life the buxom but equally elderly Maud. If any of his brothers survive (Clive is the only possibility) we have not been told of it. The title therefore must pass to a nephew. Incidentally, Clive has not been heard of for thirty-seven years and is not known to have issue. There are therefore only three candidates—the twins Claude and Eustace, and Bertie himself. One has a marked, if intangible, feeling that Bertie's father was senior to the late Uncle Henry (who died in a home, happy to the end and completely surrounded by rabbits). If so, Bertie is the heir.

The consequences of such an event would be quite incalculable. We have already touched (see **Jeeves** in WW) on the suppositional results had Bertie's manservant elected to take his talents to No. 10 Downing St. It is unthinkable that, if Bertie became eligible for a seat in the Upper House, Jeeves would fail to persuade him to take it. Britain's re-emergence as the Number One ruling power would follow as the dawn follows the night. We have seen, in the light opera *Iolanthe*, a somewhat playful interpretation of the consequences for the country, were a Fairy Queen to take up residence at Westminster. But a Fairy Queen's puissance, though limitless, tends to be directed to other than worldly issues. Not so those of a Jeeves. The vicarious takeover of Britain's domestic and international economy by such an *éminence grise* would, without doubt, precipitate the coming of the millennium (*Ed.*)

Yaxley, the Countess of: Maud Wilberforce, the bouncing lady with orange hair who once graced the bar of the old Criterion in Piccadilly Circus, m. George, Earl of Yaxley (VGJ)

Yew Alley, the: for years Angus McAllister had set before himself as his earthly goal the construction of a gravel path through the Castle's famous Yew Alley. And now, it seemed, he was at it again.

'Gravel path!' Lord Emsworth stiffened through the whole length of his stringy body. Nature, he had always maintained, intended a yew alley to be carpeted with a mossy growth. And he personally was dashed if he was going to have men with Clydeside accents and faces like dissipated potatoes coming along and mutilating that lovely expanse of green velvet. Gravel path, indeed! Why not asphalt? Why not a few hoardings with advertisements of liver pills and a filling station? That's what the man would really like (BCE)

Young Lochinvar: a shining example, in Lord Ickenham's opinion, of the lover untroubled by scruples (SS)

Yorke, Jane: 'A pill, guv'nor,' said Freddie Threepwood. 'One of the worst. A Jebusite and Amalekite. She got hold of Aggie and whisked her away and poisoned her mind. This woman, guv'nor, has got a brother in the background, and she wanted Aggie to marry the brother. And my belief is that she is trying to induce Aggie to pop over to Paris and get a divorce, so as to give the blighted brother another look in, dash him. So now is

the moment to rally round as never before. I rely on you!'
(BCE)

Z

Zachariah: listening to butler Binstead's reported views on his character and habits, George Cyril Wellbeloved feels, with the prophet, that he has been wounded in the house of his friends.

Zulu warriors: Queens of France have rarely been assaulted by, but Horace Pendlebury-Davenport, heir-presumptive to a dukedom, is arraigned at Marlborough St. Police Court, wearing a loincloth and carrying an assegai, blacked from head to foot, on a charge of prodding the more yielding surfaces of Queen Marie Antoinette with the weapon at the Bohemian Ball in the Royal Albert Hall. He later makes a spectacular appearance at the Drones Club, similarly arrayed (UFS)

Zybisco: cited by Psmith as another name in which the initial letter is given a miss-in-baulk (MP)

KEY TO THE WORKS OF P. G. WODEHOUSE, LL.D.

For those wishing to read the Blandings novels and short stories chronologically, these are listed in order of their publication. Others are arranged in the alphabetical order of the code-letters by which they are referred to in the text.

Blandings Stories

SF	SOMETHING FRESH
LIP	LEAVE IT TO PSMITH
SL	SUMMER LIGHTNING
HW	HEAVY WEATHER
BCE	BLANDINGS CASTLE AND ELSEWHERE
LEO	LORD EMSWORTH AND OTHERS
UFS	UNCLE FRED IN THE SPRINGTIME
FM	FULL MOON
NS	NOTHING SERIOUS
PHW	PIGS HAVE WINGS
SS	SERVICE WITH A SMILE
GGL	GALAHAD AT BLANDINGS
PP	PLUMPIE

Other Stories

AS	THE ADVENTURES OF SALLY
BC	BILL THE CONQUEROR
BM	BIG MONEY
BW	BARMY IN WONDERLAND
CB	THE COMING OF BILL
CC	THE CLICKING OF CUTHBERT
COJ	CARRY ON, JEEVES
CT	COCKTAIL TIME
CW	THE CODE OF THE WOOSTERS
DD	A DAMSEL IN DISTRESS
DS	DR SALLY
EBC	EGGS, BEANS AND CRUMPETS
FA	FROZEN ASSETS
FL	FRENCH LEAVE
FO	A FEW QUICK ONES
GB	THE GOLD BAT
GL	A GENTLEMAN OF LEISURE
GOB	THE GIRL ON THE BOAT
HG	THE HEART OF A GOOF
HK	THE HEAD OF KAY'S
HWA	HOT WATER
IA	THE INDISCRETIONS OF ARCHIE
IB	ICE IN THE BEDROOM
IJ	THE INIMITABLE JEEVES
IWY	IF I WERE YOU
JFS	JEEVES AND THE FEUDAL SPIRIT
JM	JOY IN THE MORNING
JO	JEEVES IN THE OFFING
JOM	JEEVES OMNIBUS
JR	JILL THE RECKLESS
LAC	LOVE AMONG THE CHICKENS

LB	THE LUCK OF THE BODKINS
LF	LOUDER AND FUNNIER
LG	LAUGHING GAS
LN	THE LITTLE NUGGET
LOB	THE LUCK OF THE BODKINS
LS	THE LUCK STONE
MB	MONEY IN THE BANK
MJ	MY MAN JEEVES
MM	MEET MR MULLINER
MMS	MR MULLINER SPEAKS
MN	MONEY FOR NOTHING
MP	MIKE AND PSMITH
MS	THE MATING SEASON
MT	THE MAN WITH TWO LEFT FEET
MU	THE MAN UPSTAIRS
MUN	MULLINER NIGHTS
MW	MIKE AT WRYKIN
OR	THE OLD RELIABLE
PB	THE PRINCE AND BETTY
PJ	PICCADILLY JIM
PSC	PSMITH IN THE CITY
PSJ	PSMITH, JOURNALIST
PU	A PREFECT'S UNCLE
QS	QUICK SERVICE
RHJ	RIGHT HO, JEEVES
RJ	RING FOR JEEVES
SA	SAM THE SUDDEN
SB	THE SMALL BACHELOR
SFE	SPRING FEVER
SFI	SOMETHING FISHY
SLJ	STIFF UPPPER LIP, JEEVES
SM	SUMMER MOONSHINE
TJ	THANK YOU, JEEVES
TP	THE POTHUNTERS
TS	THE SWOOP
TSA	TALES OF ST. AUSTIN'S
U	UKRIDGE
UD	UNCLE DYNAMITE
UM	UNEASY MONEY
VGJ	VERY GOOD, JEEVES
WEW	WEEKEND WODEHOUSE
WF	THE WHITE FEATHER
WT	WILLIAM TELL TOLD AGAIN
YMS	YOUNG MEN IN SPATS

Biographical

BG	BRING ON THE GIRLS (with Guy Bolton)
OS	OVER SEVENTY
PF	PERFORMING FLEA
PGW	P. G. WODEHOUSE (R. B. D. French)
WAW	WODEHOUSE AT WORK (Richard Usborne)

Companion

WW	WOOSTER'S WORLD (Geoffrey Jaggard)